THE NEW FOLGER LIBRARY SHAKESPEARE

Designed to make Shakespeare's great plays available to all readers, the New Folger Library edition of Shakespeare's plays provides accurate texts in modern spelling and punctuation, as well as scene-by-scene action summaries, full explanatory notes, many pictures clarifying Shakespeare's language, and notes recording all significant departures from the early printed versions. Each play is prefaced by a brief introduction, by a guide to reading Shakespeare's language, and by accounts of his life and theater. Each play is followed by an annotated list of further readings and by a "Modern Perspective" written by an expert on that particular play.

Barbara A. Mowat was Director of Research *emerita* at the Folger Shakespeare Library, Consulting Editor of *Shakespeare Quarterly,* and author of *The Dramaturgy of Shakespeare's Romances* and of essays on Shakespeare's plays and their editing.

Paul Werstine is Professor of English at the Graduate School and at King's University College at Western University. He is a general editor of the New Variorum Shakespeare and author of *Early Modern Playhouse Manuscripts and the Editing of Shakespeare* and of many papers and articles on the printing and editing of Shakespeare's plays.

The Folger Shakespeare Library

The Folger Shakespeare Library in Washington, D.C., a privately funded research library dedicated to Shakespeare and the civilization of early modern Europe, was founded in 1932 by Henry Clay and Emily Jordan Folger, and incorporated as part of Amherst College in Amherst, Massachusetts, one of the nation's oldest liberal arts colleges, from which Henry Folger had graduated in 1879. In addition to its role as the world's preeminent Shakespeare collection and its emergence as a leading center for Renaissance studies, the Folger Shakespeare Library offers a wide array of cultural and educational programs and services for the general public.

EDITORS

BARBARA A. MOWAT
Former Director of Research emerita
Folger Shakespeare Library

PAUL WERSTINE
Professor of English
King's University College
at Western University, Canada

All's Well That Ends Well

By
WILLIAM SHAKESPEARE

EDITED BY BARBARA A. MOWAT
AND PAUL WERSTINE

Simon & Schuster Paperbacks
NEW YORK LONDON TORONTO SYDNEY NEW DELHI

Simon & Schuster
1230 Avenue of the Americas
New York, NY 10020

This Simon & Schuster trade paperback edition November 2020

SIMON & SCHUSTER and colophon are registered trademarks
of Simon & Schuster, Inc.

For information about special discounts for bulk purchases,
please contact Simon & Schuster Special Sales at 1-866-506-1949
or business@simonandschuster.com.

The Simon & Schuster Speakers Bureau can bring authors to your
live event. For more information or to book an event, contact the
Simon & Schuster Speakers Bureau at 1-866-248-3049 or visit our
website at www.simonspeakers.com.

Manufactured in the United States of America

10 9 8 7 6 5 4 3 2 1

ISBN 978-1-9821-6496-6
ISBN 978-1-5011-3685-6 (ebook)

From the Director of the Folger Shakespeare Library

It is hard to imagine a world without Shakespeare. Since their composition more than four hundred years ago, Shakespeare's plays and poems have traveled the globe, inviting those who see and read his works to make them their own.

Readers of the New Folger Editions are part of this ongoing process of "taking up Shakespeare," finding our own thoughts and feelings in language that strikes us as old or unusual and, for that very reason, new. We still struggle to keep up with a writer who could think a mile a minute, whose words paint pictures that shift like clouds. These expertly edited texts, presented here with accompanying explanatory notes and up-to-date critical essays, are distinctive because of what they do: they allow readers not simply to keep up, but to engage deeply with a writer whose works invite us to think, and think again.

These New Folger Editions of Shakespeare's plays and poems are also special because of where they come from. The Folger Shakespeare Library in Washington, D.C., where the Editions are produced, is the single greatest documentary source of Shakespeare's works. An unparalleled collection of early modern books, manuscripts, and artwork connected to Shakespeare, the Folger's holdings have been consulted extensively in the preparation of these texts. The Editions also reflect the expertise gained through the regular performance of Shakespeare's works in the Folger's Elizabethan Theatre.

I want to express my deep thanks to editors Barbara Mowat and Paul Werstine for creating these indispensable editions of Shakespeare's works, which incorporate the best of textual scholarship with a richness of commentary that is both inspired and engaging. Readers who want to know more about Shakespeare and his plays can follow the paths these distinguished scholars have trod by visiting the Folger itself, where a range of physical and digital resources (available online) exists to supplement the material in these texts. I commend to you these words, and hope that they inspire.

Michael Witmore
Director, Folger Shakespeare Library

Contents

Editors' Preface

In recent years, ways of dealing with Shakespeare's texts and with the interpretation of his plays have been undergoing significant change. This edition, while retaining many of the features that have always made the Folger Shakespeare so attractive to the general reader, at the same time reflects these current ways of thinking about Shakespeare. For example, modern readers, actors, and teachers have become interested in the differences between, on the one hand, the early forms in which Shakespeare's plays were first published and, on the other hand, the forms in which editors through the centuries have presented them. In response to this interest, we have based our edition on what we consider the best early printed version of a particular play (explaining our rationale in a section called "An Introduction to This Text") and have marked our changes in the text—unobtrusively, we hope, but in such a way that the curious reader can be aware that a change has been made and can consult the "Textual Notes" to discover what appeared in the early printed version.

Current ways of looking at the plays are reflected in our brief prefaces, in many of the commentary notes, in the annotated lists of "Further Reading," and especially in each play's "Modern Perspective," an essay written by an outstanding scholar who brings to the reader his or her fresh assessment of the play in the light of today's interests and concerns.

As in the Folger Library General Reader's Shakespeare, which this edition replaces, we include explanatory notes designed to help make Shakespeare's language clearer to a modern reader, and we place the notes on the page facing the text that they explain. We also follow the earlier edition in including illustrations—of objects, of clothing, of mythological figures—from books and manuscripts in the Folger Library collection. We provide fresh accounts of the life of Shakespeare, of the publishing of his plays, and of the theaters in which his plays were performed, as well as an introduction to the text itself. We also include a section called "Reading Shakespeare's Language," in which we try to help readers learn to "break the code" of Elizabethan poetic language.

For each section of each volume, we are indebted to a host of generous experts and fellow scholars. The "Reading Shakespeare's Language" sections, for example, could not have been written had not Arthur King, of Brigham Young University, and Randall Robinson, author of *Unlocking Shakespeare's Language*, led the way in untangling Shakespearean language puzzles and shared their insights and methodologies generously with us. "Shakespeare's Life" profited by the careful reading given it by the late S. Schoenbaum; "Shakespeare's Theater" was read and strengthened by Andrew Gurr, John Astington, and William Ingram; and "The Publication of Shakespeare's Plays" is indebted to the comments of Peter W. M. Blayney. Among the texts we consulted, we found Susan Snyder's 1993 Oxford edition of the play especially helpful. We, as editors, take sole responsibility for any errors in our editions.

We are grateful to the authors of the "Modern Perspectives"; to Leeds Barroll and David Bevington for their generous encouragement; to the Huntington and Newberry Libraries for fellowship support; to King's College for the grants it has provided to Paul Werstine; to the Social Sciences and Humanities Research Council of Canada, which provided him with a Research Time Stipend for 1990–91; to R. J. Shroyer of the University of Western Ontario for essential computer support; to the Folger Institute's Center for Shakespeare Studies for its fortuitous sponsorship of a workshop on "Shakespeare's Texts for Students and Teachers" (funded by the National Endowment for the Humanities and led by Richard Knowles of the University of Wisconsin), a workshop from which we learned an enormous amount about what is wanted by college and high-school teachers of Shakespeare today; to Alice Falk for her expert copyediting; and especially to Steve Llano, our production editor at Pocket Books, whose expertise and attention to detail are essential to this project. Our biggest debt is to the Folger Shakespeare Library—to Werner Gundersheimer, Director of the Library, who made possible our edition; to Deborah Curren-Aquino, who provides extensive editorial and production support; to Jean Miller, who combs the Library holdings for illustrations, and to Julie Ainsworth, Head of the Photography Department, who carefully photographs them; to Peggy O'Brien, former Director of Education at the Folger and now Director of Education Programs at the Corporation for Public Broadcasting, who gave us expert advice about the needs being expressed by Shakespeare teachers and students (and to Martha Christian and other "master teachers" who used our texts in manuscript in their classrooms); to Allan Shnerson and Mary Bloodworth for expert computer support; to the staff of the Academic Programs Division, especially Rachel Kunkle (whose help is crucial), Mary Tonkinson, Kathleen Lynch, Carol Brobeck, Toni Krieger, Liz Pohland, Owen Williams, and Lisa Meyers; and, finally, to the generously supportive staff of the Library's Reading Room.

Barbara A. Mowat and Paul Werstine

Shakespeare's
All's Well That Ends Well

All's Well That Ends Well is, like so many of Shakespeare's comedies, about a young woman and a young man. Yet *All's Well* is in many ways Helen's story. Helen bears the name of the mythological, incredibly beautiful Helen of Troy, the object of all male desire, but the plot of *All's Well* turns on the fact that its heroine is not desired by Bertram, the man whose love she yearns for. In the face of his lack of interest and the wide gap in social standing that separates them, she sets out to win him as a husband. Having technically won him, she finds little happiness in the victory. Before they are married, he ignores her; after they are married, he shuns, deserts, and attempts to betray her. She is the one who takes all the initiative in furthering their union. Such a task is a hard one in a culture that, like Shakespeare's, consigned women to the passive role of yielding to male desire. Only by providing a spectacular, apparently miraculous, cure for the French king does she win the reward of choosing Bertram as a husband from among the young men whose fates are in the control of the King. Only through an arduous and lonely pilgrimage and a daring trick does she establish her marriage with Bertram.

In a comedy like *All's Well*, which centers on courtship and marriage, Bertram's part is largely an unsympathetic one, for, in fleeing Helen, he impedes the advancement of the plot. However, the play provides points of view from which Bertram may be perceived with some sympathy. As the play opens,

Bertram's father, like Helen's, has just died. Yet Bertram does not, as we might expect in a comedy, come into his inheritance and assume the rights and responsibilities of an autonomous male. Instead, he becomes a ward to the French king, who severely restricts Bertram's opportunities to find his own way in the world. When his young friends go off to war to seek fame, Bertram is obliged to maintain his attendance at the King's court. When Helen cures the King, the King makes Bertram available to her quite against Bertram's will. When Helen selects him, he is powerless to resist openly. To exert any control over the course of his life, he must flee the King and his native land and go to war in Italy, thereby incurring the displeasure not only of the King but also of his mother the Countess and the rest of the older generation, all of whom disapprove of his treatment of Helen and his flagrant disobedience of the King.

While Bertram finds fulfillment in his transgression, winning glory in battle and also finding sexual satisfaction, and while the play gives us reasons to understand his behavior, he continues to strike us more as an obstacle for Helen to overcome than as a sympathetic hero. The play tells Helen's fairy-tale story of incredible challenges met and overcome—though few today see a fairy-tale ending at the conclusion of her journey.

After you have read the play, we invite you to turn to the essay printed at the back of this book, "*All's Well That Ends Well*: A Modern Perspective," by Professor David McCandless of Carleton College.

Reading Shakespeare's Language: *All's Well That Ends Well*

For many people today, reading Shakespeare's language can be a problem—but it is a problem that can be solved. Those who have studied Latin (or even French or German or Spanish), and those who are used to reading poetry, will have little difficulty understanding the language of Shakespeare's poetic drama. Others, though, need to develop the skills of untangling unusual sentence structures and of recognizing and understanding poetic compressions, omissions, and wordplay. And even those skilled in reading unusual sentence structures may have occasional trouble with Shakespeare's words. Four hundred years of "static" intervene between his speaking and our hearing. Most of his immense vocabulary is still in use, but a few of his words are not, and, worse, some of his words now have meanings quite different from those they had in the sixteenth century. In the theater, most of these difficulties are solved for us by actors who study the language and articulate it for us so that the essential meaning is heard—or, when combined with stage action, is at least *felt*. When reading on one's own, one must do what each actor does: go over the lines (often with a dictionary close at hand) until the puzzles are solved and the lines yield up their poetry and the characters speak in words and phrases that are, suddenly, rewarding and wonderfully memorable.

Shakespeare's Words

As you begin to read the opening scenes of a play by
Shakespeare, you may notice occasional unfamiliar
words. Some are unfamiliar simply because we no
longer use them. In the opening scenes of *All's Well
That Ends Well*, for example, you will find the words
prejudicates (i.e., condemns in advance), *discipled* (i.e.,
trained), *approof* (i.e., proof), and *sithence* (i.e., since).
Words of this kind are explained in notes to the text
and will become familiar the more of Shakespeare's
plays you read.

In *All's Well That Ends Well*, as in all of Shakespeare's
writing, more problematic are the words that we still
use but that we use with a different meaning. In the
opening scenes of *All's Well That Ends Well*, for example, the word *want* has the meaning of "lack," *simpleness* is used where we would say "innocence,"
livelihood is used where we would say "liveliness," and
taxed where we would say "reproved" or "reprimanded." Such words will be explained in the notes to the
text, but they, too, will become familiar as you continue to read Shakespeare's language.

Some words are strange not because of the "static"
introduced by changes in language over the past centuries but because these are words that Shakespeare is
using to build dramatic worlds that have their own
space, time, and history. In the first two acts of *All's
Well That Ends Well*, for example, Shakespeare con-
jures up a number of different worlds—those of the
court, the military, and the medical profession. The
first and principal setting is that of the court, both
the provincial court of Rossillion and the royal court
of the King of France. Power relations within these
courts are determined by the accidents of birth (i.e.,

lineage or "blood") and death. Because of his father's death, Bertram, an "unseasoned courtier," is "in ward, evermore in subjection" to the King of France. Yet to Helen, by birth "a gentlewoman" to an "honorable mistress" and therefore below Bertram in social hierarchy, he is "a bright particular star." Helen laments the "difference betwixt their two estates"—between her "humble" and his "honored name"—and wishes that their "qualities were level." For Bertram, the adventure of a foreign war offers the promise of deliverance from subjection. "The Florentines and Senoys are by th' ears," and Bertram and other young courtiers who are "sick for breathing and exploit" and who desire to "wear themselves in the cap of the time" will compete to be the "bravest questant" and to survive as "well-entered soldiers." In "the Tuscan service," they will risk being forever disfigured by a "cicatrice" but will also be thrilled by "the bound and high curvet / Of Mars's fiery steed." Helen will attempt to change the fate of her birth and find "the luckiest star in heaven" through her practice of medicine or "physic," using the "applications," "prescriptions," "receipts," "appliance," and "empirics" that she has inherited from her father against the "malignant cause" from which the French king suffers. In so doing she will best the "schools" or "congregated college" of the "artists . . . both of Galen and Paracelsus," "learned and authentic fellows."

Shakespeare's Sentences

In an English sentence, meaning is quite dependent on the place given each word. "The dog bit the boy" and "The boy bit the dog" mean very different things, even though the individual words are the same. Because

English places such importance on the positions of words in sentences, on the way words are arranged, unusual arrangements can puzzle a reader. Shakespeare frequently shifts his sentences away from "normal" English arrangements—often to create the rhythm he seeks, sometimes to use a line's poetic rhythm to emphasize a particular word, sometimes to give a character his or her own speech patterns or to allow the character to speak in a special way. When we attend a good performance of the play, the actors will have worked out the sentence structures and will articulate the sentences so that the meaning is clear. In reading for ourselves, we can do as the actor does. That is, when we become puzzled by a character's speech, we can check to see if words are being presented in an unusual sequence.

Shakespeare often, for example, rearranges subjects and verbs (i.e., instead of "He goes" we find "Goes he"). In *All's Well That Ends Well*, when Bertram says of his dead father "So in approof lives not his epitaph" (1.2.57), he is using such a construction. So is Parolles when he says simply "say I" (2.3.15). The "normal" order would be "His epitaph lives not so in approof" and "I say." Shakespeare also frequently places the object before the subject and verb (i.e., instead of "I hit him," we might find "Him I hit"). The Countess's statement "Her dispositions she inherits" (1.1.41–42) is an example of such an inversion, as is the French king's "his plausive words / He scattered not in ears" (1.2.60–61). The "normal" order would be "She inherits her dispositions" and "He scattered not his plausive words in ears."

Inversions are not the only unusual sentence structures in Shakespeare's language. Often in his sentences words that would normally appear together are separated from each other. Again, this is often done to create a particular rhythm or to stress a particular word. Take, for example, "Then I confess / Here on my knee before high heaven and you / That before you and next unto high heaven / I love your son" (1.3.201–4). In these lines, the adverb "Here" and the phrase "on my knee before high heaven and you" separate the verb of the main clause ("confess") from its object (the clause "That . . . I love your son"). (Within the clause that forms the object of the main clause, the phrases "before you" and "next unto high heaven" delay the appearance of the clause's subject and verb ["I love"]. For more on delaying the appearance of the principal sentence elements, see below.) Or take the King's lines to Bertram quoting the young man's father:

> "Let me not live"—
> This his good melancholy oft began
> On the catastrophe and heel of pastime,
> When it was out—"Let me not live," quoth he,
> "After my flame lacks oil. . . ."
>
> (1.2.62–66)

Here after one sentence begins with the first quotation of Bertram's father's words, the sentence is interrupted, as marked in our text by the first dash, so that another entire sentence can be inserted ("This his good melancholy . . . was out") before the original sentence begins again. Thus Shakespeare is able to create the flavor of spontaneous conversation in the medium of blank verse.

Sometimes, although not often in *All's Well That Ends Well*, rather than separating basic sentence elements, Shakespeare simply holds them back, delaying them until other material to which he wants to give greater emphasis has been presented. Shakespeare puts this kind of construction in the mouth of the King when he again addresses Bertram, this time about Helen:

> If she be
> All that is virtuous, save what thou dislik'st—
> "A poor physician's daughter"—thou dislik'st
> Of virtue for the name.
>
> (2.3.132–35)

Holding back the essential sentence elements, the subject, the verb, and the completion of the predicate ("thou dislik'st / Of virtue for the name"), the King first establishes the terms according to which Helen is to be presented. For him, she is a paragon of virtue, "All that is virtuous"; he dismisses the issue of her inadequate lineage by reducing it to his quotation of the phrase that Bertram has earlier used to characterize her, " 'A poor physician's daughter.' " The King turns Bertram's evaluation into just so many words.

Finally, in many of Shakespeare's plays, sentences are sometimes complicated not because of unusual structures or interruptions but because Shakespeare omits words and parts of words that English sentences normally require. (In conversation, we, too, often omit words. We say, "Heard from him yet?" and our hearer supplies the missing "Have you.") Frequent reading of Shakespeare—and of other poets—trains us to supply such missing words. In *All's Well That Ends Well*, a number of speakers implicitly claim to voice wisdom by speaking in a carefully balanced elliptical way. For example, when Lafew tells the Countess and Bertram that they have nothing to fear from the French king, he states his opinion in a sentence so formulated that the very structure of his words seems a guarantee of his authority: "You shall find of the King a husband, madam; you, sir, a father" (1.1.7–8). Fully expanded the sentence would read "You shall find of the King a husband, madam; you, sir, *shall find of the King* a father," but such flabby repetition would strip it of its power to persuade. The Countess's elliptical statement at 1.3.133, "Our blood to us, this to our blood is born," shows that proverbial-sounding utterances can employ omission in a way that reverses the pattern of Lafew's statement. This time words are omitted from the first clause in the balanced structure, rather than from the second. Expanded in normal word order, the Countess's sentence would read "[As surely as] our blood is born [i.e., is innate] to us, so this is born to our blood." Again by omitting words Shakespeare lends an aura of wisdom to the Countess's declaration.

Shakespearean Wordplay

Shakespeare plays with language so often and so variously that entire books are written on the topic. Here we will mention only two kinds of wordplay, puns and metaphors. Puns in *All's Well That Ends Well* usually play on the multiple meanings of a single word. When Parolles addresses two lords on their way to war, he puns on the word *metals*: "Noble heroes, my sword and yours are kin. Good sparks and lustrous, a word, good metals" (2.1.46–47). This speech exploits *metal's* association with swords and swordsmen and its meaning (always now, but not then, conveyed under the spelling *mettle*) of "character" or "spirit." The Fool's conversation, like Parolles', is generously sprinkled with puns. When the Countess asks him, "Will your answer serve fit to all questions?" the Fool answers with a series of analogies that begins "As fit as ten groats is for the hand of an attorney, as your French crown for your taffety punk . . ." (2.2.20–22). The Fool's "French crown," as the context alerts us, refers both to a coin (just as "ten groats" also refers to money) and to syphilis, which the English represented (falsely) as of French origin. This second meaning of "French crown" is indicated by its association with a "punk" or prostitute.

A metaphor is a play on words in which one object or idea is expressed as if it were something else, something with which it shares common features. For instance, when Helen, in the context of speaking of the impossibility of her achieving the marriage to Bertram she desires, says "The hind that would be mated by the lion / Must die for love" (1.1.96–97), it is clear that she is "the hind" and he "the lion." Later, when the King quotes Bertram's father to Bertram, the speech the King recalls is itself composed of a set of metaphors:

> "Let me not live," quoth he,
> "After my flame lacks oil, to be the snuff
> Of younger spirits, whose apprehensive senses
> All but new things disdain, whose judgments are
> Mere fathers of their garments, whose constancies
> Expire before their fashions."
> (1.2.65–70)

First, vitality is compared to the oil that is burned in a lamp; once that oil is consumed, all that remains in the lamp is its wick, or "snuff," which was Bertram's father's term for himself imagined as old. Then the speech switches to a metaphorical characterization of shallow young men who care for nothing but their clothes. These men are represented as having only enough "judgment" to choose their "garments," which become the children of the otherwise childless men. In yet another metaphor, the men's "constancies" of purpose are like living things with a life span shorter than the time their clothes remain in fashion.

Implied Stage Action

Finally, in reading Shakespeare's plays we should always remember that what we are reading is a performance script. The dialogue is written to be spoken by actors who, at the same time, are moving, gesturing, picking up objects, weeping, shaking their fists. Some stage action is described in what are called "stage directions"; some is suggested within the dialogue itself. We should always try to be alert to such signals as we stage the play in our imaginations. Consider, for example, the stage action that is suggested by the following exchange between the Countess and her son Bertram in the play's first scene:

COUNTESS   . . . Farewell, Bertram.
BERTRAM   The best wishes that can be forged in your
    thoughts be servants to you. Be comfortable to my
    mother, your mistress, and make much of her.
                                        (1.1.77–81)

There are several clues in this exchange indicating that the first sentence in Bertram's speech is addressed to his mother, who then must leave the stage, the second sentence in the speech then being addressed to Helen. The clue that the Countess is about to exit is her "Farewell" to Bertram. The clue that she has exited is provided in the switch from Bertram's use of the second person to address her in the first sentence of his speech ("your . . . you") to his reference to her as "my mother, your mistress" and "her" (the third person) in the last sentence of his speech. The clue that the last sentence is addressed to Helen, and not the Countess, is Bertram's use of "your mistress" in the sentence. These indications are so clear that we, as editors, add the stage direction "*Countess exits.*" between the two sentences of Bertram's speech. This is one place, and there are others, where the dialogue allows us to be reasonably confident in adding, in brackets, a stage direction suggesting the action.

On other occasions in *All's Well That Ends Well*, the signals for stage action are not so clear. Indeed the play seems sometimes to offer a unique challenge to readers' capacity to imagine the action that accompanies its dialogue. Take, for example, the scene in which Helen addresses herself to the young lords presented to her by the King as those from among whom she can choose a husband, her reward for having healed him. There is an obvious discrepancy between the lords' actual words to Helen and Lafew's representation of their behavior. For example, when Helen says to the Second Court Lord "Love make your fortunes twenty times above / Her that so wishes [i.e., Helen herself], and her humble love," and the Second Lord replies "No better, if you please," the response appears to say frankly that he desires a wife with no greater fortune than Helen's; that is, he is perfectly happy to have her as his wife. Yet Lafew comments "Do all they deny her? An they were sons of mine, I'd have them whipped . . ." (2.3.94–95). It is hard to know whether Lafew is to be placed onstage at such a distance from Helen that he cannot actually hear the conversations about which he is commenting and that he is therefore misinterpreting

Helen's decision to pass over the Court Lords as their rejection of her, or the scene is to be staged so that the gestures and vocal inflections of the Court Lords are at odds with their words and Lafew is right to judge that they are turning her down. Because this ambiguity is undecidable, we, as editors, have added nothing to the text of the play, leaving this interpretive issue for readers, directors, and actors to judge.

It is immensely rewarding to work carefully with Shakespeare's language so that the words, the sentences, the wordplay, and the implied stage action all become clear—as readers for the past four centuries have discovered. It may be more pleasurable to attend a good performance of a play—though not everyone has thought so. But the joy of being able to stage one of Shakespeare's plays in one's imagination, to return to passages that continue to yield further meanings (or further questions) the more one reads them—these are pleasures that, for many, rival (or at least augment) those of the performed text, and certainly make it worth considerable effort to "break the code" of Elizabethan poetic drama and let free the remarkable language that makes up a Shakespeare text.

Shakespeare's Life

Surviving documents that give us glimpses into the life of William Shakespeare show us a playwright, poet, and actor who grew up in the market town of Stratford-upon-Avon, spent his professional life in London, and returned to Stratford a wealthy landowner. He was born in April 1564, died in April 1616, and is buried inside the chancel of Holy Trinity Church in Stratford.

We wish we could know more about the life of the world's greatest dramatist. His plays and poems are testaments to his wide reading—especially to his knowledge of Virgil, Ovid, Plutarch, Holinshed's *Chronicles,* and the Bible—and to his mastery of the English language, but we can only speculate about his education. We know that the King's New School in Stratford-upon-Avon was considered excellent. The school was one of the English "grammar schools" established to educate young men, primarily in Latin grammar and literature. As in other schools of the time, students began their studies at the age of four or five in the attached "petty school," and there learned to read and write in English, studying primarily the catechism from the Book of Common Prayer. After two years in the petty school, students entered the lower form (grade) of the grammar school, where they began the serious study of Latin grammar and Latin texts that would occupy most of the remainder of their school days. (Several Latin texts that Shakespeare used repeatedly in writing his plays and poems were texts that schoolboys memorized and recited.) Latin comedies were introduced early in the lower form; in the upper form, which the boys entered at age ten or eleven, students wrote their own Latin orations and declamations, studied Latin historians and rhetoricians, and began the study of Greek using the Greek New Testament.

Since the records of the Stratford "grammar school" do not survive, we cannot prove that William Shakespeare attended the school; however, every indication (his father's position as an alderman and bailiff of Stratford, the playwright's own knowledge of the Latin classics, scenes in the plays that recall grammar-school experiences—for example, *The Merry Wives of Windsor,* 4.1) suggests that he did. We also lack generally accepted documentation about Shakespeare's life after his schooling ended and his professional life in London began. His marriage in 1582 (at age eighteen) to Anne Hathaway and the subsequent births of his daughter Susanna (1583) and the twins Judith and Hamnet (1585) are recorded, but how he supported himself and where he lived are not known. Nor do we know when and why he left Stratford for the London theatrical world, nor how he rose to be the important figure in that world that he had become by the early 1590s.

We do know that by 1592 he had achieved some prominence in London as both an actor and a playwright. In that year was published a book by the playwright Robert Greene attacking an actor who had the audacity to write blank-verse drama and who was "in his own conceit [i.e., opinion] the only Shake-scene in a country." Since Greene's attack includes a parody of a line from one of Shakespeare's early plays, there is little doubt that it is Shakespeare to whom he refers, a "Shake-scene" who had aroused Greene's fury by successfully competing with university-educated dramatists like Greene himself. It was in 1593 that Shakespeare became a published poet. In that year he published his long narrative poem *Venus and Adonis;* in 1594, he followed it with *The Rape of Lucrece.* Both poems were dedicated to the young earl of Southampton (Henry Wriothesley), who may have become Shakespeare's patron.

It seems no coincidence that Shakespeare wrote these narrative poems at a time when the theaters were closed because of the plague, a contagious epidemic disease that devastated the population of London. When the theaters reopened in 1594, Shakespeare apparently resumed his double career of actor and playwright and began his long (and seemingly profitable) service as an acting-company shareholder. Records for December of 1594 show him to be a leading member of the Lord Chamberlain's Men. It was this company of actors, later named the King's Men, for whom he would be a principal actor, dramatist, and shareholder for the rest of his career.

So far as we can tell, that career spanned about twenty years. In the 1590s, he wrote his plays on English history as well as several comedies and at least two tragedies (*Titus Andronicus* and *Romeo and Juliet*). These histories, comedies, and tragedies are the plays credited to him in 1598 in a work, *Palladis Tamia*, that in one chapter compares English writers with "Greek, Latin, and Italian Poets." There the author, Francis Meres, claims that Shakespeare is comparable to the Latin dramatists Seneca for tragedy and Plautus for comedy, and calls him "the most excellent in both kinds for the stage." He also names him "Mellifluous and honey-tongued Shakespeare": "I say," writes Meres, "that the Muses would speak with Shakespeare's fine filed phrase, if they would speak English." Since Meres also mentions Shakespeare's "sugared sonnets among his private friends," it is assumed that many of Shakespeare's sonnets (not published until 1609) were also written in the 1590s.

In 1599, Shakespeare's company built a theater for themselves across the river from London, naming it the Globe. The plays that are considered by many to be Shakespeare's major tragedies (*Hamlet, Othello, King Lear,* and *Macbeth*) were written while the company was resident in this theater, as were such comedies as *Twelfth Night* and *Measure for Measure.* Many of Shakespeare's plays were performed at court (both for Queen

Elizabeth I and, after her death in 1603, for King James I), some were presented at the Inns of Court (the residences of London's legal societies), and some were doubtless performed in other towns, at the universities, and at great houses when the King's Men went on tour; otherwise, his plays from 1599 to 1608 were, so far as we know, performed only at the Globe. Between 1608 and 1612, Shakespeare wrote several plays—among them *The Winter's Tale* and *The Tempest*—presumably for the company's new indoor Blackfriars theater, though the plays seem to have been performed also at the Globe and at court. Surviving documents describe a performance of *The Winter's Tale* in 1611 at the Globe, for example, and performances of *The Tempest* in 1611 and 1613 at the royal palace of Whitehall.

Shakespeare wrote very little after 1612, the year in which he probably wrote *King Henry VIII*. (It was at a performance of *Henry VIII* in 1613 that the Globe caught fire and burned to the ground.) Sometime between 1610 and 1613 he seems to have returned to live in Stratford-upon-Avon, where he owned a large house and considerable property, and where his wife and his two daughters and their husbands lived. (His son Hamnet had died in 1596.) During his professional years in London, Shakespeare had presumably derived income from the acting company's profits as well as from his own career as an actor, from the sale of his play manuscripts to the acting company, and, after 1599, from his shares as an owner of the Globe. It was presumably that income, carefully invested in land and other property, which made him the wealthy man that surviving documents show him to have become. It is also assumed that William Shakespeare's growing wealth and reputation played some part in inclining the crown, in 1596, to grant John Shakespeare, William's

The Globe

A stylized representation of the Globe theater.
From Claes Jansz Visscher, *Londinum florentissima
Britanniae urbs* . . . [c. 1625].

father, the coat of arms that he had so long sought. William Shakespeare died in Stratford on April 23, 1616 (according to the epitaph carved under his bust in Holy Trinity Church) and was buried on April 25. Seven years after his death, his collected plays were published as *Mr. William Shakespeares Comedies, Histories, & Tragedies* (the work now known as the First Folio).

The years in which Shakespeare wrote were among the most exciting in English history. Intellectually, the discovery, translation, and printing of Greek and Roman classics were making available a set of works and worldviews that interacted complexly with Christian texts and beliefs. The result was a questioning, a vital intellectual ferment, that provided energy for the period's amazing dramatic and literary output and that fed directly into Shakespeare's plays. The Ghost in *Hamlet*, for example, is wonderfully complicated in part because he is a figure from Roman tragedy—the spirit of the dead returning to seek revenge—who at the same time inhabits a Christian hell (or purgatory); Hamlet's description of humankind reflects at one moment the Neoplatonic wonderment at mankind ("What a piece of work is a man!") and, at the next, the Christian disparagement of human sinners ("And yet, to me, what is this quintessence of dust?").

As intellectual horizons expanded, so also did geographical and cosmological horizons. New worlds—both North and South America—were explored, and in them were found human beings who lived and worshiped in ways radically different from those of Renaissance Europeans and Englishmen. The universe during these years also seemed to shift and expand. Copernicus had earlier theorized that the earth was not the center of the cosmos but revolved as a planet around the sun. Galileo's telescope, created in 1609, allowed scientists to see that Copernicus had been correct; the universe was not organized with the earth at the center, nor was it so nicely circumscribed as people had, until that time, thought. In terms of expanding horizons, the impact of these discoveries on people's beliefs—religious, scientific, and philosophical—cannot be overstated.

London, too, rapidly expanded and changed during the years (from the early 1590s to around 1610) that Shakespeare lived there. London—the center of England's government, its economy, its royal court, its overseas trade—was, during these years, becoming an exciting metropolis, drawing to it thousands of new citizens every year. Troubled by overcrowding, by poverty, by recurring epidemics of the plague, London was also a mecca for the wealthy and the aristocratic, and for those who sought advancement at court, or power in government or finance or trade. One hears in Shakespeare's plays the voices of London—the struggles for power, the fear of venereal disease, the language of buying and selling. One hears as well the voices of Stratford-upon-Avon—references to the nearby Forest of Arden, to sheepherding, to small-town gossip, to village fairs and markets. Part of the richness of Shakespeare's work is the influence felt there of the various worlds in which he lived: the world of metropolitan London, the world of small-town and rural England, the world of the theater, and the worlds of craftsmen and shepherds.

That Shakespeare inhabited such worlds we know from surviving London and Stratford documents, as well as from the evidence of the plays and poems themselves. From such records we can sketch the dramatist's life. We know from his works that he was a voracious reader. We know from legal and business documents that he was a multifaceted theater man who became a wealthy landowner. We know a bit about his family life and a fair amount about his legal and financial dealings. Most scholars today depend upon such evidence as they draw their picture of the world's greatest playwright. Such, however, has not always been the case. Until the late eighteenth century, the William Shakespeare who lived in most biographies was the creation of legend and tradition. This was the Shakespeare who was supposedly caught poaching deer at Charlecote, the estate of Sir Thomas Lucy close by Stratford; this was the Shakespeare who fled from Sir Thomas's vengeance and made his way in London by taking care of horses outside a playhouse; this was the Shakespeare who reportedly could barely read but whose natural gifts were extraordinary, whose father was a butcher who allowed his gifted son sometimes to help in the butcher shop, where William supposedly killed calves "in a high style," making a speech for the occasion. It was this legendary William Shakespeare whose Falstaff (in *1* and *2 Henry IV*) so pleased Queen Elizabeth that she demanded a play about Falstaff in love, and demanded that it be written in fourteen days (hence the existence of *The Merry Wives of Windsor*). It was this legendary Shakespeare who reached the top of his acting career in the roles of the Ghost in *Hamlet* and old Adam in *As You Like It*—and who died of a fever contracted by drinking too hard at "a merry meeting" with the poets Michael Drayton and Ben Jonson. This legendary Shakespeare is a rambunctious, undisciplined man, as attractively "wild" as his plays were seen by earlier generations to be. Unfortunately, there is no trace of evidence to support these wonderful stories.

Perhaps in response to the disreputable Shakespeare of legend—or perhaps in response to the fragmentary

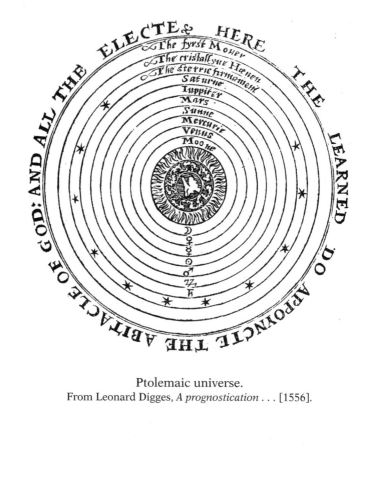

Ptolemaic universe.
From Leonard Digges, *A prognostication* . . . [1556].

and, for some, all-too-ordinary Shakespeare document-ed by surviving records—some people since the mid–nineteenth century have argued that William Shakespeare could not have written the plays that bear his name. These persons have put forward some dozen names as more likely authors, among them Queen Elizabeth, Sir Francis Bacon, Edward de Vere (earl of Oxford), and Christopher Marlowe. Such attempts to find what for these people is a more believable author of the plays is a tribute to the regard in which the plays are held. Unfortunately for their claims, the documents that exist that provide evidence for the facts of Shakespeare's life tie him inextricably to the body of plays and poems that bear his name. Unlikely as it seems to those who want the works to have been written by an aristocrat, a university graduate, or an "important" person, the plays and poems seem clearly to have been produced by a man from Stratford-upon-Avon with a very good "grammar-school" education and a life of experience in London and in the world of the London theater. How this particular man produced the works that dominate the cultures of much of the world almost four hundred years after his death is one of life's mysteries—and one that will continue to tease our imaginations as we continue to delight in his plays and poems.

Shakespeare's Theater

The actors of Shakespeare's time performed plays in a great variety of locations. They played at court (that is, in the great halls of such royal residences as Whitehall, Hampton Court, and Greenwich); they played in halls at the universities of Oxford and Cambridge, and at the Inns of Court (the residences in London of the legal societies); and they also played in the private houses of great lords and civic officials. Sometimes acting companies went on tour from London into the provinces, often (but not only) when outbreaks of bubonic plague in the capital forced the closing of theaters to reduce the possibility of contagion in crowded audiences. In the provinces the actors usually staged their plays in churches (until around 1600) or in guildhalls. While surviving records show only a handful of occasions when actors played at inns while on tour, London inns were important playing places up until the 1590s.

The building of theaters in London had begun only shortly before Shakespeare wrote his first plays in the 1590s. These theaters were of two kinds: outdoor or public playhouses that could accommodate large numbers of playgoers, and indoor or private theaters for much smaller audiences. What is usually regarded as the first London outdoor public playhouse was called simply the Theatre. James Burbage—the father of Richard Burbage, who was perhaps the most famous actor in Shakespeare's company—built it in 1576 in an area north of the city of London called Shoreditch. Among the more famous of the other public playhouses that capitalized on the new fashion were the Curtain and the Fortune (both also built north of the city), the Rose, the Swan, the Globe, and the Hope (all located on the Bankside, a region just across the Thames south of the city of London). All these playhouses had to be built outside the jurisdiction of the city of London because many civic officials were hostile to the performance of drama and repeatedly petitioned the royal council to abolish it.

The theaters erected on the Bankside (a region

under the authority of the Church of England, whose head was the monarch) shared the neighborhood with houses of prostitution and with the Paris Garden, where the blood sports of bearbaiting and bullbaiting were carried on. There may have been no clear distinction between playhouses and buildings for such sports, for the Hope was used for both plays and baiting, and Philip Henslowe, owner of the Rose and, later, partner in the ownership of the Fortune, was also a partner in a monopoly on baiting. All these forms of entertainment were easily accessible to Londoners by boat across the Thames or over London Bridge.

Evidently Shakespeare's company prospered on the Bankside. They moved there in 1599. Threatened by difficulties in renewing the lease on the land where their first playhouse (the Theatre) had been built, Shakespeare's company took advantage of the Christmas holiday in 1598 to dismantle the Theatre and transport its timbers across the Thames to the Bankside, where, in 1599, these timbers were used in the building of the Globe. The weather in late December 1598 is recorded as having been especially harsh. It was so cold that the Thames was "nigh [nearly] frozen," and there was heavy snow. Perhaps the weather aided Shakespeare's company in eluding their landlord, the snow hiding their activity and the freezing of the Thames allowing them to slide the timbers across to the Bankside without paying tolls for repeated trips over London Bridge. Attractive as this narrative is, it remains just as likely that the heavy snow hampered transport of the timbers in wagons through the London streets to the river. It also must be remembered that the Thames was, according to report, only "nigh frozen" and therefore as impassable as it ever was. Whatever the precise circumstances of this fascinating

A stage play.
From [William Alabaster,] *Roxana tragœdia* . . . (1632).

event in English theater history, Shakespeare's company was able to begin playing at their new Globe theater on the Bankside in 1599. After the first Globe burned down in 1613 during the staging of Shakespeare's *Henry VIII* (its thatch roof was set alight by cannon fire called for by the performance), Shakespeare's company immediately rebuilt on the same location. The second Globe seems to have been a grander structure than its predecessor. It remained in use until the beginning of the English Civil War in 1642, when Parliament officially closed the theaters. Soon thereafter it was pulled down.

The public theaters of Shakespeare's time were very different buildings from our theaters today. First of all, they were open-air playhouses. As recent excavations of the Rose and the Globe confirm, some were polygonal or roughly circular in shape; the Fortune, however, was square. The most recent estimates of their size put the diameter of these buildings at 72 feet (the Rose) to 100 feet (the Globe), but they were said to hold vast audiences of two or three thousand, who must have been squeezed together quite tightly. Some of these spectators paid extra to sit or stand in the two or three levels of roofed galleries that extended, on the upper levels, all the way around the theater and surrounded an open space. In this space were the stage and, perhaps, the tiring house (what we would call dressing rooms), as well as the so-called yard. In the yard stood the spectators who chose to pay less, the ones whom Hamlet contemptuously called "groundlings." For a roof they had only the sky, and so they were exposed to all kinds of weather. They stood on a floor that was sometimes made of mortar and sometimes of ash mixed with the shells of hazelnuts. The latter provided a porous and therefore dry footing for the crowd, and the shells may have been more comfortable to stand on because they were not as hard as mortar. Availability of shells may not have been a problem if hazelnuts were a favorite food for Shakespeare's audiences to munch on as they watched his plays. Archaeologists who are today unearthing the remains of theaters from this period have discovered quantities of these nutshells on theater sites.

Unlike the yard, the stage itself was covered by a roof. Its ceiling, called "the heavens," is thought to have been elaborately painted to depict the sun, moon, stars, and planets. Just how big the stage was remains hard to determine. We have a single sketch of part of the interior of the Swan. A Dutchman named Johannes de Witt visited this theater around 1596 and sent a sketch of it back to his friend, Arend van Buchel. Because van Buchel found de Witt's letter and sketch of interest, he copied both into a book. It is van Buchel's copy, adapted, it seems, to the shape and size of the page in his book, that survives. In this sketch, the stage appears to be a large rectangular platform that thrusts far out into the yard, perhaps even as far as the center of the circle formed by the surrounding galleries. This drawing, combined with the specifications for the size of the stage in the building contract for the Fortune, has led scholars to conjecture that the stage on which Shakespeare's plays were performed must have measured approximately 43 feet in width and 27 feet in depth, a vast acting area. But the digging up of a large part of the Rose by archaeologists has provided evidence of a quite different stage design. The Rose stage was a platform tapered at the corners and much shallower than what seems to be depicted in the van Buchel sketch. Indeed, its measurements seem to be about 37.5 feet across at its widest point and only 15.5

feet deep. Because the surviving indications of stage size and design differ from each other so much, it is possible that the stages in other playhouses, like the Theatre, the Curtain, and the Globe (the outdoor playhouses where Shakespeare's plays were performed), were different from those at both the Swan and the Rose.

After about 1608 Shakespeare's plays were staged not only at the Globe but also at an indoor or private playhouse in Blackfriars. This theater had been constructed in 1596 by James Burbage in an upper hall of a former Dominican priory or monastic house. Although Henry VIII had dissolved all English monasteries in the 1530s (shortly after he had founded the Church of England), the area remained under church, rather than hostile civic, control. The hall that Burbage had purchased and renovated was a large one in which Parliament had once met. In the private theater that he constructed, the stage, lit by candles, was built across the narrow end of the hall, with boxes flanking it. The rest of the hall offered seating room only. Because there was no provision for standing room, the largest audience it could hold was less than a thousand, or about a quarter of what the Globe could accommodate. Admission to Blackfriars was correspondingly more expensive. Instead of a penny to stand in the yard at the Globe, it cost a minimum of sixpence to get into Blackfriars. The best seats at the Globe (in the Lords' Room in the gallery above and behind the stage) cost sixpence; but the boxes flanking the stage at Blackfriars were half a crown, or five times sixpence. Some spectators who were particularly interested in displaying themselves paid even more to sit on stools on the Blackfriars stage.

Whether in the outdoor or indoor playhouses, the

stages of Shakespeare's time were different from ours. They were not separated from the audience by the dropping of a curtain between acts and scenes. Therefore the playwrights of the time had to find other ways of signaling to the audience that one scene (to be imagined as occurring in one location at a given time) had ended and the next (to be imagined at perhaps a different location at a later time) had begun. The customary way used by Shakespeare and many of his contemporaries was to have everyone onstage exit at the end of one scene and have one or more different characters enter to begin the next. In a few cases, where characters remain onstage from one scene to another, the dialogue or stage action makes the change of location clear, and the characters are generally to be imagined as having moved from one place to another. For example, in *Romeo and Juliet,* Romeo and his friends remain onstage in Act 1 from scene 4 to scene 5, but they are represented as having moved between scenes from the street that leads to Capulet's house into Capulet's house itself. The new location is signaled in part by the appearance onstage of Capulet's servingmen carrying napkins, something they would not take into the streets. Playwrights had to be quite resourceful in the use of hand properties, like the napkin, or in the use of dialogue to specify where the action was taking place in their plays because, in contrast to most of today's theaters, the playhouses of Shakespeare's time did not use movable scenery to dress the stage and make the setting precise. As another consequence of this difference, however, the playwrights of Shakespeare's time did not have to specify exactly where the action of their plays was set when they did not choose to do so, and much of the action of their plays is tied to no specific place.

Usually Shakespeare's stage is referred to as a "bare stage," to distinguish it from the stages of the last two or three centuries with their elaborate sets. But the stage in Shakespeare's time was not completely bare. Philip Henslowe, owner of the Rose, lists in his inventory of stage properties a rock, three tombs, and two mossy banks. Stage directions in plays of the time also call for such things as thrones (or "states"), banquets (presumably tables with plaster replicas of food on them), and beds and tombs to be pushed onto the stage. Thus the stage often held more than the actors.

The actors did not limit their performing to the stage alone. Occasionally they went beneath the stage, as the Ghost appears to do in the first act of *Hamlet*. From there they could emerge onto the stage through a trapdoor. They could retire behind the hangings across the back of the stage (or the front of the tiring house), as, for example, the actor playing Polonius does when he hides behind the arras. Sometimes the hangings could be drawn back during a performance to "discover" one or more actors behind them. When performance required that an actor appear "above," as when Juliet is imagined to stand at the window of her chamber in the famous and misnamed "balcony scene," then the actor probably climbed the stairs to the gallery over the back of the stage and temporarily shared it with some of the spectators. The stage was also provided with ropes and winches so that actors could descend from, and reascend to, the "heavens."

Perhaps the greatest difference between dramatic performances in Shakespeare's time and ours was that in Shakespeare's England the roles of women were played by boys. (Some of these boys grew up to take male roles in their maturity.) There were no women in the acting companies, only in the audience. It had not always been so in the history of the English stage. There are records of women on English stages in the thirteenth and fourteenth centuries, two hundred years before Shakespeare's plays were performed. After the accession of James I in 1603, the queen of England and her ladies took part in entertainments at court called masques, and with the reopening of the theaters in 1660 at the restoration of Charles II, women again took their place on the public stage.

The chief competitors for the companies of adult actors such as the one to which Shakespeare belonged and for which he wrote were companies of exclusively boy actors. The competition was most intense in the early 1600s. There were then two principal children's companies: the Children of Paul's (the choirboys from St. Paul's Cathedral, whose private playhouse was near the cathedral); and the Children of the Chapel Royal (the choirboys from the monarch's private chapel, who performed at the Blackfriars theater built by Burbage in 1596, which Shakespeare's company had been stopped from using by local residents who objected to crowds). In *Hamlet* Shakespeare writes of "an aerie [nest] of children, little eyases [hawks], that cry out on the top of question and are most tyrannically clapped for 't. These are now the fashion and . . . berattle the common stages [attack the public theaters]." In the long run, the adult actors prevailed. The Children of Paul's dissolved around 1606. By about 1608 the Children of the Chapel Royal had been forced to stop playing at the Blackfriars theater, which was then taken over by the King's company of players, Shakespeare's own troupe.

Acting companies and theaters of Shakespeare's time were organized in different ways. For example, Philip Henslowe owned the Rose and leased it to companies of actors, who paid him from their takings. Henslowe would act as manager of these companies, initially paying playwrights for their plays and buying properties, recovering his outlay from the actors. With the building of the Globe, Shakespeare's company, however, managed itself, with the principal actors, Shakespeare among them, having the status of "sharers" and the right to a share in the takings, as well as the responsibility for a part of the expenses. Five of the sharers, including Shakespeare, owned the Globe. As actor, as sharer in an acting company and in ownership of theaters, and as playwright, Shakespeare was about as involved in the theatrical industry as one could imagine. Although Shakespeare and his fellows prospered, their status under the law was conditional upon the protection of powerful patrons. "Common players"—those who did not have patrons or masters—were classed in the language of the law with "vagabonds and sturdy beggars." So the actors had to secure for themselves the official rank of servants of patrons. Among the patrons under whose protection Shakespeare's company worked were the lord chamberlain and, after the accession of King James in 1603, the king himself.

We are now perhaps on the verge of learning a great deal more about the theaters in which Shakespeare and his contemporaries performed—or at least of opening up new questions about them. Already about 70 percent of the Rose has been excavated, as has about 10 percent of the second Globe, the one built in 1614. It is to be hoped that soon more will be available for study. These are exciting times for students of Shakespeare's stage.

The Publication of Shakespeare's Plays

Eighteen of Shakespeare's plays found their way into print during the playwright's lifetime, but there is nothing to suggest that he took any interest in their publication. These eighteen appeared separately in editions called quartos. Their pages were not much larger than the one you are now reading, and these little books were sold unbound for a few pence. The earliest of the quartos that still survive were printed in 1594, the year that both *Titus Andronicus* and a version of the play now called *2 King Henry VI* became available. While almost every one of these early quartos displays on its title page the name of the acting company that performed the play, only about half provide the name of the playwright, Shakespeare. The first quarto edition to bear the name Shakespeare on its title page is *Love's Labor's Lost* of 1598. A few of these quartos were popular with the book-buying public of Shakespeare's lifetime; for example, quarto *Richard II* went through five editions between 1597 and 1615. But most of the quartos were far from best-sellers; *Love's Labor's Lost* (1598), for instance, was not reprinted in quarto until 1631. After Shakespeare's death, two more of his plays appeared in quarto format: *Othello* in 1622 and *The Two Noble Kinsmen*, coauthored with John Fletcher, in 1634.

In 1623, seven years after Shakespeare's death, *Mr. William Shakespeares Comedies, Histories, & Tragedies* was published. This printing offered readers in a single book thirty-six of the thirty-eight plays now thought to have been written by Shakespeare, including eighteen that had never been printed before. And it offered them in a style that was then reserved for serious literature and scholarship. The plays were arranged in double columns on pages nearly a foot high. This large page size is called "folio," as opposed to the smaller "quarto," and the 1623 volume is usually called the Shakespeare First Folio. It is reputed to have sold for the lordly price of a pound. (One copy at the Folger Library is marked fifteen shillings—that is, three-quarters of a pound.)

In a preface to the First Folio entitled "To the great Variety of Readers," two of Shakespeare's former fellow actors in the King's Men, John Heminge and Henry Condell, wrote that they themselves had collected their dead companion's plays. They suggested that they had seen his own papers: "we have scarce received from him a blot in his papers." The title page of the Folio declared that the plays within it had been printed "according to the True Original Copies." Comparing the Folio to the quartos, Heminge and Condell disparaged the quartos, advising their readers that "before you were abused with divers stolen and surreptitious copies, maimed, and deformed by the frauds and stealths of injurious impostors." Many Shakespeareans of the eighteenth and nineteenth centuries believed Heminge and Condell and regarded the Folio plays as superior to anything in the quartos.

Once we begin to examine the Folio plays in detail, it becomes less easy to take at face value the word of Heminge and Condell about the superiority of the Folio texts. For example, of the first nine plays in the Folio (one-quarter of the entire collection), four were essentially reprinted from earlier quarto printings that Heminge and Condell had disparaged; and four have now been identified as printed from copies written in the hand of a professional scribe of the 1620s named Ralph Crane; the ninth, *The Comedy of Errors*, was apparently also printed from a manuscript, but one whose origin cannot be readily identified. Evidently then, eight of the first nine plays in the First Folio were not printed, in spite of what the Folio title page announces, "according to the True Original Copies," or Shakespeare's own papers, and the source of the ninth is unknown. Since today's editors have been forced to treat Heminge and Condell's pronouncements with skepticism, they must choose whether to base their own editions upon quartos or the Folio on grounds other than Heminge and Condell's story of where the quarto and Folio versions originated.

Editors have often fashioned their own narratives to explain what lies behind the quartos and Folio. They have said that Heminge and Condell meant to criticize only a few of the early quartos, the ones that offer much shorter and sometimes quite different, often garbled, versions of plays. Among the examples of these are the 1600 quarto of *Henry V* (the Folio offers a much fuller version) or the 1603 *Hamlet* quarto (in 1604 a different, much longer form of the play got into print as a quarto). Early-twentieth-century editors speculated that these questionable texts were produced when someone in the audience took notes from the plays' dialogue during performances and then employed "hack poets" to fill out the notes. The poor results were then sold to a publisher and presented in print as Shakespeare's plays. More recently this story has given way to another in which the shorter versions are said to be re-creations from memory of Shakespeare's plays by actors who wanted to stage them in the provinces but lacked manuscript copies. Most of the quartos offer much better texts than these so-called bad quartos. Indeed, in most of the quartos we find texts that are at least equal to or better than what is printed in the Folio. Many Shakespeare enthusiasts persuaded themselves that most of the quartos were set into type directly from Shakespeare's own papers, although there is nothing on which to base this conclusion except the desire for it to be true. Thus speculation continues about how the Shakespeare plays got to be printed. All that we have are the printed texts.

The book collector who was most successful in bringing together copies of the quartos and the First Folio was Henry Clay Folger, founder of the Folger Shakespeare Library in Washington, D.C. While it is estimated that there survive around the world only about 230 copies of the First Folio, Mr. Folger was able to acquire more than seventy-five copies, as well as a large number of fragments, for the library that bears his name. He also amassed a substantial number of quartos. For example, only fourteen copies of the First Quarto of *Love's Labor's Lost* are known to exist, and three are at the Folger Shakespeare Library. As a consequence of Mr. Folger's labors, scholars visiting the Folger Library have been able to learn a great deal about sixteenth- and seventeenth-century printing and, particularly, about the printing of Shakespeare's plays. And Mr. Folger did not stop at the First Folio, but collected many copies of later editions of Shakespeare, beginning with the Second Folio (1632), the Third (1663–64), and the Fourth (1685). Each of these later folios was based on its immediate predecessor and was edited anonymously. The first editor of Shakespeare whose name we know was Nicholas Rowe, whose first edition came out in 1709. Mr. Folger collected this edition and many, many more by Rowe's successors.

An Introduction to This Text

All's Well That Ends Well was first printed in the 1623 collection of Shakespeare's plays now known as the First Folio. The present edition is based directly upon that printing.* For the convenience of the reader, we have modernized the punctuation and the spelling of the Folio. Sometimes we go so far as to modernize certain old forms of words; for example, usually when *a* means *he*, we change it to *he*; we change *mo* to *more*, and *ye* to *you*. But it is not our practice in editing any of the plays to modernize words that sound distinctly different from modern forms. For example, when the early printed texts read *sith* or *apricocks* or *porpentine*, we have not modernized to *since, apricots, porcupine.* When the forms *an, and,* or *and if* appear instead of the modern form *if,* we have reduced *and* to *an* but have not changed any of these forms to their modern equivalent, *if.* We also modernize and, where necessary, correct passages in foreign languages, unless an error in the early printed text can be reasonably explained as a joke.

Whenever we change the wording of the First Folio or add anything to its stage directions, we mark the change by enclosing it in superior half-brackets (⌐ ⌐). We want our readers to be immediately aware when we have intervened. (Only when we correct an obvious typographical error in the First Folio does the change

---

*We have also consulted the computerized text of the First Folio provided by the Text Archive of the Oxford University Computing Centre, to which we are grateful.

not get marked.) Whenever we change either the First Folio's wording or its punctuation so that meaning changes, we list the change in the textual notes at the back of the book, even if all we have done is fix an obvious error.

We, like other editors of the play, regularize the proper names. Sometimes the regularization applies only to the spelling. *Parolles*, for example, is sometimes printed as "Parolles" and sometimes as "Parrolles" in the Folio, but we always use the spelling "Parolles." Sometimes the regularization involves decisions about what the character should be called. In the Folio text, for example, more often than not the character Helen enters and speaks (according to Folio stage directions and dialogue) under the name "Helen" or "Hellen." Occasionally she appears or is addressed as "Helena" or "Helana." (Her speech prefixes are always *"Hel."* or *"Hell."*) Beginning with Nicholas Rowe in 1709, most editors have used the name "Helena" for this character throughout their editions. Since, as Susan Snyder points out in her 1993 Oxford edition of the play, the name "Helen" appears in stage directions and dialogue twenty-five times (in contrast to the four times the name "Helena" appears), we employ the proper name "Helen" throughout this edition. Two other characters, while consistently presented in the Folio under generic names ("Clown," "Steward"), are each given, on a single occasion, a proper name ("Lavatch," "Rinaldo"). Some recent editors substitute these proper names for the generic names throughout their texts. We have chosen to follow the Folio's generic designations, substituting the designation "Fool" for the Folio's "Clown." (The Folio's designation "Clown" probably indicates only that the part was played by the theatrical company's comic actor. However, the character's function in the play is that of the professional jester or Fool.)

This edition differs from many earlier ones in its efforts to aid the reader in imagining the play as a performance rather than as a series of actual events. One of the features of performance is often the refusal to differentiate onstage among secondary characters, who are frequently interchangeable. This is certainly the case with the pair of characters, variously called the "Frenchmen" or "French Captains" or "French Lords" in the Folio's stage directions, who speak in this edition after the designations FIRST LORD and SECOND LORD. Perhaps their principal task in the play is to plan and carry out the exposure of Parolles. However, only one of them can actually capture Parolles in 4.1, because the other is asked by Bertram to accompany him to his rendezvous with Diana. The Folio's initial entrance for 4.1 captures in its indeterminacy the theatrical practice of refusing to differentiate secondary characters: *"Enter one of the Frenchmen, with fiue or sixe other souldiers in ambush."* Unlike most twentieth-century editors, we have preserved the Folio's indeterminacy by altering the stage direction only slightly, changing *"Frenchmen"* to *"French Lords."* (For a detailed discussion of the editorial problem of the "French Lords" in terms of stage practice of Shakespeare's time, see Paul Werstine's *"All's Well That Ends Well* and Editorial Constructions of 'Foul Papers'"* in the 2001 volume of the journal *Archiv.*)

Whenever it is reasonably certain, in our view, that a speech is accompanied by a particular action, we provide a stage direction describing the action, setting the added direction in brackets to signal that it is not found in the Folio. (Occasional exceptions to this rule occur when the action is so obvious that to add a stage direction would insult the reader.) Stage directions for the entrance of a character in mid-scene are, with rare exceptions, placed so that they immediately precede the character's participation in the scene, even though these entrances may appear somewhat earlier in the early printed texts. Whenever we move a stage direction, we record this change in the textual notes. Latin stage directions (e.g., *Exeunt*) are translated into English (e.g., *They exit*).

We expand the often severely abbreviated forms of names used as speech headings in early printed texts into the full names of the characters. We also regularize the speakers' names in speech headings, using only a single designation for each character, even though the early printed texts sometimes use a variety of designations. Variations in the speech headings of the early printed texts are recorded in the textual notes.

In the present edition, as well, we mark with a dash any change of address within a speech, unless a stage direction intervenes. When the -ed ending of a word is to be pronounced, we mark it with an accent. Like editors for the past two centuries, we print metrically linked lines in the following way:

HELEN
   Mine honorable mistress.
COUNTESS   Nay, a mother.
                         (1.3.141–42)

However, when there are a number of short verse-lines that can be linked in more than one way, we do not, with rare exceptions, indent any of them.

The Explanatory Notes

The notes that appear on the pages facing the text are designed to provide readers with the help that they may need to enjoy the play. Whenever the meaning of a word in the text is not readily accessible in a good contemporary dictionary, we offer the meaning in a note. Sometimes we provide a note even when the relevant meaning is to be found in the dictionary but when the word has acquired since Shakespeare's time other potentially confusing meanings. In our notes, we try to offer modern synonyms for Shakespeare's words. We also try to indicate to the reader the connection between the word in the play and the modern synonym. For example, Shakespeare sometimes uses the word *head* to mean *source*, but, for modern readers, there may be no connection evident between these two words. We provide the connection by explaining Shakespeare's usage as follows: "**head:** fountainhead, source." On some occasions, a whole phrase or clause needs explanation. Then we rephrase in our own words the difficult passage, and add at the end synonyms for individual words in the passage. When scholars have been unable to determine the meaning of a word or phrase, we acknowledge the uncertainty.

ALL'S WELL
THAT ENDS WELL

Characters in the Play

HELEN, a gentlewoman of Rossillion

BERTRAM, Count of Rossillion

COUNTESS of Rossillion, Bertram's mother

STEWARD ⎫
FOOL ⎬ *in the Countess's household*
PAGE ⎭

PAROLLES, companion to Bertram

KING of France
LAFEW, a French lord
FIRST LORD ⎫ *later Captains in the*
SECOND LORD ⎭ *army of the Duke of Florence*
Other LORDS in the court of the King of France
FIRST GENTLEMAN
SECOND GENTLEMAN ⎫ *from the court of*
GENTLEMAN, a "gentle Astringer" ⎭ *the King of France*
FIRST SOLDIER, interpreter

The DUKE of Florence
A WIDOW of Florence
DIANA, the Widow's daughter
MARIANA, the Widow's neighbor

Attendants, Soldiers, Citizens of Florence, Servants

3

ALL'S WELL THAT ENDS WELL

ACT 1

1.1 Bertram, having become a ward of the court upon his father's death, departs from Rossillion. Helen, whose own physician-father has recently died, knows that her hidden love for Bertram can never be requited because of their difference in social rank, but decides that the King's disease may offer her a chance to "show her merit."

---

0 SD. Rossillion: a region in the south of France, on the border with Spain and near the Mediterranean

1. **delivering:** sending forth, handing over, surrendering (with wordplay on "giving birth")

4. **attend:** pay heed to

5. **in ward:** legally subject (Under feudal law, fatherless heirs to estates came under the guardianship of the king until reaching legal age.)

7. **of:** i.e., in the person **of**

8. **so generally:** without exception

9. **hold:** keep unbroken; **to:** toward

10. **wanted:** i.e., was lacking

14. **abandoned:** renounced

15. **practices:** professional attentions (though perhaps with wordplay on the more general sense of trickery and treacherous dealings); **persecuted time:** i.e., made his days miserable

19. **passage:** (1) event; (2) death

20–21. **had . . . would:** i.e., if his **skill** had matched his integrity, it **would**

22. **have play:** be idle; **Would:** i.e., I wish

ACT 1

Scene 1

Enter young Bertram Count of Rossillion, his mother
⌜*the Countess,*⌝ *and Helen, Lord Lafew, all in black.*

COUNTESS In delivering my son from me, I bury a second husband.

BERTRAM And I in going, madam, weep o'er my father's death anew; but I must attend his Majesty's command, to whom I am now in ward, evermore in subjection. 5

LAFEW You shall find of the King a husband, madam; you, sir, a father. He that so generally is at all times good must of necessity hold his virtue to you, whose worthiness would stir it up where it wanted rather than lack it where there is such abundance. 10

COUNTESS What hope is there of his Majesty's amendment?

LAFEW He hath abandoned his physicians, madam, under whose practices he hath persecuted time with hope, and finds no other advantage in the process but only the losing of hope by time. 15

COUNTESS This young gentlewoman had a father—O, that "had," how sad a passage 'tis!—whose skill was almost as great as his honesty; had it stretched so far, would have made nature immortal, and death should have play for lack of work. Would for 20

23. **he:** i.e., the gentlewoman's **father** (line 18)

32. **set up:** incited

35. **fistula:** long, pipelike ulcer in any part of the body (though in the story that served as Shakespeare's source, the **fistula** was on the King's breast)

37. **notorious:** public knowledge

40. **overlooking:** supervision

41. **dispositions:** mental tendencies, qualities

45–46. **simpleness:** innocence (i.e., not carried by **an unclean mind** [lines 42–43])

50. **season:** preserve, keep fresh (**Brine** is saltwater used for preserving food.)

53. **livelihood:** liveliness

54. **Go to:** an expression of impatience

55. **affect a sorrow:** (1) i.e., enjoy grieving; (2) display your grief ostentatiously; **have—:** The Folio's dash here may indicate that the Countess pauses under the effect of her own grief, since it is highly unlikely that Helen would interrupt the Countess.

56. **affect a sorrow indeed:** See longer note, page 221.

the King's sake he were living! I think it would be
the death of the King's disease.

LAFEW How called you the man you speak of,   25
madam?

COUNTESS He was famous, sir, in his profession, and it
was his great right to be so: Gerard de Narbon.

LAFEW He was excellent indeed, madam. The King
very lately spoke of him admiringly, and mourn-   30
ingly. He was skillful enough to have lived still, if
knowledge could be set up against mortality.

BERTRAM What is it, my good lord, the King lan-
guishes of?

LAFEW A fistula, my lord.   35

BERTRAM I heard not of it before.

LAFEW I would it were not notorious.—Was this gentlewoman the daughter of Gerard de Narbon?

COUNTESS His sole child, my lord, and bequeathed to
my overlooking. I have those hopes of her good   40
that her education promises. Her dispositions she
inherits, which makes fair gifts fairer; for where an
unclean mind carries virtuous qualities, there
commendations go with pity—they are virtues and
traitors too. In her they are the better for their sim-   45
pleness. She derives her honesty and achieves her
goodness.

LAFEW Your commendations, madam, get from her
tears.

COUNTESS 'Tis the best brine a maiden can season her   50
praise in. The remembrance of her father never
approaches her heart but the tyranny of her sor-
rows takes all livelihood from her cheek.—No
more of this, Helena. Go to. No more, lest it be
rather thought you affect a sorrow than to have—   55

HELEN I do affect a sorrow indeed, but I have it too.

LAFEW Moderate lamentation is the right of the dead,
excessive grief the enemy to the living.

59. **be enemy to:** i.e., resist
60. **makes . . . mortal:** i.e., quickly destroys it
62. **How . . . that:** Editors have not solved the mystery of why Lafew asks this question.
63–66. **succeed . . . birthright:** i.e., may your acquired qualities resemble your inherited graces **manners:** behavior, moral character **shape:** appearance **blood:** i.e., noble birth
67. **Be able for:** i.e., have enough power (to defeat)
68. **Rather . . . use:** i.e., in potentiality **rather than** in action
69, 70. **checked, taxed:** reproved, reprimanded
70. **more will:** i.e., determines in addition
75. **want:** lack; **best:** perhaps, **best** advice
80. **comfortable:** comforting, consoling
82. **hold:** uphold; **credit:** reputation
84. **on:** of
85. **grace his remembrance:** honor his memory (Helen may be referring to Bertram, though if so the point would have to be conveyed to the audience through a gesture, since she has not yet mentioned Bertram's name.)
86. **for him:** i.e., **for** my father at his death
88. **favor:** face, countenance
89. **undone:** lost, destroyed
90. **'Twere all one:** i.e., it would be the same
91. **That I should love:** i.e., if I loved

COUNTESS If the living be enemy to the grief, the
    excess makes it soon mortal.   60

BERTRAM Madam, I desire your holy wishes.

LAFEW How understand we that?

COUNTESS
    Be thou blessed, Bertram, and succeed thy father
    In manners as in shape. Thy blood and virtue
    Contend for empire in thee, and thy goodness   65
    Share with thy birthright. Love all, trust a few,
    Do wrong to none. Be able for thine enemy
    Rather in power than use, and keep thy friend
    Under thy own life's key. Be checked for silence,
    But never taxed for speech. What heaven more will,   70
    That thee may furnish and my prayers pluck down,
    Fall on thy head. ⌜*To Lafew.*⌝ Farewell, my lord.
    'Tis an unseasoned courtier. Good my lord,
    Advise him.

LAFEW   He cannot want the best that shall   75
    Attend his love.

COUNTESS Heaven bless him.—Farewell, Bertram.

BERTRAM The best wishes that can be forged in your
    thoughts be servants to you.   ⌜*Countess exits.*⌝
    ⌜*To Helen.*⌝ Be comfortable to my mother, your   80
    mistress, and make much of her.

LAFEW Farewell, pretty lady. You must hold the credit
    of your father.   ⌜*Bertram and Lafew exit.*⌝

HELEN
    O, were that all! I think not on my father,
    And these great tears grace his remembrance more   85
    Than those I shed for him. What was he like?
    I have forgot him. My imagination
    Carries no favor in 't but Bertram's.
    I am undone. There is no living, none,
    If Bertram be away. 'Twere all one   90
    That I should love a bright particular star
    And think to wed it, he is so above me.

93. **collateral:** attendant, accompanying

94. **his sphere:** i.e., the transparent hollow globe which carries the **star** around the earth (in the Ptolemaic image of the universe) See page xxxiv.

96. **hind:** female deer (but with possible word-play on **hind** as "servant")

97. **pretty:** pleasing; **a plague:** i.e., distressing, painful

99. **hawking:** hawklike, keen

100. **table:** perhaps, the board on which a picture is painted; or, perhaps, a table-book or tablet (See Sonnet 24: "Mine eye hath played the painter and hath stelled / Thy beauty's form in **table** of my heart.") See picture, page 120.

100–101. **capable / Of:** able to (1) take in, hold; or (2) perceive

101. **trick:** characteristic expression

106. **a great way fool:** i.e., largely **a fool**

107. **fit:** fitly, suitably

108. **take place:** find acceptance

109. **Looks:** i.e., look; **Withal:** besides

111. **Save:** i.e., God save

116. **stain:** slight trace or tinge

118. **barricado it:** i.e., fortify **it** as with barri-cades

121. **Unfold:** disclose, explain

124. **blow you up:** wordplay on (1) "destroy you by means of an explosion" and (2) "impregnate you" (Sexual double-meanings are present throughout much of this dialogue.)

In his bright radiance and collateral light
Must I be comforted, not in his sphere.
Th' ambition in my love thus plagues itself: 95
The hind that would be mated by the lion
Must die for love. 'Twas pretty, though a plague,
To see him every hour, to sit and draw
His archèd brows, his hawking eye, his curls
In our heart's table—heart too capable   100
Of every line and trick of his sweet favor.
But now he's gone, and my idolatrous fancy
Must sanctify his relics. Who comes here?

Enter Parolles.

One that goes with him. I love him for his sake,
And yet I know him a notorious liar,   105
Think him a great way fool, solely a coward.
Yet these fixed evils sit so fit in him
That they take place when virtue's steely bones
Looks bleak i' th' cold wind. Withal, full oft we see
Cold wisdom waiting on superfluous folly.   110

PAROLLES   Save you, fair queen.

HELEN   And you, monarch.

PAROLLES   No.

HELEN   And no.

PAROLLES   Are you meditating on virginity?   115

HELEN   Ay. You have some stain of soldier in you; let
me ask you a question. Man is enemy to virginity.
How may we barricado it against him?

PAROLLES   Keep him out.

HELEN   But he assails, and our virginity, though   120
valiant in the defense, yet is weak. Unfold to us
some warlike resistance.

PAROLLES   There is none. Man setting down before you
will undermine you and blow you up.

HELEN   Bless our poor virginity from underminers and   125
blowers-up! Is there no military policy how virgins
might blow up men?

129. **Marry:** i.e., indeed (originally a mild oath on the name of the Virgin Mary)

131. **politic:** judicious; expedient

133. **rational increase:** a puzzling phrase, for which editors have proposed the following meanings: (1) reasonable **increase;** (2) **increase** in the number of **rational** beings; (3) sensible profit-making

134. **got:** begotten

134–35. **That you were:** i.e., **that** which you are

135. **metal:** (1) substance, stuff (with wordplay on *mettle* meaning "disposition" or "temperament"); (2) precious **metal,** used to make coins (The connection between reproduction and coining, a familiar one, leads to further economic metaphors in lines 153–55.)

139. **stand for:** uphold, support

141. **in 't:** i.e., in its defense

142. **on the part of:** in behalf of

143. **infallible:** certain

144. **He . . . virgin:** i.e., **a virgin** is like one who commits suicide

145–46. **buried . . . limit:** Suicides were forbidden burial in consecrated ground. **limit:** i.e., ground

149. **paring:** rind; **his:** i.e., its

151. **inhibited:** forbidden, prohibited

151–52. **the canon:** i.e., ecclesiastical law

153. **Out with 't:** (1) get rid of it; (2) put it out for interest

158. **ill:** unhappily, unfortunately (Parolles responds as if Helen's **How might one do** [line 156] had meant "in what condition or state **might one** be" rather than "by what means **might one.**")

160. **lying:** remaining unused or untouched

(continued)

14

PAROLLES Virginity being blown down, man will
quicklier be blown up. Marry, in blowing him
down again, with the breach yourselves made you   130
lose your city. It is not politic in the common-
wealth of nature to preserve virginity. Loss of virginity is rational increase, and there was never
virgin ⌜got⌝ till virginity was first lost. That you
were made of is metal to make virgins. Virginity by   135
being once lost may be ten times found; by being
ever kept, it is ever lost. 'Tis too cold a companion.
Away with 't.
HELEN I will stand for 't a little, though therefore I
die a virgin.   140
PAROLLES There's little can be said in 't. 'Tis against the
rule of nature. To speak on the part of virginity is
to accuse your mothers, which is most infallible
disobedience. He that hangs himself is a virgin;
virginity murders itself and should be buried in   145
highways out of all sanctified limit as a desperate
offendress against nature. Virginity breeds mites,
much like a cheese, consumes itself to the very
paring, and so dies with feeding his own stomach.
Besides, virginity is peevish, proud, idle, made of   150
self-love, which is the most inhibited sin in the
canon. Keep it not; you cannot choose but lose by
't. Out with 't! Within ten year it will make itself
two, which is a goodly increase, and the principal
itself not much the worse. Away with 't!   155
HELEN How might one do, sir, to lose it to her own
liking?
PAROLLES Let me see. Marry, ill, to like him that ne'er
it likes. 'Tis a commodity will lose the gloss with
lying; the longer kept, the less worth. Off with 't   160
while 'tis vendible; answer the time of request. Virginity, like an old courtier, wears her cap out of
fashion, richly suited but unsuitable, just like the

161. **answer . . . request:** i.e., sell when there is demand

162. **out of:** i.e., when it is no longer in

163. **suited:** attired

164. **wear not now:** i.e., are no longer fashionable (The **toothpick** was for a time worn in the hat as an ornament.)

165–66. **Your date . . . cheek:** wordplay (on **date** as a fruit and as a season or period of time) that means, roughly, it is better to use dates in your cooking than to have age wrinkle your cheeks

170. **Will you:** do you desire or intend

172. **There:** perhaps a reference to **the court** (line 183) or perhaps to her **virginity** (Words or lines may be missing from the text after Helen's **"yet"** [line 171].)

173–79. **mother . . . disaster:** an echo of love poetry of the period, in which the **mistress** is described through extravagant figures of speech (including such oxymora as **his discord dulcet**) **phoenix:** a bird so rare that only one exists at any given time (See picture, page 40.)

179–81. **a world . . . gossips:** i.e., a vast quantity of fine, foolish names as if given by blind **Cupid** at the christenings of adopted children   **fond:** foolish **christendoms:** giving of names, "christenings" **Cupid:** Roman god of love (See picture, page 36.) **gossips:** stands godfather to, gives names to

182. **send him:** i.e., grant that he may be

187. **had not:** i.e., does not have

188. **felt:** perceived

(continued)

16

brooch and the toothpick, which wear not now.
Your date is better in your pie and your porridge   165
than in your cheek. And your virginity, your old
virginity, is like one of our French withered pears:
it looks ill, it eats dryly; marry, 'tis a withered pear.
It was formerly better, marry, yet 'tis a withered
pear. Will you anything with it?   170

HELEN   Not my virginity, yet—
There shall your master have a thousand loves,
A mother, and a mistress, and a friend,
A phoenix, captain, and an enemy,
A guide, a goddess, and a sovereign,   175
A counselor, a traitress, and a dear;
His humble ambition, proud humility,
His jarring concord, and his discord dulcet,
His faith, his sweet disaster, with a world
Of pretty, fond adoptious christendoms   180
That blinking Cupid gossips. Now shall he—
I know not what he shall. God send him well.
The court's a learning place, and he is one—

PAROLLES   What one, i' faith?

HELEN   That I wish well. 'Tis pity—   185

PAROLLES   What's pity?

HELEN
That wishing well had not a body in 't
Which might be felt, that we, the poorer born,
Whose baser stars do shut us up in wishes,
Might with effects of them follow our friends   190
And show what we alone must think, which never
Returns us thanks.

Enter Page.

PAGE   Monsieur Parolles, my lord calls for you.

PAROLLES   Little Helen, farewell. If I can remember
thee, I will think of thee at court.   195

HELEN   Monsieur Parolles, you were born under a
charitable star.

189. **baser stars:** i.e., destiny, which has condemned one to a **baser** (i.e., lower-class) life (In astrological thinking, the position of the **stars,** moon, and planets at the moment of one's birth determines the course of one's life.) See picture, page 134.

190. **effects:** outward manifestations

191. **alone must think:** i.e., can only **think**

191–92. **which . . . thanks:** i.e., for **which** we **never** receive **thanks**

196–97. **under . . . star:** i.e., when a **star** that governs kindness was in the ascendant (See note about astrology, line 189.)

198. **Mars:** i.e., the planet, which is named for the Roman god of war

201. **so kept you under:** i.e., held **you** in such subjection

202. **needs:** necessarily, inevitably

207. **for advantage:** i.e., to gain a superior position (Helen, in the following lines, plays on **advantage** as "personal benefit, increased well-being.")

209. **composition:** combination, mixture (with probable wordplay on "truce")

210. **virtue . . . wing:** i.e., power or quality of strong flight (with possible wordplay on **wing** as the name of an epaulet or shoulder flap, as is suggested in Helen's reference to his **wear,** line 211)

214. **naturalize:** familiarize, accustom

215. **capable of:** able to receive

218. **makes thee away:** i.e., does **away** with you, destroys you

223. **fated sky:** i.e., the heavens, to which we ascribe the power of fate

(continued)

PAROLLES   Under Mars, I.

HELEN   I especially think under Mars.

PAROLLES   Why under Mars?   200

HELEN   The wars hath so kept you under that you
must needs be born under Mars.

PAROLLES   When he was predominant.

HELEN   When he was retrograde, I think rather.

PAROLLES   Why think you so?   205

HELEN   You go so much backward when you fight.

PAROLLES   That's for advantage.

HELEN   So is running away, when fear proposes the
safety. But the composition that your valor and
fear makes in you is a virtue of a good wing, and I   210
like the wear well.

PAROLLES   I am so full of businesses I cannot answer
thee acutely. I will return perfect courtier, in the
which my instruction shall serve to naturalize
thee, so thou wilt be capable of a courtier's counsel   215
and understand what advice shall thrust upon
thee, else thou diest in thine unthankfulness, and
thine ignorance makes thee away. Farewell. When
thou hast leisure, say thy prayers; when thou hast
none, remember thy friends. Get thee a good hus-   220
band, and use him as he uses thee. So, farewell.

⌜*Parolles and Page exit.*⌝

HELEN

Our remedies oft in ourselves do lie
Which we ascribe to heaven. The fated sky
Gives us free scope, only doth backward pull
Our slow designs when we ourselves are dull.   225
What power is it which mounts my love so high,
That makes me see, and cannot feed mine eye?
The mightiest space in fortune nature brings
To join like likes and kiss like native things.
Impossible be strange attempts to those   230
That weigh their pains in sense and do suppose

224. **doth backward pull:** i.e., checks or retards

225. **dull:** slow in motion or action

226. **mounts . . . high:** i.e., raises the aim of **my love** to an object that is **so high**

228. **mightiest . . . fortune:** i.e., largest social disparity; **brings:** perhaps, **brings** them across or through (The syntax is awkward, but the line seems to mean "Nature brings together even those widely separated in social status.")

229. **like likes:** i.e., as if they were equals; **native:** naturally connected

230. **be strange attempts:** i.e., are rare or exceptionally great efforts

231. **in sense:** i.e., rationally; or, perhaps, in terms of what they would suffer in the attempt

1.2 The King of France refuses to take sides in the war between Siena and Florence, giving his courtiers permission to fight on either side. He welcomes Bertram to court, lamenting his own failing strength.

O SD. **Flourish cornets:** i.e., **cornets** sound a fanfare; **letters:** i.e., a letter (Latin *litterae*)

1. **Senoys:** i.e., Sienese; **by th' ears:** i.e., enemies (See longer note, page 221.)

3. **braving war: war** marked by defiance and daring

5. **We:** i.e., I (the royal "we"); **here:** a reference to the letter in his hand

6. **cousin:** a title given by princes to other princes and noblemen

(continued)

What hath been cannot be. Who ever strove
To show her merit that did miss her love?
The King's disease—my project may deceive me,
But my intents are fixed and will not leave me.   235
She exits.

⌜Scene 2⌝

Flourish cornets. Enter the King of France with letters,
⌜*two Lords,*⌝ *and divers Attendants.*

KING
   The Florentines and Senoys are by th' ears,
   Have fought with equal fortune, and continue
   A braving war.
FIRST LORD   So 'tis reported, sir.
KING
   Nay, 'tis most credible. We here receive it   5
   A certainty vouched from our cousin Austria,
   With caution that the Florentine will move us
   For speedy aid, wherein our dearest friend
   Prejudicates the business and would seem
   To have us make denial.   10
FIRST LORD   His love and wisdom,
   Approved so to your Majesty, may plead
   For amplest credence.
KING   He hath armed our answer,
   And Florence is denied before he comes.   15
   Yet for our gentlemen that mean to see
   The Tuscan service, freely have they leave
   To stand on either part.
SECOND LORD   It well may serve
   A nursery to our gentry, who are sick   20
   For breathing and exploit.

   Enter Bertram, Lafew, and Parolles.

KING   What's he comes here?

7. **the Florentine:** i.e., the Duke of Florence; **move us:** appeal to me

8. **our dearest friend:** presumably a reference to the Duke of **Austria**

9. **Prejudicates:** condemns in advance; **would seem:** i.e., thinks fit

12. **Approved:** demonstrated

15. **Florence:** i.e., the Duke of **Florence**

16–17. **to see . . . service:** i.e., to take part in the **Tuscan** war (Both Florence and Siena are in Tuscany.)

18. **To stand . . . part:** i.e., to participate on either side **To stand:** to take up an offensive or defensive position against an enemy

19. **serve:** i.e., **serve** as

20. **nursery to:** learning place for

20–21. **sick . . . exploit:** perhaps, (1) longing for exercise and military enterprise; or, perhaps, (2) in poor condition because of the lack of such activities or exertions

26. **Frank:** bounteous, generous; **curious:** careful, attentive

27. **parts:** qualities

30. **would:** i.e., wish

32. **tried:** put to the test

32–33. **look . . . service:** perhaps, have deep insight into, or long experience of, the art of warfare

33–34. **was / Discipled of:** perhaps, was trained by; or, perhaps, trained

35. **haggish:** i.e., hag-like, ugly, malicious

36. **out of act:** i.e., into inactivity

40. **unnoted:** not noticed, unremarked

(continued)

FIRST LORD
It is the Count Rossillion, my good lord,
Young Bertram.
KING   Youth, thou bear'st thy father's face.   25
Frank nature, rather curious than in haste,
Hath well composed thee. Thy father's moral parts
Mayst thou inherit too. Welcome to Paris.
BERTRAM
My thanks and duty are your Majesty's.
KING
I would I had that corporal soundness now   30
As when thy father and myself in friendship
First tried our soldiership. He did look far
Into the service of the time and was
Discipled of the bravest. He lasted long,
But on us both did haggish age steal on   35
And wore us out of act. It much repairs me
To talk of your good father. In his youth
He had the wit which I can well observe
Today in our young lords; but they may jest
Till their own scorn return to them unnoted   40
Ere they can hide their levity in honor.
So like a courtier, contempt nor bitterness
Were in his pride or sharpness; if they were,
His equal had awaked them, and his honor,
Clock to itself, knew the true minute when   45
Exception bid him speak, and at this time
His tongue obeyed his hand. Who were below him
He used as creatures of another place
And bowed his eminent top to their low ranks,
Making them proud of his humility,   50
In their poor praise he humbled. Such a man
Might be a copy to these younger times,
Which, followed well, would demonstrate them now
But goers backward.
BERTRAM   His good remembrance, sir,   55

41. **hide . . . honor:** i.e., win, by their deeds, a glory that eclipses their frivolity

42–43. **contempt . . . sharpness:** i.e., there was no **contempt** in his **pride** nor **bitterness** (i.e., asperity) in his **sharpness** (i.e., intellectual acuteness)

46. **Exception:** adverse criticism (of him)

47. **obeyed his hand:** perhaps, said no more than **his hand** was ready to put into action; **Who:** i.e., those **who**

48. **used:** treated; **as . . . place:** perhaps, as if they were of his own or higher rank; or, perhaps, with the courtesy due a foreign visitor

49. **top:** head

51. **In . . . humbled:** perhaps, **he** being **humbled** in the presence of their praises

52. **copy:** pattern, example

54. **But goers backward:** i.e., to be merely lapsing into a less perfect or developed state

55. **His good remembrance:** wordplay on **remembrance** as (1) the surviving memory of a person and (2) a memorial inscription

57. **So in approof . . . epitaph:** i.e., the inscription on his tomb is nowhere so confirmed

60. **plausive:** pleasing; commendable

64–65. **On . . . was out:** i.e., when sport or amusement was ended (See longer note, page 221.)

66. **snuff:** charred part of the wick (of a lamp or candle)

67. **apprehensive:** i.e., quick

68–69. **are . . . garments:** i.e., beget nothing but fashion

71. **I, after him:** i.e., I, succeeding **him; after him wish:** i.e., **wish** like **him**

(continued)

Lies richer in your thoughts than on his tomb.
So in approof lives not his epitaph
As in your royal speech.

KING
Would I were with him! He would always say—
Methinks I hear him now; his plausive words   60
He scattered not in ears, but grafted them
To grow there and to bear. "Let me not live"—
This his good melancholy oft began
On the catastrophe and heel of pastime,
When it was out—"Let me not live," quoth he,   65
"After my flame lacks oil, to be the snuff
Of younger spirits, whose apprehensive senses
All but new things disdain, whose judgments are
Mere fathers of their garments, whose constancies
Expire before their fashions." This he wished.   70
I, after him, do after him wish too,
Since I nor wax nor honey can bring home,
I quickly were dissolvèd from my hive
To give some laborers room.

SECOND LORD   You're lovèd, sir.   75
They that least lend it you shall lack you first.

KING
I fill a place, I know 't.—How long is 't, count,
Since the physician at your father's died?
He was much famed.

BERTRAM   Some six months since, my lord.   80

KING
If he were living, I would try him yet.—
Lend me an arm.—The rest have worn me out
With several applications. Nature and sickness
Debate it at their leisure. Welcome, count.
My son's no dearer.   85

BERTRAM   Thank your Majesty.
                         ⌜*They*⌝ *exit. Flourish.*

72. **nor wax:** i.e., neither **wax**
73. **dissolvèd:** set free, detached
76. **lend it you:** perhaps, grant you **room; lack:** miss
83. **several applications:** separate, distinct medical treatments
86 SD. **Flourish:** a fanfare (of cornets)

1.3 Bertram's mother, the Countess of Rossillion, learns of Helen's love for Bertram and forces Helen to confess this secret. When Helen reveals her plan to try to cure the King with medicines left her by her father, the Countess gives Helen permission to go to court, promising to support her in her "attempt."

O SD. **Fool:** a servant who makes his living by amusing his aristocratic patron (The character is called Clown in the Folio. See longer note, page 221.) He enters after the Countess and the Steward, or through a different entrance.
3–4. **even your content:** i.e., make your life unruffled or equable
4. **calendar:** register
9. **sirrah:** term of address to a male social inferior
10. **slowness:** lack of acuteness, stupidity
19. **go to the world:** i.e., get married
20. **woman:** i.e., serving-woman, female attendant; **do as we may:** i.e., get along as best we can (with possible wordplay on **do** as copulate)

(continued)

⌜Scene 3⌝

Enter Countess, Steward, and ⌜*Fool.*⌝

COUNTESS   I will now hear. What say you of this gentlewoman?
STEWARD   Madam, the care I have had to even your
content I wish might be found in the calendar of
my past endeavors, for then we wound our mod-   5
esty and make foul the clearness of our deservings
when of ourselves we publish them.
COUNTESS   What does this knave here? ⌜*To Fool.*⌝ Get
you gone, sirrah. The complaints I have heard of
you I do not all believe. 'Tis my slowness that I do   10
not, for I know you lack not folly to commit them
and have ability enough to make such knaveries
yours.
FOOL   'Tis not unknown to you, madam, I am a poor
fellow.   15
COUNTESS   Well, sir.
FOOL   No, madam, 'tis not so well that I am poor,
though many of the rich are damned. But if I may
have your Ladyship's good will to go to the world,
Isbel the woman and I will do as we may.   20
COUNTESS   Wilt thou needs be a beggar?
FOOL   I do beg your good will in this case.
COUNTESS   In what case?
FOOL   In Isbel's case and mine own. Service is no her-
itage, and I think I shall never have the blessing of   25
God till I have issue o' my body, for they say bairns
are blessings.
COUNTESS   Tell me thy reason why thou wilt marry.
FOOL   My poor body, madam, requires it. I am driven
on by the flesh, and he must needs go that the devil   30
drives.
COUNTESS   Is this all your Worship's reason?
FOOL   Faith, madam, I have other holy reasons, such
as they are.

24. **Isbel's case:** possible wordplay on **case** as genitals

24–25. **Service is no heritage:** proverbial, meaning "servants have little to bequeath"

26. **issue o' my body:** i.e., offspring

26–27. **bairns are blessings:** See Psalm 127.3: "children are an inheritance of the Lord and the fruit of the womb his reward."

30–31. **he . . . drives:** proverbial

33. **holy reasons:** possible wordplay on "hole" as "vagina" and **reasons** as "raisings" or erections

43. **shallow . . . in:** not deeply versed in, not knowledgeable about

45. **ears my land:** ploughs my field (i.e., copulates with my wife); **team:** draught animals (i.e., genitals) See picture, page 200.

46. **in the crop:** harvest the grain (i.e., claim the offspring); **cuckold:** a man whose wife is unfaithful to him (See picture, page 204.)

47–50. **He . . . friend:** See Ephesians 5.28–31: "So ought men to love their wives as their own bodies; he that loveth his wife loveth himself. For no man ever yet hated his own flesh, but nourisheth and cherisheth it. . . . [A] man . . . shall cleave to his wife, and they twain shall be one flesh."

50. **Ergo:** therefore (Latin)

52. **what they are:** i.e., cuckolds

53. **Charbon:** i.e., *chair bonne* (good meat)

54. **Poysam:** i.e., *poisson* (fish); **howsome'er:** however

55. **one:** the same

56. **jowl:** knock, strike; **horns:** In popular thought, the **cuckold** sprouts horns on his forehead. (See longer note, page 222, and picture, page 204.)

(continued)

COUNTESS May the world know them? 35

FOOL I have been, madam, a wicked creature, as you
and all flesh and blood are, and indeed I do marry
that I may repent.

COUNTESS Thy marriage sooner than thy wickedness.

FOOL I am out o' friends, madam, and I hope to have 40
friends for my wife's sake.

COUNTESS Such friends are thine enemies, knave.

FOOL You're shallow, madam, in great friends, for the
knaves come to do that for me which I am aweary
of. He that ears my land spares my team and gives 45
me leave to in the crop; if I be his cuckold, he's my
drudge. He that comforts my wife is the cherisher
of my flesh and blood; he that cherishes my flesh
and blood loves my flesh and blood; he that loves
my flesh and blood is my friend. *Ergo*, he that 50
kisses my wife is my friend. If men could be con-
tented to be what they are, there were no fear in
marriage, for young Charbon the Puritan and old
Poysam the Papist, howsome'er their hearts are
severed in religion, their heads are both one; they 55
may jowl horns together like any deer i' th' herd.

COUNTESS Wilt thou ever be a foul-mouthed and
calumnious knave?

FOOL A prophet I, madam, and I speak the truth the
next way: 60
⌜*Sings.*⌝ For I the ballad will repeat
      Which men full true shall find:
  Your marriage comes by destiny;
  Your cuckoo sings by kind.

COUNTESS Get you gone, sir. I'll talk with you more 65
anon.

STEWARD May it please you, madam, that he bid Helen
come to you. Of her I am to speak.

COUNTESS Sirrah, tell my gentlewoman I would speak
with her—Helen, I mean. 70

60. **next:** most direct

64. **Your cuckoo . . . kind:** i.e., the **cuckoo, by** nature, **sings** (See longer note, page 222.)

71. **face:** i.e., the **face** of **Helen** (**Helen** of Troy was considered **the cause** of the Trojan War.) See longer note, page 222, and picture, page 94.

73. **Fond:** foolishly; amorously

74. **King Priam's joy:** probably alluding to Paris, one of **Priam's** many sons and Helen of Troy's lover

75. **she:** perhaps Queen Hecuba, **Priam's** wife

77. **sentence:** opinion

81–82. **corrupt the song:** perhaps, change the words of **the song** (presumably about **Priam's** sons, only **one** of whom was not **good**)

84. **Would:** i.e., if only

86. **tithe-woman:** i.e., the "one woman in ten" (A **tithe** is a tenth part of anything, but specifically refers to the part of one's goods given to the church. Hence the reference to **the parson.**)

87. **quoth he:** i.e., did he say; **An:** if

88. **or every blazing star:** before **every** comet

89. **mend the lottery:** i.e., improve the odds (The words **draw** and **pluck** continue the image of drawing lots.) Proverbial: Marriage is a **lottery.**

94–96. **Though . . . heart:** The Fool is perhaps saying that he will hide his rebelliousness under humble obedience. (See longer note, page 223.) **big heart:** i.e., proud spirit

102–4. **Her . . . finds:** She was entrusted (**bequeathed**) **to me** by **her father** and she herself can claim the right to my love. (The Countess plays on specifically economic meanings of **bequeathed** [bestowed like property], **advantage** [pecuniary profit, interest on money lent], and **title** [legal right to the possession of property].)

FOOL ⌜*sings*⌝
> "Was this fair face the cause," quoth she,
>   "Why the Grecians sackèd Troy?
> Fond done, done fond.
>   Was this King Priam's joy?"
> With that she sighèd as she stood,   75
> With that she sighèd as she stood,
>   And gave this sentence then:
> "Among nine bad if one be good,
> Among nine bad if one be good,
>   There's yet one good in ten."   80

COUNTESS What, one good in ten? You corrupt the
song, sirrah.

FOOL One good woman in ten, madam, which is a
purifying o' th' song. Would God would serve the
world so all the year! We'd find no fault with the   85
tithe-woman if I were the parson. One in ten,
quoth he? An we might have a good woman born
but ⌜or⌝ every blazing star or at an earthquake,
'twould mend the lottery well. A man may draw his
heart out ere he pluck one.   90

COUNTESS You'll be gone, sir knave, and do as I command you!

FOOL That man should be at woman's command, and
yet no hurt done! Though honesty be no Puritan,
yet it will do no hurt; it will wear the surplice of   95
humility over the black gown of a big heart. I am
going, forsooth. The business is for Helen to come
hither.   *He exits.*

COUNTESS Well, now.

STEWARD I know, madam, you love your gentlewoman   100
entirely.

COUNTESS Faith, I do. Her father bequeathed her to
me, and she herself, without other advantage, may
lawfully make title to as much love as she finds.
There is more owing her than is paid, and more   105
shall be paid her than she'll demand.

107. **very late:** i.e., quite recently

111. **stranger sense:** i.e., ears not her own

112. **Fortune:** i.e., the **goddess** Fortuna, who personifies the cause of events in one's life (See picture, page 42.)

113. **estates:** ranks, fortunes

114. **Love:** i.e., Cupid, the Roman god of love (See picture, page 36.) **only:** except

115. **qualities:** ranks; **Dian:** i.e., Diana, goddess of chastity (See picture, page 148.)

116. **suffer:** allow; **knight:** In *Much Ado About Nothing* (5.3.13), a young woman is called Diana's "virgin **knight.**" **surprised:** captured without warning (a military term, as are **rescue, assault,** and **ransom** in line 117)

118. **touch:** note or strain

120. **withal:** with

121. **sithence:** since; **loss:** perhaps, Helen's death (a fate often predicted for virgins hopelessly in love)

122. **something:** somewhat, to some degree

123. **discharged:** performed

124. **likelihoods:** signs

126. **misdoubt:** doubt

127. **Stall:** place

131. **these:** referring, perhaps, to the things the Countess has just been told of Helen; or perhaps to the gestures or appearance of Helen as she enters

133. **Our blood to us:** i.e., just as we have **blood** in our veins; **to our blood:** i.e., to us (with wordplay on **blood** as sexual desire)

134. **show and seal:** i.e., visible evidence

136. **our:** The Countess may be referring to herself in the plural.

138. **on:** i.e., of

STEWARD   Madam, I was very late more near her than I
think she wished me. Alone she was and did communicate to herself her own words to her own
ears; she thought, I dare vow for her, they touched   110
not any stranger sense. Her matter was she loved
your son. Fortune, she said, was no goddess, that
had put such difference betwixt their two estates;
Love no god, that would not extend his might only
where qualities were level; ⌜Dian no⌝ queen of vir-   115
gins, that would suffer her poor knight surprised
without rescue in the first assault or ransom after-
ward. This she delivered in the most bitter touch
of sorrow that e'er I heard virgin exclaim in, which
I held my duty speedily to acquaint you withal,   120
sithence in the loss that may happen it concerns
you something to know it.

COUNTESS   You have discharged this honestly. Keep it
to yourself. Many likelihoods informed me of this
before, which hung so tott'ring in the balance that   125
I could neither believe nor misdoubt. Pray you
leave me. Stall this in your bosom, and I thank you
for your honest care. I will speak with you further
anon.   *Steward exits.*

Enter Helen.

⌜*Aside.*⌝
Even so it was with me when I was young.   130
    If ever we are nature's, these are ours. This thorn
Doth to our rose of youth rightly belong.
    Our blood to us, this to our blood is born.
It is the show and seal of nature's truth,
Where love's strong passion is impressed in youth.   135
By our remembrances of days foregone,
Such were our faults, or then we thought them none.
Her eye is sick on 't, I observe her now.

HELEN   What is your pleasure, madam?

146. **catalogue:** list

147. **enwombèd mine:** i.e., carried in my womb

148. **strives with:** rivals

148–49. **choice . . . seeds: Adoption** is pictured here in the metaphor of grafting a **slip** (twig) from a different plant (**foreign seeds**) onto tree stock, where it becomes part of the tree (**native**).

150. **a mother's groan:** i.e., the pains of child-birth

154–55. **That this . . . eye:** i.e., that you have tears in your eyes **distempered:** stormy; troubled **Iris:** the rainbow, messenger of the gods (with word-play on the iris of the **eye**) See below.

157. **That I am not:** Helen plays with the meaning of **daughter** (line 156) as daughter-in-law.

162. **No note . . . parents:** i.e., **no** fame or distinction attaching to **my** ancestors

169. **both our mothers:** i.e., mother of us **both**

171. **Can 't no other:** i.e., is there **no other** option

Iris, goddess of the rainbow. (1.3.155)
From Natale Conti, . . . *Mythologiae* . . . (1616).

COUNTESS
  You know, Helen, I am a mother to you.   140
HELEN
  Mine honorable mistress.
COUNTESS   Nay, a mother.
  Why not a mother? When I said "a mother,"
  Methought you saw a serpent. What's in "mother"
  That you start at it? I say I am your mother   145
  And put you in the catalogue of those
  That were enwombèd mine. 'Tis often seen
  Adoption strives with nature, and choice breeds
  A native slip to us from foreign seeds.
  You ne'er oppressed me with a mother's groan,   150
  Yet I express to you a mother's care.
  God's mercy, maiden, does it curd thy blood
  To say I am thy mother? What's the matter,
  That this distempered messenger of wet,
  The many-colored Iris, rounds thine eye?   155
  Why? That you are my daughter?
HELEN   That I am not.
COUNTESS
  I say I am your mother.
HELEN   Pardon, madam.
  The Count Rossillion cannot be my brother.   160
  I am from humble, he from honored name;
  No note upon my parents, his all noble.
  My master, my dear lord he is, and I
  His servant live and will his vassal die.
  He must not be my brother.   165
COUNTESS   Nor I your mother?
HELEN
  You are my mother, madam. Would you were—
  So that my lord your son were not my brother—
  Indeed my mother! Or were you both our mothers,
  I care no more for than I do for heaven,   170
  So I were not his sister. Can 't no other

176. **catched:** caught; **fondness:** (1) love for Bertram; (2) foolishness

177. **mystery:** secret; **loneliness:** solitariness

178. **head:** fountainhead, source; **gross:** obvious, evident

179. **Invention:** i.e., fabrication (of lies)

180. **Against:** in the face of

184. **grossly:** clearly, plainly

185. **in their kind:** according to their nature

187. **suspected:** doubted

188. **goodly clew:** fine ball of yarn

189. **howe'er:** i.e., in any case, at all events

192. **pardon me:** a phrase used in asking to be excused from doing something

197. **Go not about:** i.e., don't be evasive

200. **appeached:** given accusatory evidence

203. **before you:** i.e., even more than I do **you**

Cupid (1.1.181; 1.3.114)
From an anonymous engraving tipped into Jacques Callot,
[*La petite passion*, n.d.].

But, I your daughter, he must be my brother?
COUNTESS
    Yes, Helen, you might be my daughter-in-law.
    God shield you mean it not! "Daughter" and "mother"
    So strive upon your pulse. What, pale again?   175
    My fear hath catched your fondness! Now I see
    The mystery of your ⌐loneliness¬ and find
    Your salt tears' head. Now to all sense 'tis gross:
    You love my son. Invention is ashamed
    Against the proclamation of thy passion   180
    To say thou dost not. Therefore tell me true,
    But tell me then 'tis so, for, look, thy cheeks
    Confess it th' one to th' other, and thine eyes
    See it so grossly shown in thy behaviors
    That in their kind they speak it. Only sin   185
    And hellish obstinacy tie thy tongue
    That truth should be suspected. Speak. Is 't so?
    If it be so, you have wound a goodly clew;
    If it be not, forswear 't; howe'er, I charge thee,
    As heaven shall work in me for thine avail,   190
    To tell me truly.
HELEN   Good madam, pardon me.
COUNTESS
    Do you love my son?
HELEN   Your pardon, noble mistress.
COUNTESS
    Love you my son?   195
HELEN   Do not you love him, madam?
COUNTESS
    Go not about. My love hath in 't a bond
    Whereof the world takes note. Come, come, disclose
    The state of your affection, for your passions
    Have to the full appeached.   200
HELEN, ⌐*kneeling*¬   Then I confess
    Here on my knee before high heaven and you
    That before you and next unto high heaven

205. **friends:** relatives, family

208. **By:** with; **suit:** entreaty, courtship

211. **hope:** what can reasonably be expected

212. **captious . . . sieve:** i.e., capacious **sieve** (see below, and page 108), incapable of holding anything

213. **still:** continue to

214. **lack . . . still:** perhaps, (1) do not fail to continue losing; or, perhaps, (2) have no limit to my love and so can go on losing; **Indian-like:** See longer note, page 223.

218. **encounter with:** oppose

220. **cites:** attests to, gives evidence of

222–23. **that your Dian / . . . Love:** i.e., so that your love was both chaste and fervent

226. **that her:** i.e., **that** which **her**

231. **Wherefore:** why

234. **prescriptions:** medicines

237. **sovereignty:** excellence, efficacy; **willed:** desired, intended (with possible wordplay on *will* as bequeath)

A sieve. (1.3.212)
From Geoffrey Whitney, *A choice of emblemes* . . . (1586).

I love your son.
My friends were poor but honest; so 's my love.   205
Be not offended, for it hurts not him
That he is loved of me. I follow him not
By any token of presumptuous suit,
Nor would I have him till I do deserve him,
Yet never know how that desert should be.   210
I know I love in vain, strive against hope,
Yet in this captious and intenible sieve
I still pour in the waters of my love
And lack not to lose still. Thus, Indian-like,
Religious in mine error, I adore   215
The sun that looks upon his worshipper
But knows of him no more. My dearest madam,
Let not your hate encounter with my love
For loving where you do; but if yourself,
Whose agèd honor cites a virtuous youth,   220
Did ever in so true a flame of liking
Wish chastely and love dearly, that your Dian
Was both herself and Love, O then give pity
To her whose state is such that cannot choose
But lend and give where she is sure to lose;   225
That seeks not to find that her search implies,
But riddle-like lives sweetly where she dies.
COUNTESS
Had you not lately an intent—speak truly—
To go to Paris?
HELEN   Madam, I had.   230
COUNTESS   Wherefore?
Tell true.
HELEN, ⌜*standing*⌝
I will tell truth, by grace itself I swear.
You know my father left me some prescriptions
Of rare and proved effects, such as his reading   235
And manifest experience had collected
For general sovereignty; and that he willed me

238. **In heedfull'st . . . them:** i.e., to keep **them** carefully to myself and to employ **them   bestow:** employ

239. **faculties:** powers, properties; **inclusive:** comprehensive, all-embracing

240. **note:** reputation

241. **approved:** tested, demonstrated

242. **languishings:** attacks of languor or faintness

243. **rendered:** said to be, described as being

254. **schools:** universities

255. **Emboweled:** i.e., disemboweled, emptied; **doctrine:** learning, knowledge; **left off:** abandoned

256. **danger to itself:** i.e., disease to its own course

259. **that:** i.e., so **that; receipt:** means of cure, remedy

263. **try success:** i.e., see what **success** I might have

"A phoenix." (1.1.174)
From Geoffrey Whitney, *A choice of emblemes . . .* (1586).

In heedfull'st reservation to bestow them
As notes whose faculties inclusive were
More than they were in note. Amongst the rest   240
There is a remedy, approved, set down,
To cure the desperate languishings whereof
The King is rendered lost.

COUNTESS
This was your motive for Paris, was it? Speak.

HELEN
My lord your son made me to think of this;   245
Else Paris, and the medicine, and the King
Had from the conversation of my thoughts
Haply been absent then.

COUNTESS   But think you, Helen,
If you should tender your supposèd aid,   250
He would receive it? He and his physicians
Are of a mind: he that they cannot help him,
They that they cannot help. How shall they credit
A poor unlearnèd virgin, when the schools
Emboweled of their doctrine have left off   255
The danger to itself?

HELEN   There's something in 't
More than my father's skill, which was the great'st
Of his profession, that his good receipt
Shall for my legacy be sanctified   260
By th' luckiest stars in heaven; and would your
    Honor
But give me leave to try success, I'd venture
The well-lost life of mine on his Grace's cure
By such a day, an hour.   265

COUNTESS   Dost thou believe 't?

HELEN   Ay, madam, knowingly.

COUNTESS
Why, Helen, thou shalt have my leave and love,
Means and attendants, and my loving greetings
To those of mine in court. I'll stay at home   270

271. **into:** unto, on
273. **miss:** lack

Fortune. (1.3.112)
From *Fortunes tennis-ball* . . . (1640).

And pray God's blessing into thy attempt.
Be gone tomorrow, and be sure of this:
What I can help thee to thou shalt not miss.

They exit.

ALL'S WELL
THAT ENDS WELL

ACT 2

2.1   The King bids farewell to the French courtiers going off to war, having commanded Bertram to remain behind. Helen arrives at court and, after promising to forfeit her own life should she fail, persuades the King to let her try to cure his fatal disease. She asks, as her reward should she succeed, the hand in marriage of whichever courtier she chooses.

O SD. **the Florentine war:** i.e., the **war** between Florence and Siena (See longer note to 1.2.1.)

2. **And you:** It is possible that one group of **lords** is joining the Florentine army and the other is joining the Sienese. (See 1.2.16–18.)

4. **betwixt:** between

8. **After well-entered soldiers:** i.e., when we have been duly initiated as **soldiers**

11. **he owes:** i.e., it owns or possesses

14. **higher Italy:** perhaps, northern **Italy;** or, perhaps, Italy's social elite

15. **bated:** excepted

16. **the last monarchy:** perhaps, the Roman Empire

17. **Not:** i.e., **not** merely

18. **The bravest questant:** i.e., even **the bravest** searcher

19. **cry you loud:** i.e., proclaim **you** loudly (See picture of **Fame**, page 104.)

ACT 2

Flourish cornets. Enter the King, ⌐attended,¬ with divers
young Lords, taking leave for the Florentine war;
⌐Bertram¬ Count Rossillion, and Parolles.

KING
Farewell, young lords. These warlike principles
Do not throw from you.—And you, my lords,
   farewell.
Share the advice betwixt you. If both gain all,
The gift doth stretch itself as 'tis received   5
And is enough for both.
FIRST LORD   'Tis our hope, sir,
After well-entered soldiers, to return
And find your Grace in health.
KING
No, no, it cannot be. And yet my heart   10
Will not confess he owes the malady
That doth my life besiege. Farewell, young lords.
Whether I live or die, be you the sons
Of worthy Frenchmen. Let higher Italy—
Those bated that inherit but the fall   15
Of the last monarchy—see that you come
Not to woo honor but to wed it. When
The bravest questant shrinks, find what you seek,
That fame may cry you loud. I say farewell.

47

23–24. **Beware . . . serve:** wordplay on **captives** and **serve** as both military language and language from courtship, where "to **serve**" meant to be the lover of a lady

29. **brave:** fine, splendid

31. **here:** i.e., to remain **here; kept a coil:** i.e., annoyed

34. **An:** if; **stand to 't:** i.e., remains constant

35. **forehorse:** lead horse in a team of horses; **smock:** i.e., woman (literally, a woman's undergarment)

36. **plain:** flat, level (as opposed to an uneven battlefield) See below.

41. **accessory:** assistant, helper

"Creaking my shoes on the plain masonry." (2.1.36)
From Fabritio Caroso, *Il ballarino* . . . (1581).

FIRST LORD
  Health at your bidding serve your Majesty!   20
KING
  Those girls of Italy, take heed of them.
  They say our French lack language to deny
  If they demand. Beware of being captives
  Before you serve.
LORDS   Our hearts receive your warnings.   25
KING   Farewell.—Come hither to me.
          ⌜*The King speaks to Attendants, while Bertram,*
              Parolles, and other Lords come forward.⌝
FIRST LORD, ⌜*to Bertram*⌝
  O my sweet lord, that you will stay behind us!
PAROLLES
  'Tis not his fault, the spark.
SECOND LORD   O, 'tis brave wars.
PAROLLES
  Most admirable. I have seen those wars.   30
BERTRAM
  I am commanded here and kept a coil
  With "Too young," and "The next year," and " 'Tis
    too early."
PAROLLES
  An thy mind stand to 't, boy, steal away bravely.
BERTRAM
  I shall stay here the forehorse to a smock,   35
  Creaking my shoes on the plain masonry
  Till honor be bought up, and no sword worn
  But one to dance with. By heaven, I'll steal away!
FIRST LORD
  There's honor in the theft.
PAROLLES   Commit it, count.   40
SECOND LORD
  I am your accessory. And so, farewell.
BERTRAM   I grow to you, and our parting is a tortured
    body.

47. **metals:** wordplay on the association of *metal* with swords and therefore swordsmen, and on *metal* as *mettle*, i.e., character, spirit

49. **cicatrice:** scar

50. **sinister:** left

52. **reports:** commendations; or, perhaps, responses

56. **Stay:** wait upon, serve

58. **list:** limit

60. **wear . . . time:** i.e., are **themselves** ornaments on **the cap** of the present age

61. **muster true gait:** i.e., display the **true** course

62. **influence:** i.e., astrological power; **received:** i.e., popular or fashionable

63. **measure:** dance

64. **After:** i.e., go **after,** follow; **dilated:** prolonged, protracted

67. **like:** i.e., likely

73. **would:** i.e., wish

FIRST LORD   Farewell, captain.
SECOND LORD   Sweet Monsieur Parolles.   45
PAROLLES   Noble heroes, my sword and yours are kin.
  Good sparks and lustrous, a word, good metals.
  You shall find in the regiment of the Spinii one
  Captain Spurio ⌜with⌝ his cicatrice, an emblem of
  war, here on his sinister cheek. It was this very   50
  sword entrenched it. Say to him I live, and observe
  his reports for me.
FIRST LORD   We shall, noble captain.
PAROLLES   Mars dote on you for his novices.
                                  ⌜*Lords exit.*⌝   55
  ⌜*To Bertram.*⌝ What will you do?
BERTRAM   Stay the King.
PAROLLES   Use a more spacious ceremony to the noble
  lords. You have restrained yourself within the list
  of too cold an adieu. Be more expressive to them,
  for they wear themselves in the cap of the time;   60
  there do muster true gait; eat, speak, and move
  under the influence of the most received star, and,
  though the devil lead the measure, such are to be
  followed. After them, and take a more dilated farewell.   65
BERTRAM   And I will do so.
PAROLLES   Worthy fellows, and like to prove most
  sinewy swordmen.   ⌜*Bertram and Parolles*⌝ *exit.*

  Enter Lafew, ⌜*to the King*⌝

LAFEW, ⌜*kneeling*⌝
  Pardon, my lord, for me and for my tidings.
KING   I'll ⌜fee⌝ thee to stand up.   70
LAFEW, ⌜*standing*⌝
  Then here's a man stands that has brought his
    pardon.
  I would you had kneeled, my lord, to ask me mercy,
  And that at my bidding you could so stand up.

75. **broke thy pate:** i.e., cut open your head

77. **across:** If **across** is a response to the King's attempt at humor, it may mean "a clumsy hit" (a fencing term); if **across** is instead a continuation of Lafew's wish for the King's health (lines 73–74), it may describe the wound that Lafew is willing to sustain. (In *The Comedy of Errors*, 2.1.83, the words "break **thy pate across**" are followed by wordplay on **across** as "a cross.")

81–84. **O . . . reach them:** an allusion to the **fox** in Aesop's fable who, unable to **reach** the **grapes** he wants, declares them sour (See picture, page 60.) **will:** i.e., **will** eat   **an if:** i.e., **if**

84. **medicine:** (1) medicament; (2) doctor

86. **canary:** i.e., the canaries, a lively Spanish dance (See picture, page 72.)

88. **araise:** i.e., raise from the dead; **King Pippen:** i.e., King Pepin, who died in 768 (See picture, page 100.)

89. **Charlemagne:** Charles the Great, emperor of the West (800–814) and son of King Pepin; **pen in 's hand:** Many editors suggest a sexual meaning here, and in such words as **touch** and **araise**.

95. **light:** frivolous; **deliverance:** manner of speaking

96. **profession:** declaration (of what she is able to do)

98. **dare . . . weakness:** perhaps, can attribute to my infirmities as an old man

99. **demand:** request

102. **admiration:** object of **wonder** (line 103)

103. **take off:** do away with

(continued)

KING
   I would I had, so I had broke thy pate   75
   And asked thee mercy for 't.
LAFEW   Good faith, across.
   But, my good lord, 'tis thus: will you be cured
   Of your infirmity?
KING   No.   80
LAFEW   O, will you eat
   No grapes, my royal fox? Yes, but you will
   My noble grapes, an if my royal fox
   Could reach them. I have seen a medicine
   That's able to breathe life into a stone,   85
   Quicken a rock, and make you dance canary
   With sprightly fire and motion, whose simple touch
   Is powerful to araise King Pippen, nay,
   To give great Charlemagne a pen in 's hand
   And write to her a love line.   90
KING   What "her" is this?
LAFEW
   Why, Doctor She. My lord, there's one arrived,
   If you will see her. Now, by my faith and honor,
   If seriously I may convey my thoughts
   In this my light deliverance, I have spoke   95
   With one that in her sex, her years, profession,
   Wisdom, and constancy hath amazed me more
   Than I dare blame my weakness. Will you see her—
   For that is her demand—and know her business?
   That done, laugh well at me.   100
KING   Now, good Lafew,
   Bring in the admiration, that we with thee
   May spend our wonder too, or take off thine
   By wond'ring how thou took'st it.
LAFEW   Nay, I'll fit you,   105
   And not be all day neither.
                  ⌜*He goes to bring in Helen.*⌝
KING
   Thus he his special nothing ever prologues.

104. **took'st:** i.e., caught (with wordplay on **take** in line 103)

105. **fit:** i.e., provide

107. **nothing:** trivial or trifling remark; **prologues:** introduces, prefaces

107 SD. **Enter Helen:** Some editors have Helen enter here in disguise, thus solving the problem presented in 2.3, where Lafew seems not to have known the identity of "Doctor She."

108. **come your ways:** i.e., **come** along

113. **Cressid's uncle:** In the story of Troilus and Cressida, **Cressid's uncle** Pandarus served as go-between for the lovers. He thus became the type of the male bawd or "pander."

115. **follow us:** i.e., aim at me (the royal "we")

118. **well found:** of proven merit

120. **The rather:** the more readily

122. **receipts:** remedies, prescriptions

124. **th' only:** i.e., the most precious

125. **triple:** third

127. **touched:** infected

128. **cause:** disease

130. **appliance:** willing service

131. **bound:** i.e., dutiful

134. **leave us:** i.e., abandon me

135. **congregated college:** probably a reference to a body such as the London College of Physicians or the Faculty of Medicine in Paris

136. **art:** learning, skill (often set in opposition to **nature**)

137. **her inaidible estate:** i.e., its helpless condition; **we:** i.e., I

Enter Helen.

LAFEW, ⌜*to Helen*⌝   Nay, come your ways.
KING   This haste hath wings indeed.
LAFEW   Nay, come your ways.   110
This is his Majesty. Say your mind to him.
A traitor you do look like, but such traitors
His Majesty seldom fears. I am Cressid's uncle
That dare leave two together. Fare you well.
                                               He exits.

KING
Now, fair one, does your business follow us?   115
HELEN   Ay, my good lord,
Gerard de Narbon was my father,
In what he did profess well found.
KING   I knew him.
HELEN
The rather will I spare my praises towards him.   120
Knowing him is enough. On 's bed of death
Many receipts he gave me, chiefly one
Which, as the dearest issue of his practice,
And of his old experience th' only darling,
He bade me store up as a triple eye,   125
Safer than mine own two, more dear. I have so,
And hearing your high Majesty is touched
With that malignant cause wherein the honor
Of my dear father's gift stands chief in power,
I come to tender it and my appliance   130
With all bound humbleness.
KING   We thank you, maiden,
But may not be so credulous of cure,
When our most learnèd doctors leave us and
The congregated college have concluded   135
That laboring art can never ransom nature
From her inaidible estate. I say we must not
So stain our judgment or corrupt our hope

139. **To prostitute:** i.e., by surrendering

140. **empirics:** untrained practitioners, quacks

141. **to esteem:** i.e., by regarding as valuable

142. **when help . . . deem:** i.e., **when** I judge any remedy as beyond what is reasonable

143. **My duty:** perhaps, **my** sense of having attempted to serve you

144. **office:** service, attention

146. **A modest one:** i.e., a moderate thought (with possible wordplay on **modest** with reference to her decorous behavior); **bear me back again:** i.e., carry **back** with **me**

150. **at full:** fully

151. **art:** learning

153. **set up your rest:** i.e., bet everything (a term from the game of primero)

154–59. **He . . . denied:** These lines seem to allude to biblical passages in which the young or the weak proved wise or powerful. (See longer note, page 223.) **minister:** agent

162. **shifts:** succeeds (Many editors since the early 18th century have changed this word to "sits" or "fits," words that more easily fit the context and that maintain the rhymed couplets that dominate from line 150 until the end of the scene.)

166. **Inspirèd merit:** i.e., good works infused by divine power; **so by breath:** i.e., thus **by** words of judgment or will

168. **guess:** i.e., suppositions, conjectures

To prostitute our past-cure malady
To empirics, or to dissever so 140
Our great self and our credit to esteem
A senseless help when help past sense we deem.

HELEN
My duty, then, shall pay me for my pains.
I will no more enforce mine office on you,
Humbly entreating from your royal thoughts 145
A modest one to bear me back again.

KING
I cannot give thee less, to be called grateful.
Thou thought'st to help me, and such thanks I give
As one near death to those that wish him live.
But what at full I know, thou know'st no part, 150
I knowing all my peril, thou no art.

HELEN
What I can do can do no hurt to try
Since you set up your rest 'gainst remedy.
He that of greatest works is finisher
Oft does them by the weakest minister. 155
So holy writ in babes hath judgment shown
When judges have been babes. Great floods have flown
From simple sources, and great seas have dried
When miracles have by the great'st been denied.
Oft expectation fails, and most oft there 160
Where most it promises, and oft it hits
Where hope is coldest and despair most shifts.

KING
I must not hear thee. Fare thee well, kind maid.
Thy pains, not used, must by thyself be paid.
Proffers not took reap thanks for their reward. 165

HELEN
Inspirèd merit so by breath is barred.
It is not so with Him that all things knows
As 'tis with us that square our guess by shows;
But most it is presumption in us when

174. **against . . . aim:** i.e., contrary to what I intend (**level** here meaning, literally, the action of aiming a missile weapon)

176. **past power:** without **power**

177. **space:** i.e., of time

179. **The greatest . . . grace:** i.e., if God lends divine aid

180–81. **Ere . . . ring:** The sun's apparent circling of the earth was often pictured as the sun-god's chariot being drawn across the sky by **horses.** (See picture, page 106.)   **torcher:** one who gives light, as by carrying a torch

183. **Hesperus:** the name given by the Greeks to the planet Venus in its appearance as the evening star

184. **pilot's glass:** i.e., the hourglass used on shipboard

185. **told:** counted, reckoned; **thievish minutes:** an allusion to the commonplace that time is a thief (See Shakespeare's Sonnet 77, line 8: "Time's **thievish** progress to eternity.")

186. **sound parts:** i.e., **parts** that would then become **sound**

187. **freely:** readily

190. **Tax:** accusation

193. **otherwise:** in other ways (i.e., not only in **ballads**); **extended:** (1) stretched on an instrument of **torture** called a rack; (2) prolonged (in duration)

199. **rate:** reckon, calculate

200. **in thee hath estimate:** i.e., has a claim to be considered in your value

202. **happy:** fortunate

The help of heaven we count the act of men.   170
Dear sir, to my endeavors give consent.
Of heaven, not me, make an experiment.
I am not an impostor that proclaim
Myself against the level of mine aim,
But know I think and think I know most sure   175
My art is not past power nor you past cure.

KING
Art thou so confident? Within what space
Hop'st thou my cure?

HELEN   The greatest grace lending grace,
Ere twice the horses of the sun shall bring   180
Their fiery torcher his diurnal ring;
Ere twice in murk and occidental damp
Moist Hesperus hath quenched her sleepy lamp;
Or four and twenty times the pilot's glass
Hath told the thievish minutes, how they pass,   185
What is infirm from your sound parts shall fly,
Health shall live free, and sickness freely die.

KING
Upon thy certainty and confidence
What dar'st thou venture?

HELEN   Tax of impudence,   190
A strumpet's boldness, a divulgèd shame;
Traduced by odious ballads, my maiden's name
Seared otherwise; nay, worse of worst, extended
With vilest torture let my life be ended.

KING
Methinks in thee some blessèd spirit doth speak   195
His powerful sound within an organ weak,
And what impossibility would slay
In common sense, sense saves another way.
Thy life is dear, for all that life can rate
Worth name of life in thee hath estimate: 200
Youth, beauty, wisdom, courage, all
That happiness and prime can happy call.

204. **or monstrous:** i.e., **or** that you are very

205. **practicer:** practitioner; **physic:** medicine

207. **break time:** i.e., fail to keep **time** (musical terminology); **flinch:** give way, draw back; **property:** i.e., any attribute or quality

212. **make it even:** i.e., balance our accounts

216. **Exempted:** i.e., far removed

219. **branch . . . state:** i.e., descendant of the royal family

222. **premises:** foregoing matters (legal terminology)

225. **still:** constantly

228. **rest:** remain

229. **Unquestioned:** uninterrogated (but with wordplay on *unquestionably,* without doubt); **undoubted:** i.e., undoubtedly

231. **word:** i.e., your promise

A fox reaching for grapes. (2.1.81–84)
From Aesop, *Fabulae . . .* [1590].

Thou this to hazard needs must intimate
Skill infinite or monstrous desperate.
Sweet practicer, thy physic I will try,   205
That ministers thine own death if I die.

HELEN
If I break time or flinch in property
Of what I spoke, unpitied let me die,
And well deserved. Not helping, death's my fee.
But if I help, what do you promise me?   210

KING
Make thy demand.

HELEN   But will you make it even?

KING
Ay, by my scepter and my hopes of ⌜heaven.⌝

HELEN
Then shalt thou give me with thy kingly hand
What husband in thy power I will command.   215
Exempted be from me the arrogance
To choose from forth the royal blood of France,
My low and humble name to propagate
With any branch or image of thy state;
But such a one, thy vassal, whom I know   220
Is free for me to ask, thee to bestow.

KING
Here is my hand. The premises observed,
Thy will by my performance shall be served.
So make the choice of thy own time, for I,
Thy resolved patient, on thee still rely.   225
More should I question thee, and more I must,
Though more to know could not be more to trust:
From whence thou cam'st, how tended on; but rest
Unquestioned welcome and undoubted blessed.—
Give me some help here, ho!—If thou proceed   230
As high as word, my deed shall match thy deed.
            Flourish. ⌜*They*⌝ *exit,* ⌜*the King assisted.*⌝

2.2 The Countess sends the Fool to the court with a letter for Helen.

---

1. **put you to:** i.e., make **you** show
3. **highly . . . taught:** "Better **fed** than **taught**" was a proverbial description of a spoiled child.
5–6. **make you special:** i.e., do **you** have a high opinion of
6. **put off:** dismiss
9. **put it off:** perhaps, foist or palm **it off**
10. **a leg:** i.e., an elaborate bow
17. **barber's chair:** Proverbial: "common as **a barber's chair.**"
18. **pin-buttock:** narrow **buttock; quatch-buttock:** The meaning of **quatch** is not known.
18–19. **brawn-buttock:** fleshy **buttock**
21. **ten groats:** A groat was worth four pence. (See picture, page 64.)
22. **French crown:** (1) coin; (2) head bald from "the French disease" (syphilis); **taffety punk:** i.e., overdressed prostitute (See picture, page 170.)
23. **Tib's . . . forefinger:** Tib and Tom meant "lass and lad." **rush:** i.e., a ring made from the **rush** plant
24. **Shrove Tuesday:** the day before Lent, often called "**pancake** day"; **morris:** i.e., **morris** dance
25. **his hole:** i.e., its **hole; cuckold to his horn:** See longer note to 1.3.56, and picture, page 204.
26. **quean:** female (a term of disparagement)
26–27. **nun's . . . mouth:** A salacious distortion of the proverb "As fit as a **pudding** for a **friar's mouth.**"

(continued)

⌈Scene 2⌉

Enter Countess and ⌈*Fool.*⌉

COUNTESS   Come on, sir. I shall now put you to the
height of your breeding.

FOOL   I will show myself highly fed and lowly taught. I
know my business is but to the court.

COUNTESS   "To the court"? Why, what place make you   5
special when you put off that with such contempt?
"But to the court"?

FOOL   Truly, madam, if God have lent a man any manners, he may easily put it off at court. He that cannot make a leg, put off 's cap, kiss his hand, and   10
say nothing, has neither leg, hands, lip, nor cap;
and indeed such a fellow, to say precisely, were
not for the court. But, for me, I have an answer
will serve all men.

COUNTESS   Marry, that's a bountiful answer that fits all   15
questions.

FOOL   It is like a barber's chair that fits all buttocks:
the pin-buttock, the quatch-buttock, the brawn-
buttock, or any buttock.

COUNTESS   Will your answer serve fit to all questions?   20

FOOL   As fit as ten groats is for the hand of an attorney,
as your French crown for your taffety punk, as
Tib's rush for Tom's forefinger, as a pancake for
Shrove Tuesday, a morris for May Day, as the nail
to his hole, the cuckold to his horn, as a scolding   25
quean to a wrangling knave, as the nun's lip to the
friar's mouth, nay, as the pudding to his skin.

COUNTESS   Have you, I say, an answer of such fitness
for all questions?

FOOL   From below your duke to beneath your consta-   30
ble, it will fit any question.

COUNTESS   It must be an answer of most monstrous
size that must fit all demands.

27. **pudding to his skin:** i.e., sausage to its **skin**

34. **But a trifle neither:** i.e., nothing but **a trifle**

38. **To be young again:** As a response to "It shall do you no harm to **learn**," the Countess's words remind one of Portia's "she is not yet so old / But she may **learn**" (*Merchant of Venice* 3.2.164–65).

41. **O Lord, sir:** This empty expression used at court was mocked by other writers in Shakespeare's day. **putting off:** evasion

45. **Thick:** quickly, faster

46–47. **homely meat:** simple food

48. **put me to 't:** challenge **me; warrant:** assure

53. **very sequent to:** i.e., a proper consequence of

53–54. **answer . . . to:** wordplay on (1) reply to; and (2) suffer the consequences of

54. **bound to 't:** wordplay on (1) obliged to answer; and (2) tied up, in bonds

57. **I play . . . time:** an ironic way of saying "I'm wasting **time**" **huswife:** housewife, i.e., thrifty and efficient household manager (pronounced "hussif")

61. **a present:** an immediate

67. **again:** i.e., back **again**

The obverse and reverse of a groat. (2.2.21)
From Edward Hawkins, *The silver coins of England . . .* (1841).

FOOL   But a trifle neither, in good faith, if the learned
    should speak truth of it. Here it is, and all that   35
    belongs to 't. Ask me if I am a courtier; it shall do
    you no harm to learn.
COUNTESS   To be young again, if we could! I will be a
    fool in question, hoping to be the wiser by your
    answer. I pray you, sir, are you a courtier?   40
FOOL   O Lord, sir!—There's a simple putting off. More,
    more, a hundred of them.
COUNTESS   Sir, I am a poor friend of yours that loves
    you.
FOOL   O Lord, sir!—Thick, thick. Spare not me.   45
COUNTESS   I think, sir, you can eat none of this homely
    meat.
FOOL   O Lord, sir!—Nay, put me to 't, I warrant you.
COUNTESS   You were lately whipped, sir, as I think.
FOOL   O Lord, sir!—Spare not me.   50
COUNTESS   Do you cry "O Lord, sir!" at your whipping,
    and "spare not me"? Indeed your "O Lord, sir!" is
    very sequent to your whipping. You would answer
    very well to a whipping if you were but bound to 't.
FOOL   I ne'er had worse luck in my life in my "O Lord,   55
    sir!" I see things may serve long but not serve ever.
COUNTESS   I play the noble huswife with the time to
    entertain it so merrily with a fool.
FOOL   O Lord, sir!—Why, there 't serves well again.
COUNTESS, ⌜*giving him a paper*⌝
    ⌜An⌝ end, sir. To your business. Give Helen this,   60
    And urge her to a present answer back.
    Commend me to my kinsmen and my son.
    This is not much.
FOOL   Not much commendation to them?
COUNTESS
    Not much employment for you. You understand me.   65
FOOL   Most fruitfully. I am there before my legs.
COUNTESS   Haste you again.
                             They exit.

2.3 Having cured the King, Helen is given several courtiers from whom to choose a husband as her reward. When she selects Bertram, he objects strongly to marrying "a poor physician's daughter," but the King insists on the marriage. Bertram privately vows never to "bed" Helen and, immediately following the marriage ceremony, makes his plans to escape to the wars.

----

1. **miracles are past:** It was Protestant doctrine that **miracles** ceased soon after the establishment of the Christian church.
2. **modern:** commonplace, ordinary
3. **causeless:** not to be explained by any natural cause
4–5. **ensconcing . . . knowledge:** i.e., taking shelter behind apparent **knowledge**
6. **unknown fear:** (1) i.e., the **unknown,** which is what we most **fear;** or, (2) acknowledgment that the world is terrifyingly mysterious
7. **argument:** theme, subject
8. **shot out:** i.e., appeared like a "shooting star"; **latter times:** i.e., the time since **miracles** have ceased
10. **of the artists:** i.e., by the physicians
11. **of Galen and Paracelsus:** i.e., **of** the schools of ancient and "modern" medicine (**Galen** was a 2nd-century anatomist, physiologist, and physician; **Paracelsus** was an early-16th-century Swiss physician and alchemist.)
12. **authentic:** legally qualified, licensed
21. **in showing:** i.e., narrated

(continued)

⌜Scene 3⌝

Enter Count ⌜Bertram,⌝ Lafew, and Parolles.

LAFEW   They say miracles are past, and we have our
   philosophical persons to make modern and familiar things supernatural and causeless. Hence is it
   that we make trifles of terrors, ensconcing our-
   selves into seeming knowledge when we should   5
   submit ourselves to an unknown fear.
PAROLLES   Why, 'tis the rarest argument of wonder that
   hath shot out in our latter times.
BERTRAM   And so 'tis.
LAFEW   To be relinquished of the artists—   10
PAROLLES   So I say, both of Galen and Paracelsus.
LAFEW   Of all the learned and authentic fellows—
PAROLLES   Right, so I say.
LAFEW   That gave him out incurable—
PAROLLES   Why, there 'tis. So say I too.   15
LAFEW   Not to be helped.
PAROLLES   Right, as 'twere a man assured of a—
LAFEW   Uncertain life and sure death.
PAROLLES   Just. You say well. So would I have said.
LAFEW   I may truly say it is a novelty to the world.   20
PAROLLES   It is indeed. If you will have it in showing,
   you shall read it in what-do-you-call there.
           ⌜*He points to a paper in Lafew's hand.*⌝
LAFEW ⌜*reads*⌝ *A showing of a heavenly effect in an earth-*
   ly actor.
PAROLLES   That's it. I would have said the very same.   25
LAFEW   Why, your dolphin is not lustier. 'Fore me, I
   speak in respect—
PAROLLES   Nay, 'tis strange, 'tis very strange; that is the
   brief and the tedious of it; and he's of a most facinorous spirit that will not acknowledge it to be   30
   the—
LAFEW   Very hand of heaven.

23. **showing:** manifestation (The **wonder** [line 7] that enraptures Lafew and Parolles has apparently already been published in the broadsheet ballad whose title Lafew reads out. Such rapid publication was common in England at the time this play was written.)

26. **lustier:** more lively; **'Fore me:** a mild oath (equivalent to "by my word")

28–29. **the brief and the tedious:** a stilted way of saying "the long and the short"

29–30. **facinorous:** infamous, vile

35. **debile minister:** feeble agent

37. **use:** application

42. **Lustig:** merry, jolly; **Dutchman:** i.e., German; **maid:** young woman

44. **coranto:** lively dance

45. **Mort du vinaigre:** a meaningless "French" oath

46. **'Fore God, I think so:** On Lafew's surprise here, see note to 2.1.107 SD.

50. **repealed:** recalled (from exile or banishment)

52. **attends:** awaits

53. **parcel:** small party or company

54. **stand at my bestowing:** i.e., are mine to bestow in marriage

56. **to use:** i.e., the use of; **frank election:** unrestricted choice

57. **forsake:** refuse

59. **when Love please:** i.e., **when** it pleases the god of love; **Marry:** i.e., indeed, to be sure

60–62. **I'd . . . beard:** i.e., **I'd give** anything to be as young as these boys **bay Curtal:** i.e., my **bay** horse (named **Curtal** because of its cropped tail) **furniture:** harness and trappings **broken:** i.e., damaged by loss of teeth **writ:** perhaps, acknowledged

PAROLLES   Ay, so I say.

LAFEW   In a most weak—

PAROLLES   And debile minister. Great power, great   35
transcendence, which should indeed give us a further use to be made than alone the recov'ry of the
King, as to be—

LAFEW   Generally thankful.

Enter King, Helen, and Attendants.

PAROLLES   I would have said it. You say well. Here   40
comes the King.

LAFEW   *Lustig,* as the Dutchman says. I'll like a maid
the better whilst I have a tooth in my head. Why,
he's able to lead her a *coranto.*

PAROLLES   *Mort du vinaigre!* Is not this Helen?   45

LAFEW   'Fore God, I think so.

KING
Go, call before me all the lords in court.
⌜*An Attendant exits.*⌝
Sit, my preserver, by thy patient's side,
And with this healthful hand, whose banished sense
Thou hast repealed, a second time receive   50
The confirmation of my promised gift,
Which but attends thy naming.

Enter three or four ⌜*Court*⌝ *Lords.*

Fair maid, send forth thine eye. This youthful parcel
Of noble bachelors stand at my bestowing,
O'er whom both sovereign power and father's voice   55
I have to use. Thy frank election make.
Thou hast power to choose, and they none to forsake.

HELEN
To each of you one fair and virtuous mistress
Fall when Love please! Marry, to each but one.

LAFEW, ⌜*aside*⌝
I'd give bay Curtal and his furniture   60

69. **simply:** without qualification; **maid:** virgin

72–73. **be refused:** i.e., if you are **refused**

74. **the white death:** i.e., **death,** which turns one's **cheek** ashen

77. **Who:** i.e., whoever; **his love:** i.e., my **love** for him

78. **Dian:** i.e., Diana, goddess of chastity (See picture, page 148.)

79. **imperial Love:** i.e., Cupid (See below.)

80 SD. **addresses her to:** i.e., speaks **to;** or, perhaps, makes **her** way **to** or turns **to**

83–84. **All . . . mute:** i.e., I have nothing more to say

86. **ambs-ace:** two aces (the lowest **throw** at dice); **for my life:** perhaps, with **my life** at stake

87. **honor:** probably, the courtier's sense of family **honor,** which would be threatened by the thought of marriage to a commoner

90. **Her that so wishes:** i.e., Helen herself

91. **No better:** i.e., I wish **no better** (than your **humble love**)

Cupid, the god of love. (1.3.114; 2.3.79)
From Francesco Petrarca, *Opera* . . . (1508).

My mouth no more were broken than these boys'
And writ as little beard.
KING   Peruse them well.
  Not one of those but had a noble father.
HELEN   Gentlemen,   65
  Heaven hath through me restored the King to health.
ALL
  We understand it and thank heaven for you.
HELEN
  I am a simple maid, and therein wealthiest
  That I protest I simply am a maid.—
  Please it your Majesty, I have done already.   70
  The blushes in my cheeks thus whisper me:
  "We blush that thou shouldst choose; but, be
      refused,
  Let the white death sit on thy cheek forever;
  We'll ne'er come there again."   75
KING   Make choice and see.
  Who shuns thy love shuns all his love in me.
HELEN
  Now, Dian, from thy altar do I fly,
  And to imperial Love, that god most high,
  Do my sighs stream.   *She addresses her to a Lord.*   80
                 Sir, will you hear my suit?
FIRST ⌜COURT⌝ LORD   And grant it.
HELEN   Thanks, sir. All the
      rest is mute.
LAFEW, ⌜*aside*⌝ I had rather be in this choice than   85
      throw ambs-ace for my life.
HELEN, ⌜*to another Lord*⌝
  The honor, sir, that flames in your fair eyes
  Before I speak too threat'ningly replies.
  Love make your fortunes twenty times above
  Her that so wishes, and her humble love.   90
SECOND ⌜COURT⌝ LORD
  No better, if you please.
HELEN   My wish receive,

94–96. Do . . . eunuchs of: Lafew (here and at lines 101–3) may be unable to hear the polite responses of the courtiers, and may thus misunderstand their attitude toward Helen. On the other hand, he may instead hear and see a coldness in their responses that he correctly recognizes as a rejection.

102. bastards to: i.e., **bastards** of

103. got 'em: i.e., begot them

107–8. There's . . . wine: Using wordplay on the proverb "good **wine** makes good blood," Lafew suggests that Bertram, the fruit of his father's lineage, has good blood in his veins.

Intauolatura di Liuto del Canario.

Music for the "canario" or canaries. (2.1.86)
From Fabritio Caroso, *Il Ballarino* . . . (1581).

72

Which great Love grant, and so I take my leave.

LAFEW, ⌐*aside*⌐ Do all they deny her? An they were sons
    of mine, I'd have them whipped, or I would send   95
    them to th' Turk to make eunuchs of.

HELEN, ⌐*to another Lord*⌐
  Be not afraid that I your hand should take.
  I'll never do you wrong, for your own sake.
  Blessing upon your vows, and in your bed
  Find fairer fortune if you ever wed.   100

LAFEW, ⌐*aside*⌐ These boys are boys of ice; they'll none
    have ⌐her.⌐ Sure they are bastards to the English;
    the French ne'er got 'em.

HELEN, ⌐*to another Lord*⌐
  You are too young, too happy, and too good
  To make yourself a son out of my blood.   105

FOURTH ⌐COURT⌐ LORD   Fair one, I think not so.

LAFEW, ⌐*aside*⌐ There's one grape yet. I am sure thy
    father drunk wine. But if thou be'st not an ass, I
    am a youth of fourteen; I have known thee already.

HELEN, ⌐*to Bertram*⌐
  I dare not say I take you, but I give   110
  Me and my service ever whilst I live
  Into your guiding power.—This is the man.

KING
  Why then, young Bertram, take her. She's thy wife.

BERTRAM
  My wife, my liege? I shall beseech your Highness
  In such a business give me leave to use   115
  The help of mine own eyes.

KING   Know'st thou not,
    Bertram,
  What she has done for me?

BERTRAM   Yes, my good lord,   120
  But never hope to know why I should marry her.

KING
  Thou know'st she has raised me from my sickly bed.

125. **breeding:** upbringing, education; **charge:** expense

128. **title:** perhaps, lack of **title;** or, perhaps, the designation you gave her as **a poor physician's daughter**

131. **Would quite confound distinction:** i.e., could not be distinguished (Proverbial: "There is no difference of **bloods** in a basin.") **stands off:** i.e., are separated in quality

132. **differences:** i.e., social or class distinctions (here giving **bloods** [line 129] its meaning of lineages or ancestral descent)

135. **Of virtue:** i.e., **virtue; for:** i.e., because of

138. **additions:** titles of honor

139. **dropsied:** morbidly swollen, inflated

141. **property:** attribute or quality; **go:** be known

144. **honor's scorn:** i.e., the object of **honor's** mockery

145. **challenges itself:** i.e., lays claim to **honor; as:** i.e., **as** if

150. **trophy:** memorial

152. **honored:** i.e., honorable

153. **maid:** young woman

155. **Is:** i.e., are

BERTRAM
　　But follows it, my lord, to bring me down
　　Must answer for your raising? I know her well;
　　She had her breeding at my father's charge.　　　　125
　　A poor physician's daughter my wife? Disdain
　　Rather corrupt me ever!
KING
　　'Tis only title thou disdain'st in her, the which
　　I can build up. Strange is it that our bloods,
　　Of color, weight, and heat, poured all together,　　　130
　　Would quite confound distinction, yet stands off
　　In differences so mighty. If she be
　　All that is virtuous, save what thou dislik'st—
　　"A poor physician's daughter"—thou dislik'st
　　Of virtue for the name. But do not so.　　　　135
　　From lowest place whence virtuous things proceed,
　　The place is dignified by th' doer's deed.
　　Where great additions swell 's, and virtue none,
　　It is a dropsied honor. Good alone
　　Is good, without a name; vileness is so;　　　　140
　　The property by what ⌜it⌝ is should go,
　　Not by the title. She is young, wise, fair;
　　In these to nature she's immediate heir,
　　And these breed honor. That is honor's scorn
　　Which challenges itself as honor's born　　　　145
　　And is not like the sire. Honors thrive
　　When rather from our acts we them derive
　　Than our foregoers. The mere word's a slave
　　Debauched on every tomb, on every grave
　　A lying trophy, and as oft is dumb　　　　150
　　Where dust and damned oblivion is the tomb
　　Of honored bones indeed. What should be said?
　　If thou canst like this creature as a maid,
　　I can create the rest. Virtue and she
　　Is her own dower, honor and wealth from me.　　　155

158. **choose:** have your own way

161. **at the stake:** i.e., at risk (The term suggests both gambling [where **the stake** is the money that is hazarded] and bearbaiting [where **the stake** is the post to which the bear is tied].) **which:** i.e., **which** threat to my honor

164. **misprision:** contempt, disparagement

165. **her desert:** i.e., what she deserves

166. **We, poising us in:** i.e., I, adding my weight to; **scale:** scale-pan (The image is of a weighing apparatus consisting of a **beam** with scale-pans on each end.) See below.

167. **weigh . . . beam:** i.e., so outweigh you that your **scale** will fly up and strike **the beam**

171. **presently:** immediately

175. **staggers:** giddy confusions

180. **fancy:** preference; amorous inclination (See *The Merchant of Venice* 3.2.65–69: "Tell me where is **fancy** bred . . . ? It is engendered in the eye. . . .")

182. **late:** i.e., lately

A beam and scale-pans. (2.3.166–67)
From Silvestro Pietrasanta, . . . *Symbola heroica* . . . (1682).

BERTRAM
  I cannot love her, nor will strive to do 't.
KING
  Thou wrong'st thyself if thou shouldst strive to
    choose.
HELEN
  That you are well restored, my lord, I'm glad.
  Let the rest go.   160
KING
  My honor's at the stake, which to defeat
  I must produce my power.—Here, take her hand,
  Proud, scornful boy, unworthy this good gift,
  That dost in vile misprision shackle up
  My love and her desert; that canst not dream   165
  We, poising us in her defective scale,
  Shall weigh thee to the beam; that wilt not know
  It is in us to plant thine honor where
  We please to have it grow. Check thy contempt;
  Obey our will, which travails in thy good.   170
  Believe not thy disdain, but presently
  Do thine own fortunes that obedient right
  Which both thy duty owes and our power claims,
  Or I will throw thee from my care forever
  Into the staggers and the careless lapse   175
  Of youth and ignorance, both my revenge and hate
  Loosing upon thee in the name of justice
  Without all terms of pity. Speak. Thine answer.
BERTRAM
  Pardon, my gracious lord, for I submit
  My fancy to your eyes. When I consider   180
  What great creation and what dole of honor
  Flies where you bid it, I find that she which late
  Was in my nobler thoughts most base is now
  The praisèd of the King, who, so ennobled,
  Is as 'twere born so.   185
KING   Take her by the hand,

188–89. **counterpoise . . . replete:** (1) compensation that, even **if** it is **not** equal **to** your **estate,** will provide a more perfect **balance** between you and Helen; (2) compensation that not only will be equivalent **to** your **estate,** but will more than counterbalance it

192. **this contract:** When Bertram obeys the King's order to "take her by the hand, / And tell her she is thine" (lines 186–87), he legally betroths himself to Helen. Such a clasping of hands was known as a "handfasting," a **contract** that was, in fact, a legal marriage. The **ceremony** to follow was demanded by the church but not by the courts. The **solemn feast** (line 194) was the next customary part of the celebration of the marriage, and was usually followed by the couple being "bedded" and the marriage consummated.

193. **expedient:** fitting, appropriate; or, perhaps, expeditious; **now-born brief:** perhaps, just-issued royal mandate (This line is much debated.)

195. **more attend upon:** i.e., await; **space:** i.e., time

196. **Expecting:** i.e., anticipating the coming of; **friends:** family, relatives

197 SD. **of this wedding:** i.e., on **this** betrothal

205. **succeeding:** consequence, result

206. **companion:** often a term of contempt

207. **man:** (1) humankind; (2) manly

208. **count's man:** i.e., the servant of a **count**

210–11. **You . . . old:** i.e., I would challenge you to a duel were it not for your age (Compare lines 223–24.)

(continued)

And tell her she is thine, to whom I promise
A counterpoise, if not to thy estate,
A balance more replete.

BERTRAM   I take her hand.   190

KING
Good fortune and the favor of the King
Smile upon this contract, whose ceremony
Shall seem expedient on the now-born brief
And be performed tonight. The solemn feast
Shall more attend upon the coming space,   195
Expecting absent friends. As thou lov'st her
Thy love's to me religious; else, does err.

They exit. Parolles and Lafew stay behind,
commenting of this wedding.

LAFEW   Do you hear, monsieur? A word with you.

PAROLLES   Your pleasure, sir.

LAFEW   Your lord and master did well to make his re-   200
cantation.

PAROLLES   "Recantation"? My "lord"? My "master"?

LAFEW   Ay. Is it not a language I speak?

PAROLLES   A most harsh one, and not to be understood
without bloody succeeding. My "master"?   205

LAFEW   Are you companion to the Count Rossillion?

PAROLLES   To any count, to all counts, to what is man.

LAFEW   To what is count's man. Count's master is of
another style.

PAROLLES   You are too old, sir; let it satisfy you, you are   210
too old.

LAFEW   I must tell thee, sirrah, I write man, to which
title age cannot bring thee.

PAROLLES   What I dare too well do, I dare not do.

LAFEW   I did think thee, for two ordinaries, to be a   215
pretty wise fellow; thou didst make tolerable vent
of thy travel; it might pass. Yet the scarves and the
bannerets about thee did manifoldly dissuade me
from believing thee a vessel of too great a burden.

212. **sirrah:** term of address to a male social inferior; **write man:** i.e., am entitled by **age** (line 213) to call myself a **man**

214. **too well do:** i.e., **do** only **too well**

215. **two ordinaries:** i.e., the time it took to have two meals with you (An *ordinary* was a public meal.)

216. **make tolerable vent:** i.e., speak moderately well

217. **scarves:** i.e., military sashes (broad bands of fabric worn across the body or around the waist)

219. **burden:** carrying capacity; or, perhaps, cargo

220. **found thee:** i.e., **found** you out, discovered the truth about you

221–22. **taking up:** i.e., picking **up** (with probable wordplay on such meanings as "arresting," "opposing," "rebuking," "levying as a common soldier," "patronizing," or "hiring")

227. **window of lattice:** This complex reference perhaps begins with the scarves that cross Parolles' body, making him look like a latticework **window;** it links Parolles to the common ale-house, identified by a red **lattice,** and also signals the transparency of his deceptive military manner.

234. **dram:** i.e., tiniest bit

235. **bate thee:** i.e., deduct from what you deserve; **scruple:** tiny amount (literally, a third of a **dram**)

238. **pull at a smack:** i.e., drink a taste; **o' th' contrary:** i.e., of your own folly

241. **hold:** i.e., **hold** on to, preserve

(continued)

I have now found thee. When I lose thee again, I   220
care not. Yet art thou good for nothing but taking
up, and that thou'rt scarce worth.

PAROLLES   Hadst thou not the privilege of antiquity
upon thee—

LAFEW   Do not plunge thyself too far in anger lest thou   225
hasten thy trial, which if—Lord have mercy on
thee for a hen! So, my good window of lattice, fare
thee well; thy casement I need not open, for I look
through thee. Give me thy hand.

PAROLLES   My lord, you give me most egregious indig-   230
nity.

LAFEW   Ay, with all my heart, and thou art worthy of it.

PAROLLES   I have not, my lord, deserved it.

LAFEW   Yes, good faith, ev'ry dram of it, and I will not
bate thee a scruple.   235

PAROLLES   Well, I shall be wiser.

LAFEW   Ev'n as soon as thou canst, for thou hast to
pull at a smack o' th' contrary. If ever thou be'st
bound in thy scarf and beaten, thou ⌐shalt¬ find
what it is to be proud of thy bondage. I have a   240
desire to hold my acquaintance with thee, or
rather my knowledge, that I may say in the default
"He is a man I know."

PAROLLES   My lord, you do me most insupportable vex-
ation.   245

LAFEW   I would it were hell pains for thy sake, and my
poor doing eternal; for doing I am past, as I will by
thee in what motion age will give me leave.
                                                                              He exits.

PAROLLES   Well, thou hast a son shall take this disgrace
off me. Scurvy, old, filthy, scurvy lord! Well, I must   250
be patient; there is no fettering of authority. I'll
beat him, by my life, if I can meet him with any
convenience, an he were double and double a lord.
I'll have no more pity of his age than I would have
of—I'll beat him, an if I could but meet him again.   255

242. **in the default:** i.e., when you fail in your duty

247. **for doing:** perhaps, **for** copulation; or, perhaps, **for** manly actions

247–48. **will by thee:** i.e., **will** pass **by** you (wordplay on **I am past,** line 247)

251. **fettering:** restraining

253. **an:** i.e., even if

254. **of:** i.e., on

255. **an if:** if

259. **make some reservation of:** keep back

260. **good lord:** i.e., patron

268. **Methink'st:** i.e., it seems to me

270. **breathe themselves:** i.e., exercise **themselves** briskly

271. **measure:** treatment, punishment

276–77. **commission of:** i.e., authority derived from

277. **heraldry:** title or rank

282. **Undone:** destroyed, ruined

Enter Lafew.

LAFEW   Sirrah, your lord and master's married. There's
    news for you: you have a new mistress.
PAROLLES   I most unfeignedly beseech your Lordship
    to make some reservation of your wrongs. He is
    my good lord; whom I serve above is my master.   260
LAFEW   Who? God?
PAROLLES   Ay, sir.
LAFEW   The devil it is that's thy master. Why dost thou
    garter up thy arms o' this fashion? Dost make hose
    of thy sleeves? Do other servants so? Thou wert   265
    best set thy lower part where thy nose stands. By
    mine honor, if I were but two hours younger, I'd
    beat thee. Methink'st thou art a general offense,
    and every man should beat thee. I think thou wast
    created for men to breathe themselves upon thee.   270
PAROLLES   This is hard and undeserved measure, my
    lord.
LAFEW   Go to, sir. You were beaten in Italy for picking a
    kernel out of a pomegranate. You are a vagabond,
    and no true traveler. You are more saucy with   275
    lords and honorable personages than the commis-
    sion of your birth and virtue gives you heraldry.
    You are not worth another word; else I'd call you
    knave. I leave you.   *He exits.*
PAROLLES   Good, very good! It is so, then. Good, very   280
    good. Let it be concealed awhile.

Enter ⌜Bertram⌝ Count Rossillion.

BERTRAM
    Undone, and forfeited to cares forever!
PAROLLES   What's the matter, sweetheart?
BERTRAM
    Although before the solemn priest I have sworn,
    I will not bed her.   285

288. **Tuscan wars:** See note to 1.2.16–17.

291. **letters:** i.e., a letter

295. **box:** possible wordplay on female genitals

296. **kicky-wicky:** a word not recorded elsewhere, but perhaps related to "kicksey-winsey" (a whim or fancy) and to "kickshaws" (a trifle or toy)

297. **marrow:** vitality and strength

298. **curvet:** leap of a horse

299. **Mars's:** Mars was the Roman god of **war.**

300. **jades:** i.e., broken-down horses (See below.)

303. **hate to:** i.e., hatred of

304. **wherefore I am:** i.e., why **I** have

305. **durst not:** i.e., did not dare to

306. **furnish me to:** i.e., equip **me** with weaponry and military trappings for

308. **To:** i.e., compared **to**

309. **capriccio:** caprice, whim

311. **straight:** immediately

314. **A young . . . marred:** Proverbial: "Marrying is marring."

A jade. (2.3.300)
From Cesare Fiaschi, *Trattato dell'imbrigliare . . . caualli . . .* (1614).

PAROLLES   What, what, sweetheart?

BERTRAM
  O my Parolles, they have married me!
  I'll to the Tuscan wars and never bed her.

PAROLLES   France is a dog-hole, and it no more merits
    the tread of a man's foot. To th' wars!   290

BERTRAM   There's letters from my mother. What th'
    import is I know not yet.

PAROLLES   Ay, that would be known. To th' wars, my
    boy, to th' wars!
  He wears his honor in a box unseen   295
  That hugs his kicky-wicky here at home,
  Spending his manly marrow in her arms
  Which should sustain the bound and high curvet
  Of Mars's fiery steed. To other regions!
  France is a stable, we that dwell in 't jades.   300
  Therefore, to th' war!

BERTRAM
  It shall be so. I'll send her to my house,
  Acquaint my mother with my hate to her
  And wherefore I am fled, write to the King
  That which I durst not speak. His present gift   305
  Shall furnish me to those Italian fields
  Where noble fellows strike. Wars is no strife
  To the dark house and the ⌜detested⌝ wife.

PAROLLES
  Will this *capriccio* hold in thee? Art sure?

BERTRAM
  Go with me to my chamber, and advise me.   310
  I'll send her straight away. Tomorrow
  I'll to the wars, she to her single sorrow.

PAROLLES
  Why, these balls bound; there's noise in it. 'Tis hard.
  A young man married is a man that's marred.
  Therefore away, and leave her bravely. Go.   315
  The King has done you wrong, but hush, 'tis so.
                                            ⌜*They*⌝ *exit.*

2.4 Parolles brings Helen word that Bertram is leaving for Tuscany and that she is to get permission from the King to return to Rossillion.

---

2. **well:** wordplay, continuing through line 12, on **well** as (1) "in health"; and (2) "dead" (Proverbial: "He is **well,** since he is in **heaven**" [line 10])

4. **wants:** lacks

6. **what does she ail:** i.e., **what** is the matter with her

22. **man's:** wordplay on **man** as servant (as at 2.3.208)

23. **shakes . . . undoing:** i.e., brings about **his master's** destruction through talking too much

25. **your title:** i.e., what one is entitled to (with perhaps wordplay on **Parolles'** name, which is the French word for "words")

28. **Before:** in the presence of

29. **Before me:** a mild oath (See note to 2.3.26.)

31–32. **found thee:** i.e., **found** you out

⌜Scene 4⌝

Enter Helen ⌜*with a paper,*⌝ *and* ⌜*Fool.*⌝

HELEN   My mother greets me kindly. Is she well?

FOOL   She is not well, but yet she has her health. She's
very merry, but yet she is not well. But, thanks be
given, she's very well and wants nothing i' th' world,
but yet she is not well.   5

HELEN   If she be very well, what does she ail that she's
not very well?

FOOL   Truly, she's very well indeed, but for two things.

HELEN   What two things?

FOOL   One, that she's not in heaven, whither God send   10
her quickly; the other, that she's in earth, from
whence God send her quickly.

Enter Parolles.

PAROLLES   Bless you, my fortunate lady.

HELEN   I hope, sir, I have your good will to have mine
own good ⌜fortunes.⌝   15

PAROLLES   You had my prayers to lead them on, and to
keep them on have them still.—O my knave, how
does my old lady?

FOOL   So that you had her wrinkles and I her money, I
would she did as you say.   20

PAROLLES   Why, I say nothing.

FOOL   Marry, you are the wiser man, for many a man's
tongue shakes out his master's undoing. To say
nothing, to do nothing, to know nothing, and to
have nothing is to be a great part of your title,   25
which is within a very little of nothing.

PAROLLES   Away. Thou'rt a knave.

FOOL   You should have said, sir, "Before a knave,
thou'rt a knave"; that's "Before me, thou'rt a
knave." This had been truth, sir.   30

PAROLLES   Go to. Thou art a witty fool. I have found
thee.

33. **find me in yourself:** wordplay on (1) discover folly **in yourself;** and (2) **find me** by **yourself**

33–34. **were you taught to find me:** Parolles' response to this question apparently dropped out in the Folio printing. Editors have suggested that Parolles replies "In myself," which makes sense of the Fool's next speech.

38. **well fed:** more wordplay on the proverb "Better **fed** than taught" (See note to 2.2.3.)

41. **rite:** The consummation of the marriage was both a **rite** and a **right.** Thus either spelling would be appropriate here.

42. **time:** i.e., the present **time** (See note to 2.3.192.)

43. **to a:** i.e., because of **a**

44. **Whose want:** i.e., the lack of this **rite; sweets:** fragrant flowers

45. **curbèd time:** i.e., period of restraint

48. **What's his will else:** i.e., what **else** does he wish

50. **make:** represent

51. **apology:** excuse

52. **make . . . need:** i.e., **make** the necessity (for **haste**) seem plausible

54. **this:** i.e., **leave** or permission from the **King; presently:** for the time being

55. **Attend:** await

FOOL   Did you find me in yourself, sir, or were you
    taught to find me?
⌐PAROLLES . . . .⌐
FOOL   The search, sir, was profitable, and much fool   35
    may you find in you, even to the world's pleasure
    and the increase of laughter.
PAROLLES   A good knave, i' faith, and well fed.
    Madam, my lord will go away tonight;
    A very serious business calls on him.   40
    The great prerogative and rite of love,
    Which as your due time claims, he does acknowledge
    But puts it off to a compelled restraint,
    Whose want and whose delay is strewed with sweets,
    Which they distill now in the curbèd time   45
    To make the coming hour o'erflow with joy
    And pleasure drown the brim.
HELEN   What's his will else?
PAROLLES
    That you will take your instant leave o' th' King
    And make this haste as your own good proceeding,   50
    Strengthened with what apology you think
    May make it probable need.
HELEN   What more commands he?
PAROLLES
    That, having this obtained, you presently
    Attend his further pleasure.   55
HELEN
    In everything I wait upon his will.
PAROLLES   I shall report it so.   *Parolles exits.*
HELEN, ⌐*to Fool*⌐   I pray you, come, sirrah.
                                    ⌐*They*⌐ *exit.*

2.5 Bertram is warned that Parolles is an untrustworthy coward. Bertram gives Helen a letter and instructs her to go immediately to Rossillion to await him. He says privately that he has no intention of ever going there.

———

3. **very valiant approof:** i.e., fully demonstrated valor
4. **deliverance:** report, statement
6. **dial:** clock, watch; **true:** accurately
6–7. **took . . . bunting:** The proverb "to take a **bunting for a lark**" means to overestimate someone. Here the proverb is reversed.
9. **accordingly:** correspondingly
11–12. **my state . . . dangerous:** i.e., **my** spiritual **state** in that regard is perilous
18. **I know him:** Perhaps, Lafew pretends that Parolles' "**Sir**" (line 17) is the name of **his tailor.**
22. **away:** go **away,** leave
24. **casketed:** enclosed in a casket
28. **something:** i.e., of some value (an allusion to listening to travelers' tales as after-dinner entertainment)
30. **pass:** i.e., give currency to

⌈Scene 5⌝

Enter Lafew and Bertram.

LAFEW   But I hope your Lordship thinks not him a soldier.

BERTRAM   Yes, my lord, and of very valiant approof.

LAFEW   You have it from his own deliverance.

BERTRAM   And by other warranted testimony.   5

LAFEW   Then my dial goes not true. I took this lark for
a bunting.

BERTRAM   I do assure you, my lord, he is very great in
knowledge and accordingly valiant.

LAFEW   I have then sinned against his experience and   10
transgressed against his valor, and my state that
way is dangerous since I cannot yet find in my
heart to repent. Here he comes. I pray you make us
friends. I will pursue the amity.

Enter Parolles.

PAROLLES, ⌈*to Bertram*⌝   These things shall be done, sir.   15

LAFEW, ⌈*to Bertram*⌝   Pray you, sir, who's his tailor?

PAROLLES   Sir?

LAFEW   O, I know him well. Ay, sir, he, sir, 's a good
workman, a very good tailor.

BERTRAM, ⌈*aside to Parolles*⌝   Is she gone to the King?   20

PAROLLES   She is.

BERTRAM   Will she away tonight?

PAROLLES   As you'll have her.

BERTRAM
I have writ my letters, casketed my treasure,
Given order for our horses, and tonight,   25
When I should take possession of the bride,
⌈End⌝ ere I do begin.

LAFEW, ⌈*aside*⌝   A good traveler is something at the latter end of a dinner, but one that lies three thirds,
and uses a known truth to pass a thousand noth-   30

33. **unkindness:** ill-will, enmity

35. **run into:** i.e., incur (Lafew responds with wordplay in which **"run into"** means "rush headlong **into.**")

37. **made shift to run:** i.e., succeeded in running; or, **made** every effort **to run**

38. **like him . . . custard:** probably an allusion to the clown at civic entertainments who jumped into a huge **custard**

39–40. **suffer question for:** i.e., put up with discussion of (with possible wordplay on **question** as the application of torture as part of a judicial procedure)

40. **residence:** i.e., residing, staying

41. **mistaken:** misunderstood, taken the wrong view of (Lafew's response plays on *to mistake* as to take amiss, take offense.)

46–47. **kept of them tame:** i.e., **kept** such creatures as pets

51. **An idle:** i.e., a foolish, a silly

55. **pass:** reputation, estimation

56. **clog:** weight fastened to the leg of a prisoner

59. **present:** immediate

ings with, should be once heard and thrice beat-
en.—God save you, captain.

BERTRAM, ⌜*to Parolles*⌝ Is there any unkindness
between my lord and you, monsieur?

PAROLLES   I know not how I have deserved to run into   35
my lord's displeasure.

LAFEW   You have made shift to run into 't, boots and
spurs and all, like him that leapt into the custard;
and out of it you'll run again rather than suffer
question for your residence.   40

BERTRAM   It may be you have mistaken him, my lord.

LAFEW   And shall do so ever, though I took him at 's
prayers. Fare you well, my lord, and believe this of
me: there can be no kernel in this light nut. The
soul of this man is his clothes. Trust him not in   45
matter of heavy consequence. I have kept of them
tame and know their natures.—Farewell, monsieur. I have spoken better of you than you have or
will to deserve at my hand, but we must do good
against evil.   ⌜*He exits.*⌝   50

PAROLLES   An idle lord, I swear.

BERTRAM   I think ⌜not⌝ so.

PAROLLES   Why, do you not know him?

BERTRAM
Yes, I do know him well, and common speech
Gives him a worthy pass.   55

Enter Helen.

Here comes my clog.

HELEN
I have, sir, as I was commanded from you,
Spoke with the King and have procured his leave
For present parting. Only he desires
Some private speech with you.   60

BERTRAM   I shall obey his will.
You must not marvel, Helen, at my course,

63. **holds not color with:** is not consistent **with,** does not match; **the time:** i.e., the state of affairs at the present moment

64–65. **ministration . . . particular:** i.e., the administering of my personal duties and responsibilities

70. **respects:** motives, aims

71. **appointments:** resolutions, purposes

81. **observance:** dutiful service

82. **homely stars have:** i.e., humble destiny has (See note to **baser stars,** 1.1.189.)

85. **Hie:** hasten, go quickly

88. **owe:** i.e., own

90. **fain:** gladly

Paris and Helen of Troy. (1.3.71–74)
From Guillaume Rouillé, . . . *Promptuarii iconum* . . . (1553).

Which holds not color with the time, nor does
The ministration and requirèd office
On my particular. Prepared I was not   65
For such a business; therefore am I found
So much unsettled. This drives me to entreat you
That presently you take your way for home,
And rather muse than ask why I entreat you;
For my respects are better than they seem,   70
And my appointments have in them a need
Greater than shows itself at the first view
To you that know them not. ⌜*Giving her a paper.*⌝
    This to my mother.
'Twill be two days ere I shall see you, so   75
I leave you to your wisdom.
HELEN   Sir, I can nothing say
But that I am your most obedient servant—
BERTRAM
Come, come, no more of that.
HELEN   And ever shall   80
With true observance seek to eke out that
Wherein toward me my homely stars have failed
To equal my great fortune.
BERTRAM   Let that go.
My haste is very great. Farewell. Hie home.   85
HELEN
Pray, sir, your pardon.
BERTRAM   Well, what would you say?
HELEN
I am not worthy of the wealth I owe,
Nor dare I say 'tis mine—and yet it is—
But, like a timorous thief, most fain would steal   90
What law does vouch mine own.
BERTRAM   What would you have?
HELEN
Something, and scarce so much; nothing, indeed.

94. **what I would:** what I wish
97. **stay:** wait
103. **coraggio:** i.e., courage

"Whilst I can . . . hear the drum." (2.5.101)
From Geoffrey Whitney, *A choice of emblemes . . .* (1586).

I would not tell you what I would, my lord. Faith,
   yes: 95
Strangers and foes do sunder and not kiss.

BERTRAM
I pray you stay not, but in haste to horse.

HELEN
I shall not break your bidding, good my lord.—
Where are my other men?—Monsieur, farewell.
                                She exits.

BERTRAM
Go thou toward home, where I will never come   100
Whilst I can shake my sword or hear the drum.—
Away, and for our flight.

PAROLLES   Bravely, *coraggio!*
                         ⌜*They exit.*⌝

ALL'S WELL
THAT ENDS WELL

ACT 3

3.1   The Duke of Florence greets French courtiers who have come to fight on his side.

   O SD. **Flourish:** a trumpet blast or fanfare

   3. **Whose great decision:** i.e., the violent action of deciding which

   7. **On the:** i.e., on the part of **the**

   8. **our cousin France:** i.e., the King of **France** (**Cousin** was a title given by princes to other princes and noblemen.)

   12. **yield:** declare, communicate

   13. **But like:** except as; **outward man:** i.e., outsider

   14. **figure:** design, plan, scheme; **frames:** creates

   15. **By self-unable motion:** perhaps, out of my own inadequate imaginings

   17. **incertain:** uncertain, doubtful

"King Pippen." (2.1.88)
From Jean de Serres, *A generall historie of France* . . . (1611).

ACT 3

⌜Scene 1⌝

*Flourish. Enter the Duke of Florence, the two French
⌜Lords,⌝ with a troop of Soldiers.*

DUKE
So that from point to point now have you heard
The fundamental reasons of this war,
Whose great decision hath much blood let forth
And more thirsts after.
FIRST LORD   Holy seems the quarrel   5
Upon your Grace's part, black and fearful
On the opposer.
DUKE
Therefore we marvel much our cousin France
Would in so just a business shut his bosom
Against our borrowing prayers.   10
SECOND LORD   Good my lord,
The reasons of our state I cannot yield
But like a common and an outward man
That the great figure of a council frames
By self-unable motion; therefore dare not   15
Say what I think of it, since I have found
Myself in my incertain grounds to fail
As often as I guessed.
DUKE   Be it his pleasure.

21. **surfeit on their ease:** i.e., grow oppressed or sick through too much leisure

22. **physic:** remedy

26. **better fall:** i.e., **better** positions become vacant; **avails:** advantage, benefit, profits

3.2 The Fool returns to Rossillion with a letter from Bertram that tells the Countess of his plan to run away from the French court and his determination never to "bed" Helen. Helen enters with her own letter from Bertram, which sets seemingly impossible obstacles in the way of Bertram's ever being a husband to her. Helen decides to leave Rossillion since her presence there is keeping Bertram away and endangering his life in the war.

---

2. **save:** i.e., except

7. **ruff:** the loose turned-over portion or flap of a high boot

8. **trick:** trait, characteristic (Robert Burton's 1623 *Anatomy of Melancholy* [3.2.3] links singing to love-melancholy, but suggests that it is not so much a symptom of **melancholy** as an attempt to attract the beloved.)

12. **have no mind to:** i.e., **have no** desire for

13. **old lings:** literally, salted fish (probably a bawdy way of saying "men," with a reference to the penis)

16. **stomach:** appetite

18. **E'en that:** i.e., exactly **that** which

20. **recovered:** healed, cured; **undone:** destroyed, ruined

FIRST LORD
　But I am sure the younger of our ⌐nation,⌐   20
　That surfeit on their ease, will day by day
　Come here for physic.
DUKE   Welcome shall they be,
　And all the honors that can fly from us
　Shall on them settle. You know your places well.   25
　When better fall, for your avails they fell.
　Tomorrow to th' field.
                                   Flourish. ⌐*They exit.*⌐

⌐Scene 2⌐

Enter Countess, ⌐*with a paper,*⌐ *and* ⌐*Fool.*⌐

COUNTESS   It hath happened all as I would have had it,
　save that he comes not along with her.
FOOL   By my troth, I take my young lord to be a very
　melancholy man.
COUNTESS   By what observance, I pray you?   5
FOOL   Why, he will look upon his boot and sing, mend
　the ruff and sing, ask questions and sing, pick his
　teeth and sing. I know a man that had this trick of
　melancholy ⌐sold⌐ a goodly manor for a song.
COUNTESS   Let me see what he writes and when he   10
　means to come.   ⌐*She opens the letter.*⌐
FOOL   I have no mind to Isbel since I was at court. Our
　old lings and our Isbels o' th' country are nothing
　like your old ling and your Isbels o' th' court. The
　brains of my Cupid's knocked out, and I begin to   15
　love as an old man loves money, with no stomach.
COUNTESS   What have we here?
FOOL   E'en that you have there.   *He exits.*
⌐COUNTESS *reads.*⌐   *I have sent you a daughter-in-law.*
　She hath recovered the King and undone me. I have   20
　wedded her, not bedded her, and sworn to make the

32. **For the contempt of empire:** perhaps, **for** even an emperor to despise

33. **heavy:** weighty; sad

41. **standing to 't:** fighting courageously (with a subsequent sexual meaning in which erection is linked to the **getting** [i.e., begetting, fathering] **of children**)

45. **Save:** i.e., God **save** (a conventional greeting)

50. **quirks:** sudden strokes

51. **on the start:** perhaps, suddenly, unexpectedly

52. **woman me unto 't:** i.e., make **me** behave like a weak **woman** in the face of it

Fame with her trumpet. (2.1.19)
From August Casimir Redel, *Apophtegmata symbolica* . . . [n.d.].

"not" eternal. You shall hear I am run away. Know it
before the report come. If there be breadth enough in
the world, I will hold a long distance. My duty to
you.   25
    Your unfortunate son,
                               Bertram.

This is not well, rash and unbridled boy:
To fly the favors of so good a king,
To pluck his indignation on thy head   30
By the misprizing of a maid too virtuous
For the contempt of empire.

               Enter ⌜*Fool.*⌝

FOOL   O madam, yonder is heavy news within, be-
    tween two soldiers and my young lady.
COUNTESS   What is the matter?   35
FOOL   Nay, there is some comfort in the news, some
    comfort. Your son will not be killed so soon as I
    thought he would.
COUNTESS   Why should he be killed?
FOOL   So say I, madam, if he run away, as I hear he   40
    does. The danger is in standing to 't; that's the loss
    of men, though it be the getting of children. Here
    they come will tell you more. For my part, I only
    hear your son was run away.   ⌜*He exits.*⌝

   Enter Helen, ⌜*with a paper,*⌝ *and two Gentlemen.*

FIRST GENTLEMAN, ⌜*to Countess*⌝ Save you, good   45
    madam.
HELEN
    Madam, my lord is gone, forever gone.
SECOND GENTLEMAN   Do not say so.
COUNTESS
    Think upon patience, pray you.—Gentlemen,
    I have felt so many quirks of joy and grief   50
    That the first face of neither on the start
    Can woman me unto 't. Where is my son, I pray you?

54. **thitherward:** on the way thither

55. **dispatch in hand:** i.e., settling of business

56. **bend:** proceed, turn

57. **passport:** dismissal

68. **griefs are thine:** i.e., **griefs** that **are** (in fact) yours

71. **all my:** i.e., my only

76. **good convenience claims:** i.e., he can properly lay claim to

"The horses of the sun." (2.1.180)
From Claude François Menestrier, *L'art des emblemes* . . . (1684).

SECOND GENTLEMAN
Madam, he's gone to serve the Duke of Florence.
We met him thitherward, for thence we came,
And, after some dispatch in hand at court,　　　　55
Thither we bend again.

HELEN
Look on his letter, madam; here's my passport.
⌈*She reads.*⌉ *When thou canst get the ring upon
my finger, which never shall come off, and show me
a child begotten of thy body that I am father to, then*　　60
*call me husband. But in such a "then" I write a
"never."*
This is a dreadful sentence.

COUNTESS
Brought you this letter, gentlemen?

SECOND GENTLEMAN　　　　　　　　Ay, madam,　　　　65
And for the contents' sake are sorry for our pains.

COUNTESS
I prithee, lady, have a better cheer.
If thou engrossest all the griefs are thine,
Thou robb'st me of a moiety. He was my son,
But I do wash his name out of my blood,　　　　70
And thou art all my child.—Towards Florence is he?

SECOND GENTLEMAN　Ay, madam.

COUNTESS　And to be a soldier?

SECOND GENTLEMAN
Such is his noble purpose, and, believe 't,
The Duke will lay upon him all the honor　　　　75
That good convenience claims.

COUNTESS　　　　　　　　　　Return you thither?

FIRST GENTLEMAN
Ay, madam, with the swiftest wing of speed.

HELEN ⌈*reads*⌉
Till I have no wife I have nothing in France.
'Tis bitter.　　　　　　　　　　　　　　　　80

83. **haply:** perhaps

87. **But:** except

98. **a deal . . . much:** i.e., **a** great **deal too much of that   that:** i.e., the power to induce corruption

99. **holds:** profits

108. **Not so . . . courtesies:** i.e., you do not **serve** me except insofar as we exchange courteous behavior

Pouring "the waters of . . . love" into a sieve. (1.3.212–13)
From Guillaume de La Perrière,
Le théâtre des bon engins . . . [1539?].

COUNTESS   Find you that there?
HELEN   Ay, madam.
FIRST GENTLEMAN
  'Tis but the boldness of his hand, haply,
  Which his heart was not consenting to.
COUNTESS
  Nothing in France until he have no wife!   85
  There's nothing here that is too good for him
  But only she, and she deserves a lord
  That twenty such rude boys might tend upon
  And call her hourly mistress. Who was with him?
FIRST GENTLEMAN
  A servant only, and a gentleman   90
  Which I have sometime known.
COUNTESS   Parolles was it not?
FIRST GENTLEMAN   Ay, my good lady, he.
COUNTESS
  A very tainted fellow, and full of wickedness.
  My son corrupts a well-derivèd nature   95
  With his inducement.
FIRST GENTLEMAN   Indeed, good lady,
  The fellow has a deal of that too much
  Which holds him much to have.
COUNTESS   You're welcome,   100
    gentlemen.
  I will entreat you when you see my son
  To tell him that his sword can never win
  The honor that he loses. More I'll entreat you
  Written to bear along.   105
SECOND GENTLEMAN   We serve you, madam,
  In that and all your worthiest affairs.
COUNTESS
  Not so, but as we change our courtesies.
  Will you draw near?
                    She exits ⌜*with the Gentlemen.*⌝

115. **event:** result, outcome

117. **sportive:** amorous

118. **mark:** target

121. **still-'pearing air:** i.e., **air** that appears **still** (This phrase—spelled in the Folio "still-peering"—is much debated and often emended. Many editors substitute "still-piecing"—i.e., continually putting itself back together.)

124. **forward:** eager, spirited

125. **caitiff:** wretch

128. **ravin:** ravenous

130. **owes:** owns

132. **Whence . . . scar:** i.e., from the place where the only reward that **danger** bestows on **honor** is **a scar**

137. **officed all:** i.e., performed **all** duties

138. **pitiful:** merciful, i.e., filled with pity

139. **consolate:** console

Rumor. (3.2.138)
From Henry Peacham, *Minerua Britanna* . . . [1612].

HELEN
  "Till I have no wife I have nothing in France."   110
  Nothing in France until he has no wife.
  Thou shalt have none, Rossillion, none in France.
  Then hast thou all again. Poor lord, is 't I
  That chase thee from thy country and expose
  Those tender limbs of thine to the event   115
  Of the none-sparing war? And is it I
  That drive thee from the sportive court, where thou
  Wast shot at with fair eyes, to be the mark
  Of smoky muskets? O you leaden messengers
  That ride upon the violent speed of fire,   120
  Fly with false aim; move the still-'pearing air
  That sings with piercing; do not touch my lord.
  Whoever shoots at him, I set him there;
  Whoever charges on his forward breast,
  I am the caitiff that do hold him to 't;   125
  And though I kill him not, I am the cause
  His death was so effected. Better 'twere
  I met the ravin lion when he roared
  With sharp constraint of hunger; better 'twere
  That all the miseries which nature owes   130
  Were mine at once. No, come thou home, Rossillion,
  Whence honor but of danger wins a scar,
  As oft it loses all. I will be gone.
  My being here it is that holds thee hence.
  Shall I stay here to do 't? No, no, although   135
  The air of paradise did fan the house
  And angels officed all. I will be gone,
  That pitiful rumor may report my flight
  To consolate thine ear. Come, night; end, day;
  For with the dark, poor thief, I'll steal away.   140
                         She exits.

3.3   Bertram is put in command of the Duke of Florence's cavalry.

O SD. **Drum and Trumpets:** i.e., a drummer and trumpeters
1. **horse:** cavalry
2. **lay:** wager
2–3. **credence / Upon:** trust in, reliance on
9. **helm:** helmet
12. **file:** list, roll
14. **lover of thy drum:** The **drum,** which in Shakespeare's plays often symbolized military action or zeal, is here portrayed as the instrument of **Mars,** the god of war.

3.4   The Countess is given the letter left for her by Helen, in which Helen sets out her intention to make amends for her overambitious love by going on a pilgrimage to the shrine of St. James.

---

1. **of:** i.e., from
4. **St. Jaques' pilgrim:** i.e., a religious journeyer to the shrine of St. James (See picture, page 118.) The shrine at Compostella, where St. James the Great was presumably buried, was the most famous in Europe. (**Jaques** is pronounced as two syllables.)
7. **sainted:** sacred, holy
9. **hie:** hasten

⌜Scene 3⌝

Flourish. Enter the Duke of Florence, ⌜Bertram Count⌝
Rossillion, Drum and Trumpets, Soldiers, Parolles.

DUKE, ⌜*to Bertram*⌝
 The general of our horse thou art, and we,
 Great in our hope, lay our best love and credence
 Upon thy promising fortune.
BERTRAM   Sir, it is
 A charge too heavy for my strength, but yet   5
 We'll strive to bear it for your worthy sake
 To th' extreme edge of hazard.
DUKE   Then go thou forth,
 And Fortune play upon thy prosperous helm
 As thy auspicious mistress.   10
BERTRAM   This very day,
 Great Mars, I put myself into thy file.
 Make me but like my thoughts, and I shall prove
 A lover of thy drum, hater of love.
                                        All exit.

⌜Scene 4⌝

Enter Countess and Steward, ⌜with a paper.⌝

COUNTESS
 Alas! And would you take the letter of her?
 Might you not know she would do as she has done
 By sending me a letter? Read it again.
⌜STEWARD *reads the*⌝ *letter*
  I am Saint Jaques' pilgrim, thither gone.
   Ambitious love hath so in me offended   5
  That barefoot plod I the cold ground upon,
   With sainted vow my faults to have amended.
  Write, write, that from the bloody course of war
   My dearest master, your dear son, may hie.

12. **His . . . forgive:** i.e., ask him to **forgive me** for the **labors** he has undertaken

13. **despiteful:** malicious, spiteful; **Juno:** in Roman mythology, queen of the gods, who imposed twelve seemingly impossible **labors** on Hercules

14. **camping foes:** i.e., enemies housed in tents

15. **dogs:** i.e., dog, pursue

17. **Whom:** i.e., **death**

19. **advice:** judgment; wisdom

20. **spoke:** i.e., spoken

22. **prevented:** forestalled, anticipated

24. **at overnight:** i.e., last night

27. **angel:** guardian or attendant spirit

32. **unworthy . . . wife:** i.e., **husband unworthy of** his **wife**

33. **weigh heavy of:** i.e., speak emphatically about

34. **weigh:** esteem, value

37. **When haply:** i.e., perhaps **when**

41. **in sense:** perhaps, in estimation or perception

Bless him at home in peace, whilst I from far   10
  His name with zealous fervor sanctify.
His taken labors bid him me forgive;
  I, his despiteful Juno, sent him forth
From courtly friends, with camping foes to live
  Where death and danger dogs the heels of worth.   15
He is too good and fair for death and me,
Whom I myself embrace to set him free.

⌜COUNTESS⌝
Ah, what sharp stings are in her mildest words!
Rinaldo, you did never lack advice so much
As letting her pass so. Had I spoke with her,   20
I could have well diverted her intents,
Which thus she hath prevented.

STEWARD   Pardon me, madam.
If I had given you this at overnight,
She might have been o'erta'en. And yet she writes   25
Pursuit would be but vain.

COUNTESS   What angel shall
Bless this unworthy husband? He cannot thrive
Unless her prayers, whom heaven delights to hear
And loves to grant, reprieve him from the wrath   30
Of greatest justice. Write, write, Rinaldo,
To this unworthy husband of his wife.
Let every word weigh heavy of her worth
That he does weigh too light. My greatest grief,
Though little he do feel it, set down sharply.   35
Dispatch the most convenient messenger.
When haply he shall hear that she is gone,
He will return; and hope I may that she,
Hearing so much, will speed her foot again,
Led hither by pure love. Which of them both   40
Is dearest to me, I have no skill in sense
To make distinction. Provide this messenger.
My heart is heavy, and mine age is weak.
Grief would have tears, and sorrow bids me speak.
                        They exit.

3.5 Helen, on her pilgrimage, meets Diana, whom Bertram has been attempting to seduce.

O SD. **tucket:** trumpet signal

7. **the Duke's:** presumably, the Duke of Siena's

12. **earl:** i.e., nobleman; **maid:** young woman; virgin; **name:** reputation

13. **honesty:** chastity (the standard meaning of **honesty** in Shakespeare's day when applied to a woman)

14. **my neighbor:** i.e., **Mariana**

18. **filthy officer:** i.e., one who performs a **filthy** office (by soliciting for Bertram); **suggestions:** temptations, incitements to evil

21. **engines:** instruments, agents; **go under:** i.e., are known by

23. **the misery:** i.e., of the **seduced** maids; **is example:** i.e., illustrates; **so:** i.e., such; **shows in:** i.e., exhibitions or displays of

25. **succession:** i.e., the act of following the same course of conduct; **limed:** trapped as if with birdlime, a sticky substance applied to bushes to catch birds; **twigs:** i.e., the **twigs** forming birch rods used for flogging

27. **grace:** virtue; honor

30. **fear:** be apprehensive about

⌜Scene 5⌝

A tucket afar off. Enter old Widow of Florence, her
daughter ⌜*Diana,*⌝ *and Mariana, with other Citizens.*

WIDOW   Nay, come, for if they do approach the city, we
    shall lose all the sight.
DIANA   They say the French count has done most hon-
    orable service.
WIDOW   It is reported that he has taken their great'st   5
    commander, and that with his own hand he slew
    the Duke's brother. ⌜*A trumpet sounds.*⌝ We have
    lost our labor. They are gone a contrary way. Hark,
    you may know by their trumpets.
MARIANA   Come, let's return again and suffice ourselves   10
    with the report of it.—Well, Diana, take heed of
    this French earl. The honor of a maid is her name,
    and no legacy is so rich as honesty.
WIDOW, ⌜*to Diana*⌝   I have told my neighbor how you
    have been solicited by a gentleman, his com-   15
    panion.
MARIANA   I know that knave, hang him! One Parolles, a
    filthy officer he is in those suggestions for the
    young earl.—Beware of them, Diana. Their prom-
    ises, enticements, oaths, tokens, and all these   20
    engines of lust are not the things they go under.
    Many a maid hath been seduced by them; and
    the misery is example that so terrible shows in the
    wrack of maidenhood cannot for all that dissuade
    succession, but that they are limed with the twigs   25
    that threatens them. I hope I need not to advise
    you further, but I hope your own grace will keep
    you where you are, though there were no further
    danger known but the modesty which is so lost.
DIANA   You shall not need to fear me.   30
WIDOW   I hope so.

32. **lie:** stay for a night or a short while

36. **Saint Jaques le Grand:** See note to 3.4.4.

37. **palmers:** i.e., pilgrims (The word usually designated travelers who had been to the Holy Land, but here has its more general meaning.)

38. **port:** city gate

39 SD. **march:** i.e., drum beats accompanying marching troops

44. **The rather for:** i.e., all the sooner because

45. **ample:** i.e., amply, fully

47. **If you shall please so:** a polite statement of agreement

48. **stay upon:** i.e., await

57. **Whatsome'er:** i.e., whatever

58. **bravely taken:** well esteemed

A pilgrim to the shrine of "St. Jaques." (3.4.4)
From Henry Peacham, *Minerua Britanna* . . . [1612].

Enter Helen ⌜as a pilgrim.⌝

Look, here comes a pilgrim. I know she will lie at
my house; thither they send one another. I'll ques-
tion her.—God save you, pilgrim. Whither are
bound?   35
HELEN, ⌜*as pilgrim*⌝ To Saint Jaques le Grand.
  Where do the palmers lodge, I do beseech you?
WIDOW
  At the Saint Francis here beside the port.
HELEN, ⌜*as pilgrim*⌝ Is this the way?   *A march afar.*
WIDOW
  Ay, marry, is 't.—Hark you, they come this way.—   40
  If you will tarry, holy pilgrim,
  But till the troops come by,
  I will conduct you where you shall be lodged,
  The rather for I think I know your hostess
  As ample as myself.   45
HELEN, ⌜*as pilgrim*⌝   Is it yourself?
WIDOW   If you shall please so, pilgrim.
HELEN, ⌜*as pilgrim*⌝
  I thank you, and will stay upon your leisure.
WIDOW
  You came I think from France?
HELEN, ⌜*as pilgrim*⌝   I did so.   50
WIDOW
  Here you shall see a countryman of yours
  That has done worthy service.
HELEN, ⌜*as pilgrim*⌝   His name, I pray you?
DIANA
  The Count Rossillion. Know you such a one?
HELEN, ⌜*as pilgrim*⌝
  But by the ear, that hears most nobly of him.   55
  His face I know not.
DIANA   Whatsome'er he is,
  He's bravely taken here. He stole from France,

59. **for:** because
61. **mere:** merely, purely
66. **with him:** i.e., as he does
67. **In argument:** i.e., as a subject or theme; **to:** i.e., in comparison **to**
68. **mean:** inferior, undistinguished
69. **All her deserving:** i.e., her only merit
70. **reservèd honesty:** cold or reticent chastity
78. **A shrewd turn:** an injury
83. **brokes:** bargains, negotiates
86. **honestest:** most chaste

"To sit and draw . . ." (1.1.98–100)
From Geoffrey Whitney, *A choice of emblemes* . . . (1586).

As 'tis reported, for the King had married him
Against his liking. Think you it is so?   60
HELEN, ⌜*as pilgrim*⌝
Ay, surely, mere the truth. I know his lady.
DIANA
There is a gentleman that serves the Count
Reports but coarsely of her.
HELEN, ⌜*as pilgrim*⌝   What's his name?
DIANA
Monsieur Parolles.   65
HELEN, ⌜*as pilgrim*⌝   O, I believe with him.
In argument of praise, or to the worth
Of the great count himself, she is too mean
To have her name repeated. All her deserving
Is a reservèd honesty, and that   70
I have not heard examined.
DIANA   Alas, poor lady,
'Tis a hard bondage to become the wife
Of a detesting lord.
WIDOW
I ⌜warrant,⌝ good creature, wheresoe'er she is,   75
Her heart weighs sadly. This young maid might do
    her
A shrewd turn if she pleased.
HELEN, ⌜*as pilgrim*⌝   How do you mean?
Maybe the amorous count solicits her   80
In the unlawful purpose?
WIDOW   He does indeed,
And brokes with all that can in such a suit
Corrupt the tender honor of a maid,
But she is armed for him and keeps her guard   85
In honestest defense.
MARIANA
The gods forbid else!

87 SD. **Drum and Colors:** i.e., a drummer and soldiers bearing the regimental flags

94. **honester:** more honorable

99. **lady:** i.e., wife

104. **Lose our drum:** Since the regimental **drum** was decorated with the regiment's colors, its loss was symbolically humiliating, equivalent to losing the regiment's flag.

105. **shrewdly:** seriously, intensely

108. **courtesy:** low bow

108–9. **ring-carrier:** go-between, pander

111. **host:** lodge; **enjoined penitents:** those directed to perform a penance (in this case, a pilgrimage)

115. **Please it:** i.e., if **it please**

116–17. **the charge and thanking / Shall be for me:** i.e., I will gratefully pay the expense

Drum and Colors. Enter ⌐Bertram¬ Count Rossillion,
Parolles, and the whole Army.

WIDOW   So, now they come.
  That is Antonio, the Duke's eldest son;
  That, Escalus.   90
HELEN, ⌐*as pilgrim*¬ Which is the Frenchman?
DIANA   He,
  That with the plume. 'Tis a most gallant fellow.
  I would he loved his wife. If he were honester,
  He were much goodlier. Is 't not a handsome   95
    gentleman?
HELEN, ⌐*as pilgrim*¬   I like him well.
DIANA
  'Tis pity he is not honest. Yond's that same knave
  That leads him to these places. Were I his lady,
  I would poison that vile rascal.   100
HELEN, ⌐*as pilgrim*¬   Which is he?
DIANA
  That jackanapes with scarves. Why is he melancholy?
HELEN, ⌐*as pilgrim*¬ Perchance he's hurt i' th' battle.
PAROLLES Lose our drum? Well.
MARIANA He's shrewdly vexed at something. Look, he 105
  has spied us.
WIDOW, ⌐*to Parolles*¬ Marry, hang you.
MARIANA, ⌐*to Parolles*¬ And your courtesy, for a ring-
  carrier.
               ⌐*Bertram, Parolles, and the army*¬ *exit.*
WIDOW
  The troop is passed. Come, pilgrim, I will bring you 110
  Where you shall host. Of enjoined penitents
  There's four or five, to Great Saint Jaques bound,
  Already at my house.
HELEN, ⌐*as pilgrim*¬   I humbly thank you.
  Please it this matron and this gentle maid   115
  To eat with us tonight, the charge and thanking

118. **of:** i.e., on
119. **Worthy the note:** i.e., worth her attention

3.6 The French lords in Florence decide that Parolles' unhappiness about the loss of the troop's drum can be used as a way to trick him into revealing his cowardice to Bertram. Bertram agrees to go along with the plot. He then goes to seek out Diana.

O SD. **as at first:** i.e., the **French Lords** who appeared earlier
1. **put him to 't:** i.e., test **him,** challenge **him**
2. **have his way:** i.e., be given scope
3. **hilding:** contemptible good-for-nothing
9. **as my:** i.e., **as** if he were **my**
12. **entertainment:** employment; support
13–14. **reposing too far in:** placing **too** much confidence **in**
15. **main:** serious; significant
18. **try:** test
19. **fetch off:** rescue
23. **surprise:** capture
25. **hoodwink:** blindfold

Shall be for me. And to requite you further,
I will bestow some precepts of this virgin
Worthy the note.
BOTH   We'll take your offer kindly.   120

They exit.

⌐Scene 6¬

*Enter ⌐Bertram¬ Count Rossillion and the French
⌐Lords,¬ as at first.*

FIRST LORD   Nay, good my lord, put him to 't. Let him
have his way.
SECOND LORD   If your Lordship find him not a hilding,
· hold me no more in your respect.
FIRST LORD   On my life, my lord, a bubble.   5
BERTRAM   Do you think I am so far deceived in him?
FIRST LORD   Believe it, my lord. In mine own direct
knowledge, without any malice, but to speak of
him as my kinsman, he's a most notable coward,
an infinite and endless liar, an hourly promise-   10
breaker, the owner of no one good quality worthy
your Lordship's entertainment.
SECOND LORD   It were fit you knew him, lest, reposing
too far in his virtue, which he hath not, he might
at some great and trusty business in a main danger   15
fail you.
BERTRAM   I would I knew in what particular action to
try him.
SECOND LORD   None better than to let him fetch off his
drum, which you hear him so confidently under-   20
take to do.
FIRST LORD   I, with a troop of Florentines, will suddenly surprise him. Such I will have whom I am sure
he knows not from the enemy. We will bind and
hoodwink him so, that he shall suppose no other   25

26. **leaguer:** military camp

36. **bottom:** reality, truth

38–39. **if you . . . entertainment:** i.e., **if you** do not throw him out (a proverbial expression)

39. **inclining:** favorable inclination, bias

43. **in any hand:** i.e., in **any** case, at **any** rate

46. **A pox on 't:** an exclamation of irritation or impatience (**Pox** was the name used for various diseases, including syphilis.) **but:** only

49. **horse:** cavalry; **wings:** divisions on each side of the center in a battle array

51. **in:** i.e., on

52. **service:** military engagement

53. **Caesar:** i.e., Julius **Caesar,** famous for his generalship (See below.)

55–56. **our success:** i.e., what befell us; or, the outcome

Julius Caesar. (3.6.53)
From Plutarch, *The liues of the noble Grecians
and Romanes . . .* (1579).

but that he is carried into the leaguer of the adversary's when we bring him to our own tents. Be but
your Lordship present at his examination. If he do
not for the promise of his life, and in the highest
compulsion of base fear, offer to betray you and   30
deliver all the intelligence in his power against
you, and that with the divine forfeit of his soul
upon oath, never trust my judgment in anything.

SECOND LORD   O, for the love of laughter, let him fetch
his drum. He says he has a stratagem for 't. When   35
your Lordship sees the bottom of ⌜his⌝ success in
't, and to what metal this counterfeit lump of ⌜ore⌝
will be melted, if you give him not John Drum's
entertainment, your inclining cannot be removed.
Here he comes.   40

Enter Parolles.

FIRST LORD, ⌜*aside to Bertram*⌝   O, for the love of laughter, hinder not the honor of his design. Let him
fetch off his drum in any hand.

BERTRAM, ⌜*to Parolles*⌝ How now, monsieur? This
drum sticks sorely in your disposition.   45

SECOND LORD   A pox on 't! Let it go. 'Tis but a drum.

PAROLLES   But a drum! Is 't but a drum? A drum so
lost! There was excellent command, to charge in
with our horse upon our own wings and to rend
our own soldiers!   50

SECOND LORD   That was not to be blamed in the command of the service. It was a disaster of war that
Caesar himself could not have prevented if he had
been there to command.

BERTRAM   Well, we cannot greatly condemn our suc-   55
cess. Some dishonor we had in the loss of that
drum, but it is not to be recovered.

PAROLLES   It might have been recovered.

BERTRAM   It might, but it is not now.

60. **But:** i.e., except for the fact

63. **hic jacet:** i.e., I'll die trying (literally, "here lies," the first two words of a Latin epitaph)

64. **stomach:** i.e., appetite or desire (with perhaps a pun on **stomach** as "courage")

65. **mystery:** skill

66. **his:** its

67. **magnanimous:** courageous, valiant

68. **grace:** countenance

69. **speed:** prosper

75. **about:** i.e., go **about**

76. **pen down:** perhaps, contain, confine; or, perhaps, write **down**

77. **put myself . . . preparation:** perhaps, arm myself; or, perhaps, prepare for my own death

81. **success:** outcome

83. **possibility:** capacity, ability

84. **subscribe for:** i.e., countenance, support

89. **damns:** dooms, condemns; **better:** rather

PAROLLES   It is to be recovered. But that the merit of   60
service is seldom attributed to the true and exact
performer, I would have that drum or another, or
hic jacet.
BERTRAM   Why, if you have a stomach, to 't, monsieur!
If you think your mystery in stratagem can bring   65
this instrument of honor again into his native
quarter, be magnanimous in the enterprise and go
on. I will grace the attempt for a worthy exploit. If
you speed well in it, the Duke shall both speak of it
and extend to you what further becomes his great-   70
ness, even to the utmost syllable of your worthiness.
PAROLLES   By the hand of a soldier, I will undertake it.
BERTRAM   But you must not now slumber in it.
PAROLLES   I'll about it this evening, and I will presently   75
pen down my dilemmas, encourage myself in my
certainty, put myself into my mortal preparation;
and by midnight look to hear further from me.
BERTRAM   May I be bold to acquaint his Grace you are
gone about it?   80
PAROLLES   I know not what the success will be, my
lord, but the attempt I vow.
BERTRAM   I know thou 'rt valiant, and to the possibility
of thy soldiership will subscribe for thee. Farewell.
PAROLLES   I love not many words.   *He exits.*   85
FIRST LORD   No more than a fish loves water. Is not this
a strange fellow, my lord, that so confidently seems
to undertake this business which he knows is not
to be done, damns himself to do, and dares better
be damned than to do 't?   90
SECOND LORD   You do not know him, my lord, as we do.
Certain it is that he will steal himself into a man's
favor and for a week escape a great deal of discoveries, but when you find him out, you have him
ever after.   95

100. **invention:** fiction; **clap upon you:** i.e., stick you with; **probable:** plausible

101. **embossed:** cornered, driven to extremity (hunting terminology that continues in lines 104–6)

105. **case:** skin; **smoked:** perhaps, driven out of hiding as if with smoke

107. **sprat:** small fish (a term of contempt)

109. **look my twigs:** i.e., find the **twigs** smeared with birdlime (Parolles is being compared to a bird about to be trapped. See note to 3.5.25.)

115. **honest:** chaste

116. **all the fault:** i.e., **all** that's wrong

118. **coxcomb:** (1) fool, simpleton; (2) conceited fop; **we have i' th' wind:** i.e., **we have** under observation (a hunting phrase that means, literally, he is downwind of us)

119. **re-send:** send back again, return

BERTRAM Why, do you think he will make no deed at
all of this that so seriously he does address himself
unto?

FIRST LORD None in the world, but return with an
invention and clap upon you two or three probable 100
lies. But we have almost embossed him. You shall
see his fall tonight; for indeed he is not for your
Lordship's respect.

SECOND LORD We'll make you some sport with the fox
ere we case him. He was first smoked by the old 105
Lord Lafew. When his disguise and he is parted,
tell me what a sprat you shall find him, which you
shall see this very night.

FIRST LORD I must go look my twigs. He shall be
caught. 110

BERTRAM Your brother he shall go along with me.

⌜FIRST⌝ LORD As 't please your Lordship. I'll leave you.
⌜*He exits.*⌝

BERTRAM
Now will I lead you to the house and show you
The lass I spoke of.

⌜SECOND⌝ LORD   But you say she's honest. 115

BERTRAM
That's all the fault. I spoke with her but once
And found her wondrous cold. But I sent to her,
By this same coxcomb that we have i' th' wind,
Tokens and letters, which she did re-send.
And this is all I have done. She's a fair creature. 120
Will you go see her?

⌜SECOND⌝ LORD   With all my heart, my lord.
They exit.

3.7 Helen enlists Diana's mother in contriving to meet Bertram's conditions. Diana will agree to sleep with Bertram on the condition that he give her his ancestral ring. Helen will then substitute herself for Diana in the darkness of Diana's bedroom.

---

3. **But I shall lose:** i.e., without losing
4. **estate:** rank, fortune
9. **give me trust:** i.e., believe **me** that
10. **counsel:** secrecy, confidence
12. **By:** as concerns, with regard to
15. **approves:** proves, demonstrates
16. **fortune:** position and wealth
20. **found it:** i.e., received **your help**
22. **Lays down . . . before:** i.e., lustfully besieges
23. **carry her:** win **her** (as if by military assault); **in fine:** finally; or, perhaps, in short
24. **bear it:** i.e., carry **it** out
25. **important:** importunate, urgent; **blood:** sexual appetite
26. **County:** Count
27. **downward . . . house:** i.e., has been passed down in his family
29–30. **holds / In most rich choice:** i.e., highly esteems **choice:** special value, estimation
30. **idle fire:** i.e., mad passion
31. **will:** carnal desire or appetite

⌜Scene 7⌝

Enter Helen and Widow.

HELEN
  If you misdoubt me that I am not she,
  I know not how I shall assure you further
  But I shall lose the grounds I work upon.
WIDOW
  Though my estate be fall'n, I was well born,
  Nothing acquainted with these businesses,   5
  And would not put my reputation now
  In any staining act.
HELEN   Nor would I wish you.
  First give me trust the Count he is my husband,
  And what to your sworn counsel I have spoken   10
  Is so from word to word; and then you cannot,
  By the good aid that I of you shall borrow,
  Err in bestowing it.
WIDOW   I should believe you,
  For you have showed me that which well approves 15
  You're great in fortune.
HELEN   Take this purse of gold,
  And let me buy your friendly help thus far,
  Which I will overpay and pay again
  When I have found it. The Count he woos your   20
    daughter,
  Lays down his wanton siege before her beauty,
  ⌜Resolved⌝ to carry her. Let her in fine consent
  As we'll direct her how 'tis best to bear it.
  Now his important blood will naught deny   25
  That she'll demand. A ring the County wears
  That downward hath succeeded in his house
  From son to son some four or five descents
  Since the first father wore it. This ring he holds
  In most rich choice. Yet, in his idle fire,   30
  To buy his will it would not seem too dear,
  Howe'er repented after.

33. **bottom:** nature, fundamental character
34. **lawful:** i.e., as **lawful**
36. **Desires:** demands; **encounter:** assignation
37. **In fine:** finally
39. **To marry her:** i.e., for her dowry
42. **persever:** proceed (accent on second syllable)
46. **To her unworthiness:** i.e., **to her,** even though she is unworthy (The Widow may be commenting on Diana's lower-class status, or she may be speaking as a mother who modestly dispraises her own child.)
51. **wicked . . . deed:** i.e., Bertram's **meaning** will be illicit but his actions will be **lawful**
52. **lawful . . . act:** i.e., Helen's intentions and actions will both be **lawful**
53. **both not:** i.e., neither Bertram nor Helen; **fact:** action, deed

Astrologers determining a baby's "stars." (1.1.189; 2.5.82)
From Jakob Ruff, *De conceptu et generatione hominis* . . . (1580).

WIDOW
Now I see the bottom of your purpose.
HELEN
You see it lawful, then. It is no more
But that your daughter, ere she seems as won,   35
Desires this ring, appoints him an encounter,
In fine, delivers me to fill the time,
Herself most chastely absent. After,
To marry her, I'll add three thousand crowns
To what is passed already.   40
WIDOW   I have yielded.
Instruct my daughter how she shall persever
That time and place with this deceit so lawful
May prove coherent. Every night he comes
With musics of all sorts and songs composed   45
To her unworthiness. It nothing steads us
To chide him from our eaves, for he persists
As if his life lay on 't.
HELEN   Why then tonight
Let us assay our plot, which, if it speed,   50
Is wicked meaning in a lawful deed,
And lawful meaning in a lawful act,
Where both not sin, and yet a sinful fact.
But let's about it.
                                        ⌜*They exit.*⌝

ALL'S WELL
THAT ENDS WELL

ACT 4

4.1 Parolles is captured and blindfolded by a French lord and soldiers pretending to be the enemy who can speak to him only through an interpreter. He offers to give away military secrets in exchange for his life.

O SD. **in ambush:** i.e., preparing to lie **in ambush**

5. **unless:** i.e., except for

11. **linsey-woolsey:** nonsense, gibberish (literally, material woven of wool and flax)

14. **strangers:** foreigners

15. **entertainment:** employment

17. **not to know:** i.e., **not** knowing

18. **So we seem to know:** i.e., provided that **we seem to** understand each other

19–20. **chough's language:** i.e., inarticulate chatter (A *chough* is any of the small chattering crows, but the name is most often applied to the jackdaw, which could be taught to imitate human speech.)

21. **politic:** probably, wise, judicious (rather than crafty or cunning)

22. **couch:** i.e., hide, lie in ambush

ACT 4

⌜Scene 1⌝

Enter one of the French ⌜Lords,⌝ with five or six other
Soldiers in ambush.

LORD He can come no other way but by this hedge
corner. When you sally upon him, speak what ter-
rible language you will. Though you understand it
not yourselves, no matter. For we must not seem to
understand him, unless some one among us whom   5
we must produce for an interpreter.
FIRST SOLDIER Good captain, let me be th' interpreter.
LORD Art not acquainted with him? Knows he not thy
voice?
FIRST SOLDIER No, sir, I warrant you.   10
LORD But what linsey-woolsey hast thou to speak to
us again?
FIRST SOLDIER E'en such as you speak to me.
LORD He must think us some band of strangers i' th'
adversary's entertainment. Now, he hath a smack   15
of all neighboring languages. Therefore we must
every one be a man of his own fancy, not to know
what we speak one to another. So we seem to know
is to know straight our purpose: choughs' language, gabble enough and good enough. As for   20
you, interpreter, you must seem very politic. But
couch, ho! Here he comes to beguile two hours in

139

23. **swear:** i.e., **swear** to

25. **Within these three hours:** i.e., after no more than **three hours**

27. **plausive:** plausible

28. **carries it:** i.e., will carry **it** off; **smoke me:** i.e., **smoke me** out; force me out into the open; or perhaps, drive me out of hiding (as if with smoke)

31. **his creatures:** i.e., soldiers (and perhaps swords, muskets, etc.)

32. **daring:** i.e., **daring** to carry out

39. **in exploit:** in action or combat

41. **Wherefore:** why

42. **instance:** proof (that I fought for the drum)

42–43. **butter-woman's:** dairy-woman's

43. **another of:** i.e., **another** (**tongue**) from

44. **Bajazeth's mule:** perhaps a printing or scribal error; perhaps an allusion to a lost story

46. **that:** i.e., **that** which

47. **would:** wish

48. **turn:** purpose

50. **afford you so:** i.e., spare **you** on such grounds

51. **baring:** i.e., shaving

a sleep and then to return and swear the lies he
forges.   ⌜*They move aside.*⌝

Enter Parolles.

PAROLLES Ten o'clock. Within these three hours 'twill   25
be time enough to go home. What shall I say I have
done? It must be a very plausive invention that
carries it. They begin to smoke me, and disgraces
have of late knocked too often at my door. I find
my tongue is too foolhardy, but my heart hath the   30
fear of Mars before it, and of his creatures, not
daring the reports of my tongue.
LORD, ⌜*aside*⌝ This is the first truth that e'er thine own
tongue was guilty of.
PAROLLES What the devil should move me to under-   35
take the recovery of this drum, being not ignorant
of the impossibility and knowing I had no such
purpose? I must give myself some hurts and say I
got them in exploit. Yet slight ones will not carry it.
They will say "Came you off with so little?" And   40
great ones I dare not give. Wherefore? What's the
instance? Tongue, I must put you into a butter-
woman's mouth and buy myself another of
Bajazeth's mule if you prattle me into these perils.
LORD, ⌜*aside*⌝ Is it possible he should know what he is,   45
and be that he is?
PAROLLES I would the cutting of my garments would
serve the turn, or the breaking of my Spanish
sword.
LORD, ⌜*aside*⌝ We cannot afford you so.   50
PAROLLES Or the baring of my beard, and to say it was
in stratagem.
LORD, ⌜*aside*⌝ 'Twould not do.
PAROLLES Or to drown my clothes and say I was
stripped.   55
LORD, ⌜*aside*⌝ Hardly serve.

65. **anon:** soon

66 SD. **Alarum:** a signal calling upon men to arm (here, presumably, the sound of a **drum,** as promised at line 66)

72. **Muskos':** perhaps, Muscovites' (i.e., from Moscow)

73. **want:** lack

76. **discover:** reveal; **undo:** destroy

78–79. **betake . . . faith:** i.e., pray (literally, commend yourself to your **faith** in God)

82, 84. **reuania, voliuorco:** more easily pronounced as "revania" and "volivorco"

86. **hoodwinked:** blindfolded; **lead thee on:** perhaps, direct your comments

87. **gather:** gain; **Haply:** perhaps; **inform:** report

A poniard. (4.1.79)
From Louis de Gaya, *A treatise of the arms . . .* (1678).

PAROLLES   Though I swore I leapt from the window of
   the citadel—
LORD, ⌐*aside*⌐ How deep?
PAROLLES   Thirty fathom.   60
LORD, ⌐*aside*⌐ Three great oaths would scarce make
   that be believed.
PAROLLES   I would I had any drum of the enemy's. I
   would swear I recovered it.
LORD, ⌐*aside*⌐ You shall hear one anon.   65
PAROLLES   A drum, now, of the enemy's—
                                             Alarum within.
LORD, ⌐*advancing*⌐ *Throca movousus, cargo, cargo,*
   cargo.
ALL   *Cargo, cargo, cargo, villianda par corbo, cargo.*
                                             ⌐*They seize him.*⌐
PAROLLES   O ransom, ransom! Do not hide mine eyes.   70
                                             ⌐*They blindfold him.*⌐
FIRST SOLDIER   *Boskos thromuldo boskos.*
PAROLLES
   I know you are the Muskos' regiment,
   And I shall lose my life for want of language.
   If there be here German or Dane, Low Dutch,
   Italian, or French, let him speak to me.   75
   I'll discover that which shall undo the Florentine.
FIRST SOLDIER   *Boskos vauvado,* I understand thee and
   can speak thy tongue. *Kerelybonto,* sir, betake thee
   to thy faith, for seventeen poniards are at thy
   bosom.   80
PAROLLES   O!
FIRST SOLDIER   O, pray, pray, pray! *Manka reuania*
   dulche.
LORD   *Oscorbidulchos voliuorco.*
FIRST SOLDIER
   The General is content to spare thee yet   85
   And, hoodwinked as thou art, will lead thee on
   To gather from thee. Haply thou mayst inform
   Something to save thy life.

98. **woodcock:** i.e., dupe (The **woodcock** is a bird easily snared and therefore considered foolish.) See below.

99. **muffled:** blindfolded

4.2 Diana agrees to lie with Bertram after he reluctantly gives her his ancestral ring.

---

3. **Titled goddess:** i.e., you have the name of a **goddess** (See picture, page 148.)

4. **addition:** i.e., more or greater titles (with possible wordplay on the word's meaning of "title of honor")

5. **hath love no quality:** i.e., is **love** not an attribute

6. **mind:** disposition, intention, inclination

"We have caught the woodcock." (4.1.98)
From Henry Parrot, *Laquei ridiculosi* . . . (1613).

PAROLLES   O, let me live,
    And all the secrets of our camp I'll show,   90
    Their force, their purposes. Nay, I'll speak that
    Which you will wonder at.
FIRST SOLDIER   But wilt thou faithfully?
PAROLLES   If I do not, damn me.
FIRST SOLDIER   *Acordo linta.* Come on, thou ⌜art⌝   95
    granted space.
                    He exits ⌜*with Parolles under guard.*⌝
                              A short alarum within.
LORD
    Go tell the Count Rossillion and my brother
    We have caught the woodcock and will keep him
        muffled
    Till we do hear from them.   100
⌜SECOND⌝ SOLDIER   Captain, I will.
LORD
    He will betray us all unto ourselves.
    Inform on that.
⌜SECOND⌝ SOLDIER   So I will, sir.
LORD
    Till then I'll keep him dark and safely locked.   105
                                        ⌜*They*⌝ *exit.*

                          ⌜Scene 2⌝

              Enter Bertram and the maid called Diana.

BERTRAM
    They told me that your name was Fontibell.
DIANA
    No, my good lord, Diana.
BERTRAM   Titled goddess,
    And worth it, with addition. But, fair soul,
    In your fine frame hath love no quality?   5
    If the quick fire of youth light not your mind,

7. **monument:** statue, effigy

11. **got:** begotten, conceived

12. **honest:** chaste (i.e., not engaged in unlawful sex)

13. **should:** i.e., would

18. **prithee:** pray thee; **vows:** possibly his oath never to be Helen's husband, but more likely his **vows** to dedicate himself to Diana (discussed in lines 26–38)

21. **rights:** perhaps "rites" as well as **rights** (See note to **rite** at 2.4.41.) **service:** the condition of being the servant of the lady one loves

23. **serve you:** i.e., satisfy **you** (sexually); **roses:** Since the Middle Ages, the rose was used in allegorical poetry to figure virginity, and the plucking of the rose was the sexual conquest of the virgin.

30. **take . . . witness:** i.e., **swear by** that which is most **holy**

32. **Jove's:** Jove was king of the Roman gods. (For Diana's swearing by **Jove's great attributes,** see longer note, page 224.)

34. **ill:** perhaps, wickedly, sinfully; perhaps, badly; **holding:** i.e., power to bind or constrain; or, perhaps, validity

37. **conditions:** contracts; **unsealed:** not formally confirmed or ratified

You are no maiden but a monument.
When you are dead, you should be such a one
As you are now, for you are cold and stern,
And now you should be as your mother was   10
When your sweet self was got.

DIANA
  She then was honest.

BERTRAM   So should you be.

DIANA   No.
  My mother did but duty—such, my lord,   15
  As you owe to your wife.

BERTRAM   No more o' that.
  I prithee do not strive against my vows.
  I was compelled to her, but I love thee
  By love's own sweet constraint, and will forever   20
  Do thee all rights of service.

DIANA   Ay, so you serve us
  Till we serve you. But when you have our roses,
  You barely leave our thorns to prick ourselves
  And mock us with our bareness.   25

BERTRAM   How have I sworn!

DIANA
  'Tis not the many oaths that makes the truth,
  But the plain single vow that is vowed true.
  What is not holy, that we swear not by,
  But take the high'st to witness. Then pray you, tell   30
    me,
  If I should swear by Jove's great attributes
  I loved you dearly, would you believe my oaths
  When I did love you ill? This has no holding
  To swear by him whom I protest to love   35
  That I will work against him. Therefore your oaths
  Are words, and poor conditions but unsealed,
  At least in my opinion.

BERTRAM   Change it, change it.
  Be not so holy-cruel. Love is holy,   40

42. **Stand no more off:** i.e., do not continue to be aloof or distant

43. **sick:** yearning

44. **Who then recovers:** i.e., which **then** recover

45. **persever:** accent on second syllable

51. **honor:** i.e., object to which family **honor** is attached

53. **were:** i.e., would be

55. **honor's:** chastity is

59. **own proper:** i.e., very own

64. **bid:** commanded

67. **order take:** make arrangements (so that)

68. **band:** i.e., bonds

"Dian." (1.3.115; 2.3.78; 4.2.3)
From Robert Whitcombe, *Janua divorum* . . . (1678).

And my integrity ne'er knew the crafts
That you do charge men with. Stand no more off,
But give thyself unto my sick desires,
Who then recovers. Say thou art mine, and ever
My love as it begins shall so persever.   45

DIANA
I see that men ⌜may⌝ rope 's in such a ⌜snare⌝
That we'll forsake ourselves. Give me that ring.

BERTRAM
I'll lend it thee, my dear, but have no power
To give it from me.

DIANA   Will you not, my lord?   50

BERTRAM
It is an honor 'longing to our house,
Bequeathèd down from many ancestors,
Which were the greatest obloquy i' th' world
In me to lose.

DIANA   Mine honor's such a ring.   55
My chastity's the jewel of our house,
Bequeathèd down from many ancestors,
Which were the greatest obloquy i' th' world
In me to lose. Thus your own proper wisdom
Brings in the champion Honor on my part   60
Against your vain assault.

BERTRAM   Here, take my ring.
My house, mine honor, yea, my life be thine,
And I'll be bid by thee.

DIANA
When midnight comes, knock at my chamber   65
    window.
I'll order take my mother shall not hear.
Now will I charge you in the band of truth,
When you have conquered my yet maiden bed,
Remain there but an hour, nor speak to me.   70
My reasons are most strong, and you shall know them
When back again this ring shall be delivered.

75. **token:** represent, signify

77. **done:** finished, ended

80. **You may so in the end:** This line has different resonances depending on whether it is said to Bertram (as our placement of his exit suggests) or in soliloquy (with the exit placed at the end of line 79). The Folio does not give Bertram an exit direction.

82. **in 's:** i.e., in his

83. **the like:** the same kind of

85. **braid:** perhaps, deceitful (a word not recorded elsewhere as an adjective or past participle)

86. **that:** i.e., whoever; **maid:** virgin, unmarried woman

87. **disguise:** deception

4.3 News comes to the Duke of Florence's court that Bertram's wife has died while on pilgrimage. When Bertram enters, he has received this news, he has made his plans to return to Rossillion, and he has (he thinks) lain with Diana. A blindfolded Parolles gives away military secrets and betrays Bertram and the other French lords, and is then himself abandoned by them.

———————

6. **worthy:** deserved

9. **even:** quite, fully

11. **darkly:** in secrecy, secretly

And on your finger in the night I'll put
Another ring, that what in time proceeds
May token to the future our past deeds.   75
Adieu till then; then, fail not. You have won
A wife of me, though there my hope be done.

BERTRAM
A heaven on earth I have won by wooing thee.

DIANA
For which live long to thank both heaven and me!
You may so in the end.   ⌐*He exits.*⌐   80
My mother told me just how he would woo
As if she sat in 's heart. She says all men
Have the like oaths. He had sworn to marry me
When his wife's dead. Therefore I'll lie with him
When I am buried. Since Frenchmen are so braid,   85
Marry that will, I live and die a maid.
Only, in this disguise I think 't no sin
To cozen him that would unjustly win.
                                              She exits.

⌐Scene 3⌐

*Enter the two French ⌐Lords⌐ and some two
or three Soldiers.*

FIRST LORD   You have not given him his mother's letter?

SECOND LORD   I have delivered it an hour since. There
is something in 't that stings his nature, for on the
reading it he changed almost into another man.   5

FIRST LORD   He has much worthy blame laid upon him
for shaking off so good a wife and so sweet a lady.

SECOND LORD   Especially he hath incurred the everlast-
ing displeasure of the King, who had even tuned
his bounty to sing happiness to him. I will tell you   10
a thing, but you shall let it dwell darkly with you.

16. **fleshes his will:** i.e., gratifies his lust (See longer note, page 224.)

17. **monumental:** perhaps, serving as a memento; or, perhaps, ancestral

18. **made:** successful; **unchaste composition:** lascivious contract

19. **delay:** retard, hinder; or, perhaps, quench; **our rebellion:** i.e., the **rebellion** of **our** flesh

20. **ourselves:** i.e., in or by **ourselves** (without God's aid)

21. **Merely:** absolutely, entirely

22. **still:** always; **them:** i.e., **traitors**

24. **ends:** i.e., (1) aims; (2) punishments by torture and death (While both meanings would apply to **traitors,** only the first applies to Bertram.)

25–26. **in his proper . . . himself:** a very difficult metaphor paraphrased by Samuel Johnson as "betrays his own secrets in his own talk" **proper:** (one's) own

27. **Is it not meant damnable:** perhaps, does **it not** show a **damnable** meaning

30–31. **dieted to his hour:** i.e., regulated or restricted by the appointment he has set

33. **company:** i.e., companion

35. **curiously:** elaborately or carefully (The metaphor is of placing a **counterfeit** precious stone in an elaborate setting.)

36. **him:** i.e., Parolles; **he:** i.e., Bertram

37. **his presence:** i.e., the **presence** of the one

44. **higher:** perhaps, farther

45. **demand:** question

46. **of his counsel:** i.e., in his confidence

47–48. **a great deal of his act:** i.e., an accessory to his misconduct (literally, a large part of his deed)

FIRST LORD   When you have spoken it, 'tis dead, and I
am the grave of it.

SECOND LORD   He hath perverted a young gentlewoman here in Florence of a most chaste renown,   15
and this night he fleshes his will in the spoil of her
honor. He hath given her his monumental ring and
thinks himself made in the unchaste composition.

FIRST LORD   Now God delay our rebellion! As we are
ourselves, what things are we!   20

SECOND LORD   Merely our own traitors. And, as in the
common course of all treasons we still see them
reveal themselves till they attain to their abhorred
ends, so he that in this action contrives against his
own nobility, in his proper stream o'erflows him-   25
self.

FIRST LORD   Is it not meant damnable in us to be trumpeters of our unlawful intents? We shall not, then,
have his company tonight?

SECOND LORD   Not till after midnight, for he is dieted to   30
his hour.

FIRST LORD   That approaches apace. I would gladly
have him see his company anatomized, that he
might take a measure of his own judgments
wherein so curiously he had set this counterfeit.   35

SECOND LORD   We will not meddle with him till he
come, for his presence must be the whip of the
other.

FIRST LORD   In the meantime, what hear you of these
wars?   40

SECOND LORD   I hear there is an overture of peace.

FIRST LORD   Nay, I assure you, a peace concluded.

SECOND LORD   What will Count Rossillion do then?
Will he travel higher or return again into France?

FIRST LORD   I perceive by this demand you are not alto-   45
gether of his counsel.

SECOND LORD   Let it be forbid, sir! So should I be a
great deal of his act.

50. **pretense:** purpose, intention
54. **in fine:** i.e., in short, she
56. **justified:** supported by evidence
57. **letters:** i.e., letter
58. **point:** instant
60. **office:** part, function
75. **crimes:** sins
80. **will:** i.e., **will** leave

A "gallant knave" in the stocks. (4.3.104–5)
From Geoffrey Whitney, *A choice of emblemes* . . . (1586).

154

FIRST LORD   Sir, his wife some two months since fled
from his house. Her pretense is a pilgrimage to   50
Saint Jaques le Grand, which holy undertaking
with most austere sanctimony she accomplished.
And, there residing, the tenderness of her nature
became as a prey to her grief; in fine, made a groan
of her last breath, and now she sings in heaven.   55
SECOND LORD   How is this justified?
FIRST LORD   The stronger part of it by her own letters,
which makes her story true even to the point of her
death. Her death itself, which could not be her
office to say is come, was faithfully confirmed by   60
the rector of the place.
SECOND LORD   Hath the Count all this intelligence?
FIRST LORD   Ay, and the particular confirmations, point
from point, to the full arming of the verity.
SECOND LORD   I am heartily sorry that he'll be glad of   65
this.
FIRST LORD   How mightily sometimes we make us
comforts of our losses.
SECOND LORD   And how mightily some other times we
drown our gain in tears. The great dignity that his   70
valor hath here acquired for him shall at home be
encountered with a shame as ample.
FIRST LORD   The web of our life is of a mingled yarn,
good and ill together. Our virtues would be proud
if our faults whipped them not, and our crimes   75
would despair if they were not cherished by our
virtues.

Enter a ⌜*Servant.*⌝

How now? Where's your master?
SERVANT   He met the Duke in the street, sir, of whom
he hath taken a solemn leave. His Lordship will   80
next morning for France. The Duke hath offered
him letters of commendations to the King.

89–90. **By an . . . success:** i.e., to summarize the **businesses** I have **dispatched** in succession, or with success

90. **congeed with:** i.e., taken ceremonious leave of

91. **his nearest:** i.e., those **nearest** him

92–93. **entertained:** hired

93–94. **parcels of dispatch:** i.e., items of business

94. **nicer needs:** i.e., more delicate pieces of business

99. **as fearing:** i.e., in that I fear

102. **module:** i.e., image; **has:** i.e., he **has**

103. **double-meaning:** ambiguous, riddling (The witches in *Macbeth* (5.8.24) are accused of "palter[ing]" with Macbeth "in a double sense" in their equivocal prophecies about his future.)

104. **stocks:** an instrument of punishment and public shaming that imprisoned the legs in a heavy wooden frame (See picture, page 154.)

107. **usurping his spurs:** i.e., pretending to be valiant (To win one's **spurs** was to attain distinction through valor.) There is also wordplay here on **spurs** as worn on the **heels** (line 106) in horseback riding. **carry:** comport, conduct

112. **shed:** spilled (Proverbial: "To cry for spilt **milk.**")

112–13. **Morgan:** This is presumably either a soldier or the Second Lord's brother (i.e., First Lord). The name does not appear elsewhere in the play.

113–14. **the time of his remembrance:** i.e., as far back as he can remember

115. **setting:** i.e., being set

SECOND LORD   They shall be no more than needful
there, if they were more than they can commend.
They cannot be too sweet for the King's tartness.   85

Enter ⌜*Bertram*⌝ *Count Rossillion.*

Here's his Lordship now.—How now, my lord? Is 't
not after midnight?

BERTRAM   I have tonight dispatched sixteen businesses, a month's length apiece. By an abstract of
success: I have congeed with the Duke, done my   90
adieu with his nearest, buried a wife, mourned for
her, writ to my lady mother I am returning, entertained my convoy, and between these main parcels
of dispatch effected many nicer needs. The last
was the greatest, but that I have not ended yet.   95

SECOND LORD   If the business be of any difficulty, and
this morning your departure hence, it requires
haste of your Lordship.

BERTRAM   I mean the business is not ended as fearing
to hear of it hereafter. But shall we have this dia-   100
logue between the Fool and the Soldier? Come,
bring forth this counterfeit module; has deceived
me like a double-meaning prophesier.

SECOND LORD   Bring him forth. Has sat i' th' stocks all
night, poor gallant knave.   ⌜*Soldiers exit.*⌝ 105

BERTRAM   No matter. His heels have deserved it in
usurping his spurs so long. How does he carry
himself?

SECOND LORD   I have told your Lordship already: the
stocks carry him. But to answer you as you would   110
be understood: he weeps like a wench that had
shed her milk. He hath confessed himself to Morgan, whom he supposes to be a friar, from the time
of his remembrance to this very instant disaster of
his setting i' th' stocks. And what think you he hath   115
confessed?

124. **Hoodman:** the blindfolded player in the game of blindman's buff (See below.)

129. **pasty:** meat pie

135. **note:** written statement

138. **how many . . . strong:** i.e., what is the strength of the Duke's cavalry

145. **take the Sacrament on 't:** i.e., confirm the truth of my statement by receiving Holy Communion

147. **All's one:** i.e., it's all the same

"Hoodman comes." (4.3.124–25)
From *Officium beate Marie v[ir]ginis ad vsum saru[m]* . . . [c. 1512].

BERTRAM   Nothing of me, has he?

SECOND LORD   His confession is taken, and it shall be
read to his face. If your Lordship be in 't, as I
believe you are, you must have the patience to   120
hear it.

Enter Parolles, ⌜blindfolded,⌝ with his Interpreter,
⌜*the First Soldier.*⌝

BERTRAM   A plague upon him! Muffled! He can say
nothing of me.

FIRST LORD, ⌜*aside to Bertram*⌝   Hush, hush. Hoodman
comes.—*Portotartarossa.*   125

FIRST SOLDIER, ⌜*to Parolles*⌝   He calls for the tortures.
What will you say without 'em?

PAROLLES   I will confess what I know without constraint. If you pinch me like a pasty, I can say no
more.   130

FIRST SOLDIER   *Bosko Chimurcho.*

⌜FIRST⌝ LORD   *Boblibindo chicurmurco.*

FIRST SOLDIER   You are a merciful general.—Our general bids you answer to what I shall ask you out of a
note.   135

PAROLLES   And truly, as I hope to live.

FIRST SOLDIER, ⌜*as if reading a note*⌝   *First, demand of
him how many horse the Duke is strong.*—What say
you to that?

PAROLLES   Five or six thousand, but very weak and   140
unserviceable. The troops are all scattered, and the
commanders very poor rogues, upon my reputation and credit, and as I hope to live.

FIRST SOLDIER   Shall I set down your answer so?

PAROLLES   Do. I'll take the Sacrament on 't, how and   145
which way you will.

BERTRAM, ⌜*aside*⌝   All's one to him. What a past-saving
slave is this!

FIRST LORD, ⌜*aside to Bertram*⌝   You're deceived, my

151. **militarist:** one who studies military science

152. **theoric:** theory

153. **practice:** i.e., **practice** of **war** (Describing the knowledge of war in terms of **theoric** and **practice** was commonplace. See below.) **chape:** metal plate on a sheath

154–55. **for keeping:** i.e., because he keeps

162. **con him no thanks:** i.e., do not thank **him**

173. **so many:** i.e., the same number

177. **muster-file:** i.e., muster-roll, the official list of officers and men

179. **poll:** i.e., individuals (literally, head)

180. **cassocks:** military cloaks

184. **Demand of him:** i.e., ask **him** about

THEORIQVE
AND PRACTISE
OF WARRE.

Written to Don Philip Prince of Caſtil,
by Don BERNARDINO de
Mendoza.

Tranſlated out of the Caſtilian tonge into Engliſhe,
by Sʳ. *EDWARDE HOBY*
Knight.

Directed to Sʳ. *GEORGE CAREW*
Knight.

1597.

"The whole theoric of war." (4.3.151–52)
From Bernardino de Mendoza, *Theorique and practise of warre . . . translated . . . by Sr. Edwarde Hoby . . .* (1597).

160

lord. This is Monsieur Parolles, the gallant   150
militarist—that was his own phrase—that had the
whole theoric of war in the knot of his scarf, and
the practice in the chape of his dagger.

SECOND LORD, ⌜*aside*⌝   I will never trust a man again for
keeping his sword clean, nor believe he can have   155
everything in him by wearing his apparel neatly.

FIRST SOLDIER, ⌜*to Parolles*⌝   Well, that's set down.

PAROLLES   "Five or six thousand horse," I said—I will
say true—"or thereabouts" set down, for I'll speak
truth.   160

FIRST LORD, ⌜*aside*⌝   He's very near the truth in this.

BERTRAM, ⌜*aside*⌝   But I con him no thanks for 't, in the
nature he delivers it.

PAROLLES   "Poor rogues," I pray you say.

FIRST SOLDIER   Well, that's set down.   165

PAROLLES   I humbly thank you, sir. A truth's a truth.
The rogues are marvelous poor.

FIRST SOLDIER, ⌜*as if reading a note*⌝   *Demand of him of
what strength they are o' foot.*—What say you to
that?   170

PAROLLES   By my troth, sir, if I were to live ⌜but⌝ this
present hour, I will tell true. Let me see: Spurio a
hundred and fifty, Sebastian so many, Corambus
so many, Jaques so many; Guiltian, Cosmo,
Lodowick and Gratii, two hundred fifty each; mine   175
own company, Chitopher, Vaumond, Bentii, two
hundred fifty each; so that the muster-file, rotten
and sound, upon my life amounts not to fifteen
thousand poll, half of the which dare not shake the
snow from off their cassocks lest they shake them-   180
selves to pieces.

BERTRAM, ⌜*aside*⌝   What shall be done to him?

FIRST LORD, ⌜*aside*⌝   Nothing but let him have thanks.
(⌜*Aside to First Soldier.*⌝) Demand of him my condition and what credit I have with the Duke.   185

191. **well-weighing:** i.e., weighty (both heavy and influential)

194–95. **particular of the inter'gatories:** i.e., individual questions **inter'gatories:** interrogatories

197. **a botcher's prentice:** i.e., an apprentice to a cobbler or to a tailor who mends clothes

199. **shrieve's fool:** i.e., mentally retarded girl in the custody of the sheriff; **dumb:** i.e., mute

201–2. **hold your hands:** i.e., don't attack him

202–3. **his brains . . . falls:** i.e., he will surely soon meet a sudden and violent death

210. **for no other but:** i.e., as nothing more than

212. **band:** i.e., army

214. **Marry:** i.e., indeed

215. **In good sadness:** i.e., in all seriousness

FIRST SOLDIER, ⌜*to Parolles*⌝   Well, that's set down. ⌜*Pretending to read:*⌝ *You shall demand of him whether one Captain Dumaine be i' th' camp, a Frenchman; what his reputation is with the Duke, what his valor, honesty, and expertness in wars; or whether he* 190 *thinks it were not possible with well-weighing sums of gold to corrupt him to a revolt.*—What say you to this? What do you know of it?

PAROLLES   I beseech you let me answer to the particular of the inter'gatories. Demand them singly.   195

FIRST SOLDIER   Do you know this Captain Dumaine?

PAROLLES   I know him. He was a botcher's prentice in Paris, from whence he was whipped for getting the shrieve's fool with child, a dumb innocent that could not say him nay.   200

BERTRAM, ⌜*aside to First Lord*⌝   Nay, by your leave, hold your hands, though I know his brains are forfeit to the next tile that falls.

FIRST SOLDIER   Well, is this captain in the Duke of Florence's camp?   205

PAROLLES   Upon my knowledge he is, and lousy.

FIRST LORD, ⌜*aside to Bertram*⌝   Nay, look not so upon me. We shall hear of your ⌜Lordship⌝ anon.

FIRST SOLDIER   What is his reputation with the Duke?

PAROLLES   The Duke knows him for no other but a   210 poor officer of mine, and writ to me this other day to turn him out o' th' band. I think I have his letter in my pocket.

FIRST SOLDIER   Marry, we'll search.
                    ⌜*They search Parolles' pockets.*⌝

PAROLLES   In good sadness, I do not know. Either it is   215 there, or it is upon a file with the Duke's other letters in my tent.

FIRST SOLDIER   Here 'tis; here's a paper. Shall I read it to you?

PAROLLES   I do not know if it be it or no.   220

226. **advertisement:** warning; **a proper:** i.e., an excellent, admirable

239. **scores:** obtains goods (usually food or drink) on credit; **the score:** i.e., what he owes

240–41. **Half . . . make it:** perhaps, **make** your bargain while you are not yet **won   is match:** i.e., **is** a bargain   **Match:** i.e., **match** him, be equal (to him)   **make it:** i.e., achieve the **match** (There is wordplay on **match** as "mate" or "lover.")

244. **mell:** (1) associate; (2) copulate

245. **count of:** i.e., **count** on, depend on

252. **armipotent:** i.e., valiant

254. **cat:** See *The Merchant of Venice* 4.1.48–49: "Some men . . . are mad if they behold a **cat.**"

256. **fain:** obliged

Nessus abducting the wife of Hercules. (4.3.268)
From Gabriele Simeoni, *La vita . . .* (1559).

BERTRAM, ⌐*aside*¬ Our interpreter does it well.

FIRST LORD, ⌐*aside*¬ Excellently.

FIRST SOLDIER ⌐*reads*¬ *Dian, the Count's a fool and full of gold—*

PAROLLES That is not the Duke's letter, sir. That is an 225
advertisement to a proper maid in Florence, one
Diana, to take heed of the allurement of one Count
Rossillion, a foolish idle boy, but for all that very
ruttish. I pray you, sir, put it up again.

FIRST SOLDIER Nay, I'll read it first, by your favor. 230

PAROLLES My meaning in 't, I protest, was very honest
in the behalf of the maid, for I knew the young
count to be a dangerous and lascivious boy, who is
a whale to virginity and devours up all the fry it
finds. 235

BERTRAM, ⌐*aside*¬ Damnable both-sides rogue!

FIRST SOLDIER ⌐*reads*¬
When he swears oaths, bid him drop gold, and
take it.
After he scores, he never pays the score.
Half won is match well made. Match, and well 240
make it.
He ne'er pays after-debts. Take it before.
And say a soldier, Dian, told thee this:
Men are to mell with; boys are not to kiss.
For count of this: the Count's a fool, I know it, 245
Who pays before, but not when he does owe it.
                    Thine, as he vowed to thee in thine ear,
                                              Parolles.

BERTRAM, ⌐*aside*¬ He shall be whipped through the
army with this rhyme in 's forehead. 250

SECOND LORD, ⌐*aside*¬ This is your devoted friend, sir,
the manifold linguist and the armipotent soldier.

BERTRAM, ⌐*aside*¬ I could endure anything before but a
cat, and now he's a cat to me.

FIRST SOLDIER, ⌐*to Parolles*¬ I perceive, sir, by ⌐our¬ 255
general's looks we shall be fain to hang you.

259. **repent out:** i.e., live **out** in repentance

260, 262. **so:** i.e., provided that

268. **Nessus:** the centaur who attempted to ravish the wife of **Hercules** (line 270), a hero of extraordinary strength and courage (See picture, page 164.) Centaurs were mythological monsters who were bestial below the waist, and, in *King Lear*, symbols of lust.

269. **professes:** makes a profession of, practices

271. **truth were a fool:** Autolycus, the clever con man in *The Winter's Tale*, says after filling his purse with others' money, "What **a fool** honesty is" (4.4.711).

274. **they:** i.e., his servants

275. **conditions:** i.e., condition

284–85. **led . . . tragedians:** i.e., his soldiership is mere acting (Traveling acting companies, like **English** companies on the Continent, used drums and trumpets to announce their presence in a city.)

285. **belie:** tell lies about

286–87. **that country:** i.e., England

288. **Mile End: Mile End** Green was used as a drilling ground for the London citizen militia, mocked in other of Shakespeare's plays. (See, e.g., *2 Henry IV* 3.2.289.)

288–89. **the doubling of files:** a simple drill maneuver

292. **rarity:** i.e., excellence

PAROLLES   My life, sir, in any case! Not that I am afraid
to die, but that, my offenses being many, I would
repent out the remainder of nature. Let me live,
sir, in a dungeon, i' th' stocks, or anywhere, so I   260
may live.

FIRST SOLDIER   We'll see what may be done, so you confess freely. Therefore once more to this Captain
Dumaine: you have answered to his reputation
with the Duke, and to his valor. What is his hon-   265
esty?

PAROLLES   He will steal, sir, an egg out of a cloister. For
rapes and ravishments, he parallels Nessus. He
professes not keeping of oaths. In breaking 'em he
is stronger than Hercules. He will lie, sir, with such   270
volubility that you would think truth were a fool.
Drunkenness is his best virtue, for he will be
swine-drunk, and in his sleep he does little harm,
save to his bedclothes about him; but they know
his conditions and lay him in straw. I have but   275
little more to say, sir, of his honesty; he has everything that an honest man should not have; what an
honest man should have, he has nothing.

FIRST LORD, ⌜*aside*⌝   I begin to love him for this.

BERTRAM, ⌜*aside*⌝   For this description of thine hon-   280
esty? A pox upon him! For me, he's more and more
a cat.

FIRST SOLDIER   What say you to his expertness in war?

PAROLLES   Faith, sir, has led the drum before the English tragedians. To belie him I will not, and more   285
of his soldiership I know not, except in that country he had the honor to be the officer at a place
there called Mile End, to instruct for the doubling
of files. I would do the man what honor I can, but
of this I am not certain.   290

FIRST LORD, ⌜*aside*⌝   He hath out-villained villainy so
far that the rarity redeems him.

297. **cardecu:** an old French silver coin, worth a quarter of an *ecu,* and thus of little value (pronounced "kar-de-kew")

297–300. **sell . . . perpetually:** i.e., **sell** all present and future rights to his soul's **salvation fee-simple:** absolute possession of a property **remainders:** residual interests in an estate

309. **lackey:** i.e., running footman (one who ran alongside his master's coach); **coming on:** advancing (as opposed to **in a retreat** [lines 308–9])

319. **supposition:** imagination, fancy

325. **discovered:** revealed

326. **held:** regarded

"For he will be swine-drunk." (4.3.272–73)
From Jean Jacques Boissard, *Theatrum vitae humanae . . .* [1596].

BERTRAM, ⌐*aside*⌐ A pox on him! He's a cat still.

FIRST SOLDIER   His qualities being at this poor price,
    I need not to ask you if gold will corrupt him to   295
    revolt.

PAROLLES   Sir, for a cardecu he will sell the fee-simple
    of his salvation, the inheritance of it, and cut th'
    entail from all remainders, and a perpetual succes-
    sion for it perpetually.   300

FIRST SOLDIER   What's his brother, the other Captain
    Dumaine?

SECOND LORD, ⌐*aside*⌐ Why does he ask him of me?

FIRST SOLDIER   What's he?

PAROLLES   E'en a crow o' th' same nest: not altogether   305
    so great as the first in goodness, but greater a great
    deal in evil. He excels his brother for a coward, yet
    his brother is reputed one of the best that is. In a
    retreat he outruns any lackey. Marry, in coming on
    he has the cramp.   310

FIRST SOLDIER   If your life be saved, will you undertake
    to betray the Florentine?

PAROLLES   Ay, and the captain of his horse, Count
    Rossillion.

FIRST SOLDIER   I'll whisper with the General and know   315
    his pleasure.

PAROLLES, ⌐*aside*⌐ I'll no more drumming. A plague of
    all drums! Only to seem to deserve well, and to
    beguile the supposition of that lascivious young
    boy the Count, have I run into this danger. Yet who   320
    would have suspected an ambush where I was
    taken?

FIRST SOLDIER   There is no remedy, sir, but you must
    die. The General says you that have so traitorously
    discovered the secrets of your army and made   325
    such pestiferous reports of men very nobly held
    can serve the world for no honest use. Therefore
    you must die.—Come, headsman, off with his
    head.

338. **will you:** i.e., do you wish to send
339. **for:** i.e., on my way to
341. **sonnet:** love poem
342. **An:** if
344. **undone:** ruined (with wordplay in line 345 on "untied")
348. **but:** only
349. **impudent:** shameless
356. **Who:** i.e., he who

A "taffety punk." (2.2.22)
From *Roxburghe ballads* (printed in 1895).

PAROLLES   O Lord, sir, let me live, or let me see my   330
    death!
FIRST SOLDIER   That shall you, and take your leave of
    all your friends. ⌜*He removes the blindfold.*⌝ So,
    look about you. Know you any here?
BERTRAM   Good morrow, noble captain.   335
SECOND LORD   God bless you, Captain Parolles.
FIRST LORD   God save you, noble captain.
SECOND LORD   Captain, what greeting will you to my
    Lord Lafew? I am for France.
FIRST LORD   Good captain, will you give me a copy of   340
    the sonnet you writ to Diana in behalf of the Count
    Rossillion? An I were not a very coward, I'd com-
    pel it of you. But fare you well.
                            ⌜*Bertram and Lords*⌝ *exit.*
FIRST SOLDIER   You are undone, captain—all but your
    scarf; that has a knot on 't yet.   345
PAROLLES   Who cannot be crushed with a plot?
FIRST SOLDIER   If you could find out a country where
    but women were that had received so much
    shame, you might begin an impudent nation. Fare
    you well, sir. I am for France too. We shall speak of   350
    you there.   *He exits.*
PAROLLES
  Yet am I thankful. If my heart were great,
  'Twould burst at this. Captain I'll be no more,
  But I will eat and drink, and sleep as soft
  As captain shall. Simply the thing I am   355
  Shall make me live. Who knows himself a braggart,
  Let him fear this, for it will come to pass
  That every braggart shall be found an ass.
  Rust, sword; cool, blushes; and Parolles live
  Safest in shame. Being fooled, by fool'ry thrive.   360
  There's place and means for every man alive.
  I'll after them.   *He exits.*

4.4 Helen sets out with Diana and Diana's mother to seek the King of France in Marseilles.

---

6. **which gratitude:** i.e., **gratitude** for **which**
7. **flinty Tartar's bosom:** Tartars (or Tatars) were peoples who, under Mongol leadership, overran much of Europe in the 13th century. In *The Merchant of Venice*, Tartars are linked to "brassy bosoms and rough hearts of flint," and are described as "never trained to offices of tender courtesy" (4.1.32–34).
10. **convenient convoy:** i.e., appropriate escort
11. **breaking:** disbanding
22. **motive:** instrument
25. **saucy:** lascivious
27. **for:** i.e., taking it **for**
31. **death and honesty:** i.e., a chaste **death**
32. **impositions:** orders, commands
33. **Upon . . . suffer:** i.e., **to suffer** as you wish

A Tartar. (4.4.7)
From Balthasar Küchler, *Repraesentatio der
fürstlichen Auffzug* (1611).

⌜Scene 4⌝

Enter Helen, Widow, and Diana.

HELEN
That you may well perceive I have not wronged you,
One of the greatest in the Christian world
Shall be my surety, 'fore whose throne 'tis needful,
Ere I can perfect mine intents, to kneel.
Time was, I did him a desirèd office   5
Dear almost as his life, which gratitude
Through flinty Tartar's bosom would peep forth
And answer thanks. I duly am informed
His Grace is at Marseilles, to which place
We have convenient convoy. You must know   10
I am supposèd dead. The army breaking,
My husband hies him home, where, heaven aiding
And by the leave of my good lord the King,
We'll be before our welcome.
WIDOW   Gentle madam,   15
You never had a servant to whose trust
Your business was more welcome.
HELEN   Nor ⌜you,⌝ mistress,
Ever a friend whose thoughts more truly labor
To recompense your love. Doubt not but heaven   20
Hath brought me up to be your daughter's dower,
As it hath fated her to be my motive
And helper to a husband. But O, strange men,
That can such sweet use make of what they hate
When saucy trusting of the cozened thoughts   25
Defiles the pitchy night! So lust doth play
With what it loathes for that which is away.
But more of this hereafter.—You, Diana,
Under my poor instructions yet must suffer
Something in my behalf.   30
DIANA   Let death and honesty
Go with your impositions, I am yours
Upon your will to suffer.

35. **But:** only, merely; **word:** motto, maxim
38. **revives:** i.e., will revive
39. **Still:** always; **the fine's:** i.e., **the** conclusion is
40. **course:** process

4.5 The Countess, who has learned of Helen's death, receives word that the King of France is approaching Rossillion and then that Bertram himself has arrived. Lord Lafew proposes that Bertram marry Lafew's daughter, to which the Countess agrees.

––––––––––––

1. **with:** i.e., by
2. **snipped-taffeta:** i.e., wearing **taffeta** sleeves slashed so that another color of material shows
2–3. **saffron:** The dried orange-yellow stigma of the **saffron** plant was used to color foodstuffs and starch.
5. **had been:** i.e., would have **been**
7. **humble-bee:** i.e., bumble-bee
11. **dearest:** i.e., most heartfelt; or, perhaps, most severe or dire
18. **herb of grace:** rue (See picture, page 178.)
19–20. **nose-herbs:** i.e., **herbs** for smelling (as opposed to **herbs** for eating)
21. **Nebuchadnezzar:** a biblical king who went mad and "ate **grass** like an ox" (Daniel 4.32) See picture, page 180.
22. **grass:** See longer note, page 225.
23. **Whether:** i.e., which of the two

HELEN   Yet, I pray you—
But with the word "The time will bring on summer,"   35
When briers shall have leaves as well as thorns
And be as sweet as sharp. We must away.
Our wagon is prepared, and time revives us.
All's well that ends well. Still the fine's the crown.
Whate'er the course, the end is the renown.   40
They exit.

⌜Scene 5⌝

Enter ⌜Fool, Countess,⌝ and Lafew.

LAFEW   No, no, no, your son was misled with a
snipped-taffeta fellow there, whose villainous saffron would have made all the unbaked and doughy
youth of a nation in his color. Your daughter-in-
law had been alive at this hour, and your son here   5
at home, more advanced by the King than by that
red-tailed humble-bee I speak of.

COUNTESS   I would I had not known him. It was the
death of the most virtuous gentlewoman that ever
nature had praise for creating. If she had partaken   10
of my flesh and cost me the dearest groans of a
mother, I could not have owed her a more rooted
love.

LAFEW   'Twas a good lady, 'twas a good lady. We may
pick a thousand salads ere we light on such an-   15
other herb.

FOOL   Indeed, sir, she was the sweet marjoram of the
salad, or rather the herb of grace.

LAFEW   They are not herbs, you knave. They are nose-
herbs.   20

FOOL   I am no great Nebuchadnezzar, sir. I have not
much skill in ⌜grass.⌝

LAFEW   Whether dost thou profess thyself, a knave or a
fool?

33. **subscribe:** i.e., vouch

41. **phys'nomy:** i.e., physiognomy, face

43. **The black prince:** i.e., **the devil,** but also an allusion to England's famous "Black Prince," Edward III's oldest son, who made war on **France** (The **prince** thus has an **English name** [line 40].)

46. **suggest:** tempt, seduce

49–50. **keeps a good fire:** The connection between **the devil** and hellfire is made in Matthew (25.41) and in Revelation (20.10).

50. **prince of the world:** a name given **the devil** in the Gospel of John (12.31; 14.30; 16.11)

51. **his Nobility:** a mock-title modeled on the form of "his Lordship"

51–56. **I am for . . . great fire:** The concluding section of Jesus' "Sermon on the Mount" describes **the way that leads to** salvation (by **the narrow gate**) as contrasted to **the broad gate** that **the many** will enter on their **way** to destruction. (See Matthew 7.13–14.)

A Fool with his mock-scepter, or bauble. (4.5.31)
From Stephen Batman, *The trauayled pylgrime* . . . (1569).

FOOL   A fool, sir, at a woman's service, and a knave at a   25
man's.

LAFEW   Your distinction?

FOOL   I would cozen the man of his wife and do his
service.

LAFEW   So you were a knave at his service indeed.   30

FOOL   And I would give his wife my bauble, sir, to do
her service.

LAFEW   I will subscribe for thee, thou art both knave
and fool.

FOOL   At your service.   35

LAFEW   No, no, no.

FOOL   Why, sir, if I cannot serve you, I can serve as
great a prince as you are.

LAFEW   Who's that, a Frenchman?

FOOL   Faith, sir, he has an English ⌜name,⌝ but his   40
phys'nomy is more hotter in France than there.

LAFEW   What prince is that?

FOOL   The black prince, sir, alias the prince of darkness, alias the devil.

LAFEW, ⌜*giving him money*⌝ Hold thee, there's my   45
purse. I give thee not this to suggest thee from thy
master thou talk'st of. Serve him still.

FOOL   I am a woodland fellow, sir, that always loved a
great fire, and the master I speak of ever keeps a
good fire. But sure he is the prince of the world; let   50
his Nobility remain in 's court. I am for the house
with the narrow gate, which I take to be too little
for pomp to enter. Some that humble themselves
may, but the many will be too chill and tender, and
they'll be for the flow'ry way that leads to the   55
broad gate and the great fire.

LAFEW   Go thy ways. I begin to be aweary of thee. And
I tell thee so before because I would not fall out
with thee. Go thy ways. Let my horses be well
looked to, without any tricks.   60

61–63. **If . . . nature:** wordplay on (1) the cheating **tricks** played by grooms and stablemen; on (2) **jades' tricks** as the actions of untrustworthy horses; and on (3) **jades** as **horses**

64. **shrewd:** railing, scolding; **unhappy:** unfortunate (although the present-day meaning may also be intended)

68. **has no pace:** i.e., he **runs** in an undisciplined way (language used to describe the gait of a horse)

73. **moved:** urged

74–75. **in the minority of them both:** i.e., when they were **both** under age

75–76. **a self-gracious remembrance:** i.e., a thoughtful recollection that came from himself

82. **post:** i.e., speedily (as if by post-horse)

84. **him that:** i.e., someone who

91. **admitted:** i.e., allowed (to remain here)

92–93. **honorable privilege:** i.e., the **privilege** that goes with your honor

94. **that:** i.e., my **privilege**

"Sweet marjoram" and rue, or "herb of grace." (4.5.17, 18)
From John Gerard, *The herball* . . . (1597).

FOOL   If I put any tricks upon 'em, sir, they shall be
jades' tricks, which are their own right by the law
of nature.   *He exits.*

LAFEW   A shrewd knave and an unhappy.

COUNTESS   So he is. My lord that's gone made himself   65
much sport out of him. By his authority he
remains here, which he thinks is a patent for his
sauciness, and indeed he has no pace, but runs
where he will.

LAFEW   I like him well. 'Tis not amiss. And I was about   70
to tell you, since I heard of the good lady's death
and that my lord your son was upon his return
home, I moved the King my master to speak in the
behalf of my daughter, which in the minority of
them both his Majesty out of a self-gracious   75
remembrance did first propose. His Highness hath
promised me to do it, and to stop up the displeasure he hath conceived against your son there is
no fitter matter. How does your Ladyship like it?

COUNTESS   With very much content, my lord, and I   80
wish it happily effected.

LAFEW   His Highness comes post from Marseilles, of
as able body as when he numbered thirty. He will
be here tomorrow, or I am deceived by him that in
such intelligence hath seldom failed.   85

COUNTESS   It rejoices me that, I hope, I shall see him
ere I die. I have letters that my son will be here
tonight. I shall beseech your Lordship to remain
with me till they meet together.

LAFEW   Madam, I was thinking with what manners I   90
might safely be admitted.

COUNTESS   You need but plead your honorable privilege.

LAFEW   Lady, of that I have made a bold charter. But I
thank my God it holds yet.   95

97. **patch of velvet:** used to cover both **a scar** won in battle and the marks of syphilitic ulcers

99–100. **two pile and a half:** i.e., thick **velvet**

101. **liv'ry:** i.e., livery, uniform

102. **belike:** probably

103. **carbonadoed:** slashed

The mad Nebuchadnezzar. (4.5.21)
From Conrad Lycosthenes, *Prodigiorum* . . . [1557].

Enter ⌐Fool.⌐

FOOL   O madam, yonder's my lord your son with a
patch of velvet on 's face. Whether there be a scar
under 't or no, the velvet knows, but 'tis a goodly
patch of velvet. His left cheek is a cheek of two pile
and a half, but his right cheek is worn bare.   100

LAFEW   A scar nobly got, or a noble scar, is a good liv'ry
of honor. So belike is that.

FOOL   But it is your carbonadoed face.

LAFEW   Let us go see your son, I pray you. I long to talk
with the young noble soldier.   105

FOOL   'Faith, there's a dozen of 'em, with delicate fine
hats, and most courteous feathers which bow the
head and nod at every man.

They exit.

ALL'S WELL
THAT ENDS WELL

ACT 5

5.1   Helen finds herself unable to petition the King because he has already departed for Rossillion.

─────────

5. **bold:** confident, sure

6 SD. **Astringer:** i.e., an austringer or ostreger, a keeper of goshawks (See longer note, page 225, and picture below.)

16. **nice:** i.e., fastidious, punctilious

16–17. **put . . . use of:** i.e., call upon **you** to use

"A gentle Astringer." (5.1.6 SD)
From George Turberville, *The booke of faulconrie . . .* (1575).

ACT 5

⌜Scene 1⌝

Enter Helen, Widow, and Diana, with two Attendants.

HELEN
   But this exceeding posting day and night
   Must wear your spirits low. We cannot help it.
   But since you have made the days and nights as one
   To wear your gentle limbs in my affairs,
   Be bold you do so grow in my requital   5
   As nothing can unroot you.

     Enter ⌜a Gentleman,⌝ a gentle Astringer.

                    In happy time!
   This man may help me to his Majesty's ear,
   If he would spend his power.—God save you, sir.
GENTLEMAN   And you.   10
HELEN
   Sir, I have seen you in the court of France.
GENTLEMAN   I have been sometimes there.
HELEN
   I do presume, sir, that you are not fall'n
   From the report that goes upon your goodness,
   And therefore, goaded with most sharp occasions   15
   Which lay nice manners by, I put you to
   The use of your own virtues, for the which
   I shall continue thankful.

185

27. **removed:** departed
28. **use:** habit
36. **like:** likely
37. **Commend:** commit
41. **Our means . . . means:** i.e., **our** resources will contrive for us
44. **falls:** happens

GENTLEMAN   What's your will?
HELEN, ⌐*taking out a paper*⌐   That it will please you   20
  To give this poor petition to the King
  And aid me with that store of power you have
  To come into his presence.
GENTLEMAN
  The King's not here.
HELEN   Not here, sir?   25
GENTLEMAN   Not indeed.
  He hence removed last night, and with more haste
  Than is his use.
WIDOW   Lord, how we lose our pains!
HELEN   All's well that ends well yet,   30
  Though time seem so adverse and means unfit.—
  I do beseech you, whither is he gone?
GENTLEMAN
  Marry, as I take it, to Rossillion,
  Whither I am going.
HELEN, ⌐*giving him the paper*⌐   I do beseech you, sir,   35
  Since you are like to see the King before me,
  Commend the paper to his gracious hand,
  Which I presume shall render you no blame
  But rather make you thank your pains for it.
  I will come after you with what good speed   40
  Our means will make us means.
GENTLEMAN   This I'll do for you.
HELEN
  And you shall find yourself to be well thanked
  Whate'er falls more. We must to horse again.—
  Go, go, provide.   45
                            ⌐*They exit.*⌐

5.2 Parolles arrives at Rossillion and persuades Lafew to take him into his service.

---

2. **Lavatch:** the Fool's name, which is not mentioned elsewhere in the play. (See longer note to 1.3.0 SD, page 221.)

5. **mood:** anger

9. **eat . . . butt'ring:** Parolles' use of the word **muddied** (line 5) triggers a series of comments playing on the proverb "**Fish** bred up in dirty pools will stink of mud." See lines 21–23, below.

16. **deliver me:** i.e., **deliver**

18. **close-stool:** enclosed chamber pot

19. **purr:** the playing card called the **knave** (line 25) in the obsolete card game Post and Pair (with wordplay on the sound made by **Fortune's cat,** as well as on more obscure meanings of **purr** as male child and as animal dung) The primary meaning of **knave** may be a reminder of Parolles' earlier attacks on the Fool as a **knave** (in 2.4) and a preparation for Lafew's attack on Parolles as a **knave** in lines 31–33.

20–21. **not a musk-cat:** i.e., **not** sweet-smelling (The **musk-cat** is any animal, usually the musk-deer, which provides **musk,** from which perfume is made. The term was associated with sweet smells and was also applied to fops and other perfumed creatures.) See picture, page 208.

⌜Scene 2⌝

Enter ⌜Fool⌝ and Parolles.

PAROLLES, ⌜*holding out a paper*⌝ Good Monsieur
Lavatch, give my lord Lafew this letter. I have ere
now, sir, been better known to you, when I have
held familiarity with fresher clothes. But I am
now, sir, muddied in Fortune's mood, and smell   5
somewhat strong of her strong displeasure.

FOOL   Truly, Fortune's displeasure is but sluttish if it
smell so strongly as thou speak'st of. I will hence-
forth eat no fish of Fortune's butt'ring. Prithee,
allow the wind.   10

PAROLLES   Nay, you need not to stop your nose, sir. I
spake but by a metaphor.

FOOL   Indeed, sir, if your metaphor stink I will stop my
nose, or against any man's metaphor. Prithee, get
thee further.   15

PAROLLES   Pray you, sir, deliver me this paper.

FOOL   Foh! Prithee, stand away. A paper from Fortune's close-stool, to give to a nobleman!

Enter Lafew.

Look, here he comes himself.—Here is a purr of
Fortune's, sir, or of Fortune's cat—but not a   20
musk-cat—that has fall'n into the unclean fish-
pond of her displeasure and, as he says, is muddied withal. Pray you, sir, use the carp as you may,
for he looks like a poor, decayed, ingenious, foolish, rascally knave. I do pity his distress in my   25
smiles of comfort, and leave him to your Lordship.
⌜*He exits.*⌝

PAROLLES   My lord, I am a man whom Fortune hath
cruelly scratched.

LAFEW   And what would you have me to do? 'Tis too
late to pare her nails now. Wherein have you   30

34. **cardecu:** See note to 4.3.297. **justices:** perhaps, the **justices** of the peace, who had responsibility for beggars; or, perhaps, the judges who would decide the case if Parolles took **Fortune** to court

41. **more than a word:** Parolles' name suggests the plural of **word** in French (*paroles*).

41–42. **Cock's my passion:** i.e., by God's (or Christ's) **passion** (*Cock* was sometimes used in oaths in place of *God.*)

44. **found me:** i.e., **found me** out

45. **lost:** destroyed, ruined

48. **grace:** favor (but used by Lafew in the phrase **in grace** [line 51] to mean "into salvation"); **out:** i.e., **out** of favor

49. **Out upon thee:** an interjection of reproach

51. **out:** i.e., **out** of salvation

53. **Sirrah:** As a term of address to a male social inferior, the word indicates how far Parolles has fallen.

5.3 The King forgives Bertram and agrees to a marriage between Bertram and Lafew's daughter. Bertram gives Lafew a ring, which is then recognized by Lafew and the King as Helen's. Bertram's claim that it was thrown to him from a window leads to his arrest for Helen's murder. Diana appears claiming Bertram for her husband, and her statements about Bertram's promises are supported by Parolles. Bertram claims, in turn, that Diana is a prostitute, but her possession of his ancestral ring invalidates that claim. As charges and counter-charges mount, a pregnant Helen enters and tells

(continued)

190

played the knave with Fortune that she should
scratch you, who of herself is a good lady and
would not have knaves thrive long under ⌜her?⌝
There's a cardecu for you. Let the justices make
you and Fortune friends. I am for other business.   35

PAROLLES   I beseech your Honor to hear me one single
word.

LAFEW   You beg a single penny more. Come, you shall
ha 't. Save your word.

PAROLLES   My name, my good lord, is Parolles.   40

LAFEW   You beg more than ⌜a⌝ word, then. Cock's my
passion; give me your hand. How does your drum?

PAROLLES   O my good lord, you were the first that
found me.

LAFEW   Was I, in sooth? And I was the first that lost   45
thee.

PAROLLES   It lies in you, my lord, to bring me in some
grace, for you did bring me out.

LAFEW   Out upon thee, knave! Dost thou put upon me
at once both the office of God and the devil? One   50
brings thee in grace, and the other brings thee out.
⌜*Trumpets sound.*⌝ The King's coming. I know by
his trumpets. Sirrah, inquire further after me. I
had talk of you last night. Though you are a fool
and a knave, you shall eat. Go to, follow.   55

PAROLLES   I praise God for you.

⌜*They exit.*⌝

⌜Scene 3⌝

*Flourish. Enter King, ⌜Countess,⌝ Lafew, the two French
Lords, with Attendants.*

KING
We lost a jewel of her, and our esteem
Was made much poorer by it. But your son,

Bertram that she has met his seemingly impossible demands.

---

1. **of:** i.e., in; **our esteem:** i.e., my value, worth
3. **As:** i.e., **as** if, **as** though
4. **estimation:** valuation; **home:** fully
6. **make:** consider
7. **i' th' blade of:** i.e., in unripened (The phrase *in the blade* describes a cereal plant like wheat, before the ears of grain form.)
12. **high bent:** The image is of a bow tightly drawn and ready **to shoot** (line 13).
13. **watched:** waited for
15. **my pardon:** i.e., that you pardon me
26. **repetition:** rehearsal (of the past), further mention
30. **A stranger:** i.e., as if he were someone new to me
34. **hath reference to:** i.e., is referred **to,** is to be decided by
35. **letters:** i.e., a letter

As mad in folly, lacked the sense to know
Her estimation home.
COUNTESS   'Tis past, my liege,   5
And I beseech your Majesty to make it
Natural rebellion done i' th' blade of youth,
When oil and fire, too strong for reason's force,
O'erbears it and burns on.
KING   My honored lady,   10
I have forgiven and forgotten all,
Though my revenges were high bent upon him
And watched the time to shoot.
LAFEW   This I must say—
But first I beg my pardon: the young lord   15
Did to his Majesty, his mother, and his lady
Offense of mighty note, but to himself
The greatest wrong of all. He lost a wife
Whose beauty did astonish the survey
Of richest eyes, whose words all ears took captive,   20
Whose dear perfection hearts that scorned to serve
Humbly called mistress.
KING   Praising what is lost
Makes the remembrance dear. Well, call him hither.
We are reconciled, and the first view shall kill   25
All repetition. Let him not ask our pardon.
The nature of his great offense is dead,
And deeper than oblivion we do bury
Th' incensing relics of it. Let him approach
A stranger, no offender, and inform him   30
So 'tis our will he should.
GENTLEMAN   I shall, my liege. ⌜*He exits.*⌝
KING
What says he to your daughter? Have you spoke?
LAFEW
All that he is hath reference to your Highness.
KING
Then shall we have a match. I have letters sent me   35
That sets him high in fame.

38. **of season:** i.e., **of** any one **season**

40–41. **to the brightest . . . give way:** i.e., divided **clouds** yield to sunshine (Proverbial: "After black **clouds,** clear weather.")

47. **take . . . top:** i.e., seize the moment (**The forward top,** or forelock, alludes to the proverb "Seize occasion by the forelock," i.e., before it passes by.) See picture, page 196.

53–60. **I stuck . . . object:** i.e., her image so impressed **my heart** that the face and form of **every other** woman was distorted **stuck:** fixed **infixing:** fixing or fastening on **his:** i.e., its **perspective:** optical glass that distorts images (accent on first syllable) **favor:** face **fair color:** i.e., beautiful complexion **expressed it stol'n:** i.e., rendered or portrayed **it** as artificial, not natural **proportions:** figures, forms **To:** i.e., into

61. **she:** i.e., Helen

65. **scores:** debts

66. **compt:** account (both "reckoning of what you owe" and "statement regarding your moral conduct")

68. **turns:** i.e., **turns** into

70. **Make trivial price of:** i.e., devalue

Enter Count Bertram.

LAFEW   He looks well on 't.

KING   I am not a day of season,
For thou mayst see a sunshine and a hail
In me at once. But to the brightest beams   40
Distracted clouds give way. So stand thou forth.
The time is fair again.

BERTRAM   My high-repented blames,
Dear sovereign, pardon to me.

KING   All is whole.   45
Not one word more of the consumèd time.
Let's take the instant by the forward top,
For we are old, and on our quick'st decrees
Th' inaudible and noiseless foot of time
Steals ere we can effect them. You remember   50
The daughter of this lord?

BERTRAM   Admiringly, my liege. At first
I stuck my choice upon her, ere my heart
Durst make too bold a herald of my tongue;
Where the impression of mine eye infixing,   55
Contempt his scornful perspective did lend me,
Which warped the line of every other favor,
Scorned a fair color or expressed it stol'n,
Extended or contracted all proportions
To a most hideous object. Thence it came   60
That she whom all men praised and whom myself,
Since I have lost, have loved, was in mine eye
The dust that did offend it.

KING   Well excused.
That thou didst love her strikes some scores away   65
From the great compt. But love that comes too late,
Like a remorseful pardon slowly carried,
To the great sender turns a sour offense,
Crying "That's good that's gone!" Our rash faults
Make trivial price of serious things we have,   70

73. **after:** i.e., afterwards; **dust:** i.e., death ("Thou art **dust,** and to **dust** shalt thou return." Genesis 3.19)

81. **ere they meet:** perhaps, before the marriage days intersect (in unhappiness); **cesse:** i.e., cease

82. **son:** i.e., future son-in-law

83. **digested:** dissolved, assimilated (since the daughter would take the husband's name)

89. **last:** i.e., **last** time; **took her leave:** i.e., **took leave** of **her**

96. **Necessitied to help:** i.e., in need of **help**

98. **reave:** rob, deprive

Taking Occasion "by the forward top." (5.3.47)
From Jean Jacques Boissard, . . . *Emblemes Latins* . . . (1588).

196

Not knowing them until we know their grave.
Oft our displeasures, to ourselves unjust,
Destroy our friends and after weep their dust.
Our own love, waking, cries to see what's done,
While shameful hate sleeps out the afternoon.   75
Be this sweet Helen's knell, and now forget her.
Send forth your amorous token for fair Maudlin.
The main consents are had, and here we'll stay
To see our widower's second marriage day.

⌜COUNTESS⌝

Which better than the first, O dear heaven, bless,   80
Or, ere they meet, in me, O nature, cesse!

LAFEW

Come on, my son, in whom my house's name
Must be digested, give a favor from you
To sparkle in the spirits of my daughter,
That she may quickly come.   85
                          ⌜*Bertram gives him a ring.*⌝
                    By my old beard
And ev'ry hair that's on 't, Helen that's dead
Was a sweet creature. Such a ring as this,
The last that e'er I took her leave at court,
I saw upon her finger.   90

BERTRAM   Hers it was not.

KING

Now, pray you, let me see it, for mine eye,
While I was speaking, oft was fastened to 't.
                    ⌜*Lafew passes the ring to the King.*⌝
This ring was mine, and when I gave it Helen,
I bade her if her fortunes ever stood   95
Necessitied to help, that by this token
I would relieve her. ⌜*To Bertram*⌝ Had you that craft to
     reave her
Of what should stead her most?

BERTRAM   My gracious   100
     sovereign,

106. **rate:** value, worth

112. **ungaged:** free, not bound to another

112–13. **subscribed . . . fortune:** i.e., acknowledged my situation

114. **that course of honor:** i.e., as honorable a way

116. **heavy satisfaction:** i.e., sorrowful acceptance of the truth

118–19. **Plutus . . . med'cine: Plutus,** the god of riches, here pictured as an alchemist who **knows** the deepest secrets of **nature's mystery** (line 120) **tinct:** tincture, quintessence **multiplying med'cine:** i.e., the elixir that turns metals into gold (thus **multiplying** the precious metal)

120. **science:** knowledge

125. **to:** i.e., as her

129. **Upon her great disaster:** i.e., if something disastrous happened to **her**

133. **fain:** gladly; rather

Howe'er it pleases you to take it so,
The ring was never hers.
COUNTESS   Son, on my life,
I have seen her wear it, and she reckoned it   105
At her life's rate.
LAFEW   I am sure I saw her wear it.
BERTRAM
You are deceived, my lord. She never saw it.
In Florence was it from a casement thrown me,
Wrapped in a paper which contained the name   110
Of her that threw it. Noble she was, and thought
I stood ⸢ungaged,⸣ but when I had subscribed
To mine own fortune and informed her fully
I could not answer in that course of honor
As she had made the overture, she ceased   115
In heavy satisfaction and would never
Receive the ring again.
KING   Plutus himself,
That knows the tinct and multiplying med'cine,
Hath not in nature's mystery more science   120
Than I have in this ring. 'Twas mine, 'twas Helen's,
Whoever gave it you. Then if you know
That you are well acquainted with yourself,
Confess 'twas hers and by what rough enforcement
You got it from her. She called the saints to surety   125
That she would never put it from her finger
Unless she gave it to yourself in bed,
Where you have never come, or sent it us
Upon her great disaster.
BERTRAM   She never saw it.   130
KING
Thou speak'st it falsely, as I love mine honor,
And mak'st conjectural fears to come into me
Which I would fain shut out. If it should prove
That thou art so inhuman—'twill not prove so,
And yet I know not. Thou didst hate her deadly,   135

139. **My forepast proofs:** i.e., evidence already in **my** possession

140. **tax my fears of little vanity:** i.e., not accuse **my fears** of having no worth or value

141. **Having vainly:** i.e., since I foolishly

144. **easy:** i.e., easily

151. **for four . . . short:** i.e., because **four or five** times (she) arrived too late, after the court had already moved on

152. **tender:** present

154. **this:** i.e., **this** time, now

155. **looks:** perhaps, shows itself

156. **importing:** i.e., urgent

157. **verbal brief:** i.e., oral summary or abstract

166. **undone:** ruined, destroyed

Earing (plowing) the land. (1.3.45)
From Joseph Blagrave, *The epitomie of the art of husbandry . . .* (1685).

And she is dead, which nothing but to close
Her eyes myself could win me to believe
More than to see this ring.—Take him away.
My forepast proofs, howe'er the matter fall,
Shall tax my fears of little vanity,   140
Having vainly feared too little. Away with him.
We'll sift this matter further.

BERTRAM   If you shall prove
This ring was ever hers, you shall as easy
Prove that I husbanded her bed in Florence,   145
Where yet she never was.   ⌜*He exits, under guard.*⌝

KING
I am wrapped in dismal thinkings.

                    Enter a Gentleman.

GENTLEMAN   Gracious sovereign,
Whether I have been to blame or no, I know not.
                    ⌜*He gives the King a paper.*⌝
Here's a petition from a Florentine   150
Who hath for four or five removes come short
To tender it herself. I undertook it,
Vanquished thereto by the fair grace and speech
Of the poor suppliant, who, by this, I know
Is here attending. Her business looks in her   155
With an importing visage, and she told me,
In a sweet verbal brief, it did concern
Your Highness with herself.

⌜KING *reads*⌝ *Upon his many protestations to marry me*
  when his wife was dead, I blush to say it, he won 160
  me. Now is the Count Rossillion a widower, his
  vows are forfeited to me and my honor's paid to him.
  He stole from Florence, taking no leave, and I follow
  him to his country for justice. Grant it me, O king.
  In you it best lies. Otherwise a seducer flourishes, 165
  and a poor maid is undone.
                              Diana Capilet.

168. **in a fair:** Since fairs were notorious for the sale of stolen goods, Lafew seems to be implying that he could find a **son-in-law** better than Bertram almost anywhere he looked.

168–69. **toll for this:** i.e., sell this one (literally, register this one in the toll-book at the market)

169. **I'll none of:** i.e., I do not want

171. **suitors:** petitioners

177. **fly them as:** i.e., flee from **them** just **as** soon as; **swear them lordship:** i.e., marry **them**

178. **Yet:** still

181. **Derivèd:** descended

"An old courtier." (1.1.162)
From Cesare Vecellio, *Degli habiti antichi et moderni . . .* (1590).

LAFEW   I will buy me a son-in-law in a fair, and toll for
    this. I'll none of him.

KING
    The heavens have thought well on thee, Lafew,   170
    To bring forth this discov'ry.—Seek these suitors.
    Go speedily, and bring again the Count.
                   ⌜*Gentleman and Attendants exit.*⌝
    I am afeard the life of Helen, lady,
    Was foully snatched.

COUNTESS   Now justice on the doers!   175

         Enter Bertram ⌜under guard.⌝

KING
    I wonder, sir, ⌜since⌝ wives are monsters to you
    And that you fly them as you swear them lordship,
    Yet you desire to marry.

         Enter Widow ⌜and⌝ Diana.

               What woman's that?

DIANA
    I am, my lord, a wretched Florentine,   180
    Derivèd from the ancient Capilet.
    My suit, as I do understand, you know
    And therefore know how far I may be pitied.

WIDOW
    I am her mother, sir, whose age and honor
    Both suffer under this complaint we bring,   185
    And both shall cease without your remedy.

KING
    Come hither, count. Do you know these women?

BERTRAM
    My lord, I neither can nor will deny
    But that I know them. Do they charge me further?

DIANA
    Why do you look so strange upon your wife?   190

193. **this hand:** i.e., your **hand** (which, as a part of the betrothal ceremony, is pledged to the betrothed)

199. **comes too short:** is inadequate

201. **fond:** (1) foolish; (2) doting

206. **for:** i.e., as **for; you have them ill to friend:** i.e., they are not on your side

213. **impudent:** shameless, lacking decency

214. **gamester:** i.e., player of sexual "games," prostitute

218. **rich validity:** i.e., great value

220. **commoner:** i.e., common harlot, prostitute

A cuckold. (1.3.46; 2.2.25)
From *Bagford ballads* (printed in 1878).

204

BERTRAM
  She's none of mine, my lord.
DIANA   If you shall marry,
  You give away this hand, and that is mine;
  You give away heaven's vows, and those are mine;
  You give away myself, which is known mine,   195
  For I by vow am so embodied yours
  That she which marries you must marry me,
  Either both or none.
LAFEW, ⌜*to Bertram*⌝ Your reputation comes too short
  for my daughter. You are no husband for her.   200
BERTRAM, ⌜*to the King*⌝
  My lord, this is a fond and desp'rate creature
  Whom sometime I have laughed with. Let your
    Highness
  Lay a more noble thought upon mine honor
  Than for to think that I would sink it here.   205
KING
  Sir, for my thoughts, you have them ill to friend
  Till your deeds gain them. Fairer prove your honor
  Than in my thought it lies.
DIANA   Good my lord,
  Ask him upon his oath if he does think   210
  He had not my virginity.
KING
  What sayst thou to her?
BERTRAM   She's impudent, my lord,
  And was a common gamester to the camp.
DIANA
  He does me wrong, my lord. If I were so,   215
  He might have bought me at a common price.
  Do not believe him. O, behold this ring,
  Whose high respect and rich validity
  Did lack a parallel. Yet for all that
  He gave it to a commoner o' th' camp,   220
  If I be one.

225. **owed:** i.e., owned

234. **quoted for:** i.e., noted or set down as

235. **taxed:** censured; **debauched:** disparaged, vilified

236. **but:** i.e., merely, simply

237. **or that:** i.e., either **that; for:** because of

241. **boarded:** made advances to

242. **distance:** a technical term from fencing (the interval of space to be maintained between two combatants), here applied to the game of seduction

243. **Madding:** exciting, enraging

244. **fancy's:** i.e., desire's

245. **motives:** causes, instigators; **in fine:** finally

246. **modern grace:** ordinary charm

247. **rate:** i.e., terms

251. **turned off:** dismissed

252. **diet me:** i.e., limit the satisfaction you'll offer **me**

COUNTESS   He blushes, and 'tis hit.
  Of six preceding ancestors that gem,
  Conferred by testament to th' sequent issue,
  Hath it been owed and worn. This is his wife.   225
  That ring's a thousand proofs.
KING, ⌜*to Diana*⌝   Methought you said
  You saw one here in court could witness it.
DIANA
  I did, my lord, but loath am to produce
  So bad an instrument. His name's Parolles.   230
LAFEW
  I saw the man today, if man he be.
KING
  Find him, and bring him hither.   ⌜*Attendant exits.*⌝
BERTRAM   What of him?
  He's quoted for a most perfidious slave,
  With all the spots o' th' world taxed and debauched,   235
  Whose nature sickens but to speak a truth.
  Am I or that or this for what he'll utter,
  That will speak anything?
KING   She hath that ring of yours.
BERTRAM
  I think she has. Certain it is I liked her   240
  And boarded her i' th' wanton way of youth.
  She knew her distance and did angle for me,
  Madding my eagerness with her restraint,
  As all impediments in fancy's course
  Are motives of more fancy; and in fine   245
  Her ⌜infinite cunning⌝ with her modern grace
  Subdued me to her rate. She got the ring,
  And I had that which any inferior might
  At market price have bought.
DIANA   I must be patient.   250
  You that have turned off a first so noble wife
  May justly diet me. I pray you yet—
  Since you lack virtue, I will lose a husband—

254. **Send:** Since Diana is wearing or holding this **ring** (line 217), she here must mean "ask." **home:** i.e., to its **home,** to its owner

261. **goes false:** i.e., is untrue that

265. **starts:** startles

270. **on your just proceeding:** i.e., if you behave honorably; **keep off:** hinder from touching you, ward **off**

271. **By, by:** concerning, about

279–80. **a woman:** The distinction here between **gentleman** and **woman** suggests that **a gentleman** would love someone of his own social status (a gentlewoman or lady) differently than he would love someone beneath him (**a woman**).

A musk-cat or musk-deer. (5.2.21)
From Edward Topsell, *The historie of*
foure-footed beastes . . . (1607).

Send for your ring. I will return it home,
And give me mine again.   255
BERTRAM   I have it not.
KING, ⌐*to Diana*⌐   What ring was yours, I pray you?
DIANA
Sir, much like the same upon your finger.
KING
Know you this ring? This ring was his of late.
DIANA
And this was it I gave him, being abed.   260
KING
The story, then, goes false you threw it him
Out of a casement?
DIANA   I have spoke the truth.

Enter Parolles.

BERTRAM
My lord, I do confess the ring was hers.
KING
You boggle shrewdly. Every feather starts you.—   265
Is this the man you speak of?
DIANA   Ay, my lord.
KING
Tell me, sirrah—but tell me true, I charge you,
Not fearing the displeasure of your master,
Which, on your just proceeding, I'll keep off—   270
By him and by this woman here what know you?
PAROLLES   So please your Majesty, my master hath
    been an honorable gentleman. Tricks he hath had
    in him which gentlemen have.
KING   Come, come, to th' purpose. Did he love this   275
    woman?
PAROLLES   Faith, sir, he did love her, but how?
KING   How, I pray you?
PAROLLES   He did love her, sir, as a gentleman loves a
    woman.   280

284. **companion:** fellow (often, as here, a term of contempt)

287. **drum:** drummer; **naughty:** bad, inferior

295. **of Satan . . . furies:** i.e., **of** the torment he was in **limbo:** i.e., Hell **furies:** avenging goddesses (See below.)

296. **in that credit with them:** i.e., so much in their confidence

298. **motions:** proposals

302. **fine:** subtle, refined

The Furies. (5.3.295)
From Vincenzo Cartari, *Le vere e noue imagini . . .* (1615).

KING How is that?

PAROLLES He loved her, sir, and loved her not.

KING As thou art a knave and no knave. What an equivocal companion is this!

PAROLLES I am a poor man, and at your Majesty's 285 command.

LAFEW He's a good drum, my lord, but a naughty orator.

DIANA Do you know he promised me marriage?

PAROLLES Faith, I know more than I'll speak. 290

KING But wilt thou not speak all thou know'st?

PAROLLES Yes, so please your Majesty. I did go between them, as I said; but more than that he loved her, for indeed he was mad for her, and talked of Satan and of limbo and of furies and I 295 know not what. Yet I was in that credit with them at that time, that I knew of their going to bed and of other motions, as promising her marriage, and things which would derive me ill will to speak of. Therefore I will not speak what I know. 300

KING Thou hast spoken all already, unless thou canst say they are married. But thou art too fine in thy evidence. Therefore stand aside.

⌈*To Diana.*⌉

This ring you say was yours?

DIANA   Ay, my good lord. 305

KING

Where did you buy it? Or who gave it you?

DIANA

It was not given me, nor I did not buy it.

KING

Who lent it you?

DIANA   It was not lent me neither.

KING

Where did you find it then? 310

DIANA   I found it not.

326. **customer:** prostitute
328. **Wherefore:** why
330. **maid:** virgin

Hercules' words taking "all ears . . . captive." (5.3.20)
From Vincenzo Cartari, *Le vere e noue imagini . . .* (1615).

KING
  If it were yours by none of all these ways,
  How could you give it him?
DIANA   I never gave it him.
LAFEW   This woman's an easy glove, my lord; she goes   315
  off and on at pleasure.
KING
  This ring was mine. I gave it his first wife.
DIANA
  It might be yours or hers for aught I know.
KING, ⌐to Attendants⌐
  Take her away. I do not like her now.
  To prison with her, and away with him.—   320
  Unless thou tell'st me where thou hadst this ring,
  Thou diest within this hour.
DIANA   I'll never tell you.
KING
  Take her away.
DIANA   I'll put in bail, my liege.   325
KING
  I think thee now some common customer.
DIANA, ⌐to Bertram⌐
  By Jove, if ever I knew man, 'twas you.
KING
  Wherefore hast thou accused him all this while?
DIANA
  Because he's guilty and he is not guilty.
  He knows I am no maid, and he'll swear to 't.   330
  I'll swear I am a maid, and he knows not.
  Great king, I am no strumpet. By my life,
  I am either maid or else this old man's wife.
KING
  She does abuse our ears. To prison with her.
DIANA
  Good mother, fetch my bail. ⌐Widow exits.⌐ Stay,   335
  royal sir.

337. **owes:** owns
338. **surety:** i.e., be surety for
339. **he knows himself:** i.e., **he himself knows**
340. **quit:** (1) acquit; (2) repay
344. **quick:** (1) alive; (2) pregnant
346. **exorcist:** conjuror (who has summoned this spirit)
347. **Beguiles the truer office:** i.e., deludes the more trustworthy function
350. **shadow:** spectral form (that might be called up by an **exorcist**), with wordplay on (1) a form from which the substance has departed; and (2) a delusive semblance or image
355. **look you:** i.e., see
364. **mother:** i.e., mother-in-law
366. **Tom Drum:** probably an allusion to the proverbial **Tom** (or John) **Drum's entertainment** (See note to 3.6.38–39.)
366–67. **handkercher:** i.e., handkerchief

The jeweler that owes the ring is sent for,
And he shall surety me. But for this lord
Who hath abused me as he knows himself,
Though yet he never harmed me, here I quit him.   340
He knows himself my bed he hath defiled,
And at that time he got his wife with child.
Dead though she be, she feels her young one kick.
So there's my riddle: one that's dead is quick.
And now behold the meaning.   345

       Enter Helen and Widow.

KING   Is there no exorcist
Beguiles the truer office of mine eyes?
Is 't real that I see?
HELEN   No, my good lord,
'Tis but the shadow of a wife you see,   350
The name and not the thing.
BERTRAM   Both, both. O, pardon!
HELEN
O, my good lord, when I was like this maid,
I found you wondrous kind. There is your ring,
And, look you, here's your letter. ⌜*She takes out a*   355
    paper.⌝ This it says:
When from my finger you can get this ring
And ⌜*are*⌝ *by me with child, etc.* This is done.
Will you be mine now you are doubly won?
BERTRAM
If she, my liege, can make me know this clearly,   360
I'll love her dearly, ever, ever dearly.
HELEN
If it appear not plain and prove untrue,
Deadly divorce step between me and you.—
O my dear mother, do I see you living?
LAFEW
Mine eyes smell onions. I shall weep anon.—   365
   ⌜*To Parolles.*⌝ Good Tom Drum, lend me a hand-

368. **make sport:** i.e., amuse myself; **courtesies:** low bows

371. **even:** exact, precise

372. **fresh uncroppèd flower:** i.e., virgin

377. **Resolvedly:** perhaps, so as to resolve doubt or uncertainty

378. **meet:** fitly, properly

379. **past:** i.e., being **past**

kercher. So, I thank thee. Wait on me home.
I'll make sport with thee. Let thy courtesies alone.
They are scurvy ones.

KING
Let us from point to point this story know,   370
To make the even truth in pleasure flow.
⌜*To Diana.*⌝ If thou be'st yet a fresh uncroppèd flower,
Choose thou thy husband, and I'll pay thy dower.
For I can guess that by thy honest aid
Thou kept'st a wife herself, thyself a maid.   375
Of that and all the progress more and less,
Resolvedly more leisure shall express.
All yet seems well, and if it end so meet,
The bitter past, more welcome is the sweet.
                                        Flourish.

_____

4. **strift:** striving

5. **Ours . . . patience:** i.e., we will take on the role of listening patiently; **yours our parts:** i.e., you (by applauding) will take over **our parts** as actors

_____

Giletta of Narbona

⁋Giletta a **Phiſicians** doughter of Narbon, healed the **Frenche King** of a **Fiſtula**, for reward wherof ſhe demaūded Beltramo **Coūte** of Roſsiglioneto huſbande. **The Counte** being maried againſte his wil, for deſpite fled to Florence, and loued an other. Giletta his wife, by pollicie founde meanes to lye with her huſbande, in place of his louer, and was begotten with child of twoo ſoones : whiche knowen to her huſbande, he receiued her againe, and afterwardes ſhe liued in great honoꝛ and felicitie.

Gileta, a physician's daughter of Narbon, healed the French king of a fistula, for reward whereof she demanded Beltramo Count of Rossillion to husband. The Count being married against his will, for despite fled to Florence and loved another. Giletta, his wife, by policy found means to lie with her husband in place of his lover, and was begotten with child of two sons, which known to her husband he received her again, and afterwards she lived in great honor and felicity.

Synopsis of the plot of "Giletta of Narbona," the primary source for *All's Well That Ends Well*.
From William Painter, *The pallace of pleasure . . .* (1569).

⌐EPILOGUE¬

The King's a beggar, now the play is done.
All is well ended if this suit be won,
That you express content, which we will pay,
With strift to please you, day exceeding day.
Ours be your patience, then, and yours our parts.   5
Your gentle hands lend us, and take our hearts.

All exit.

Longer Notes

1.1.56. **affect a sorrow indeed:** The exchange between Helen and the Countess about Helen's display of grief is reminiscent of that between Gertrude and Hamlet about Hamlet's mourning clothes and his obvious sorrow for his dead father (*Hamlet* 1.2.70–89). Hamlet insists that his "suits of solemn black" and his sighs and tears, "the trappings and the suits of woe," are indeed "actions that a man might play." But he goes on to insist: "But I have that within which passes show." Helen's version of this is "I do affect a sorrow indeed, but I have it too."

1.2.1. **The Florentines and Senoys are by th' ears:** Shakespeare would have found the war between Florence and Siena in the short story the play dramatizes, Boccaccio's "Gileta of Narbonne," as translated by William Painter (1566). The line there reads "The Florentines and Senois were at wars." The play seems to be referring to no specific historical war.

1.2.64–65. **On . . . was out:** Both **catastrophe** and **heel** mean "conclusion," but there may also be wordplay on the phrase "**out** at **heel**"—with stockings or shoes worn through at the **heel;** and the word **out,** in its meaning of "no longer alight," may also look forward to the metaphor of the lamp at line 66.

1.3.0 SD. **Fool:** This character's designation throughout the Folio stage directions and speech headings as "Clown" may indicate merely that his part was played

221

by the theatrical company's comic actor. His function seems to be that of the professional jester or Fool—namely, to entertain his aristocratic mistress through his skillful playing with language—and at several points in the dialogue his role as Fool is commented upon. (See, for example, 2.2.58, 2.4.31–37, 4.5.23–34.) He is once called "Monsieur Lavatch" (5.2.1–2), which leads some recent editors to call him "Lavatch" throughout their editions.

1.3.56. **horns:** The Fool's speech (lines 43–56) makes the commonplace connection between beasts with horns and the fate of the married man, whose wife, according to the Fool, will certainly be unfaithful, making the husband a cuckold, or horned man. The association of cuckolds with horns growing from the man's forehead goes back to ancient times and may originate with the early and prevalent practice of "grafting the spurs of a castrated cock on the root of the excised comb, where they grew and became horns, sometimes of several inches long" (*OED*, s.v. "horn," 7a).

1.3.64. **Your cuckoo sings by kind:** Because the cuckoo does not build nests but leaves its eggs for other birds to hatch and feed, its song of "cuckoo" is linked to "cuckold," a man whose wife is unfaithful. The cuckoo's song was considered a mocking cry directed to married men.

1.3.71. **face:** The first two lines of the song (lines 71–72) recall the famous speech addressed by Faustus to the image of Helen of Troy in Christopher Marlowe's *Doctor Faustus*: "Was this the face that launched a thousand ships / And burnt the topless towers of Ilium?"

1.3.94–96. **Though . . . heart:** Anglican ministers were required, when officiating, to wear a **surplice** (a white linen vestment); Puritans who wished to **do no hurt** (i.e., not offend authority) put a **surplice** over their Genevan **black gown.**

1.3.214. **Indian-like:** In *Love's Labor's Lost,* Shakespeare has a character refer to "a rude and savage man of Ind" who "At the first op'ning of the gorgeous East, / Bows . . . his vassal head and . . . / Kisses the base ground with obedient breast" (4.3.243–45). In earlymodern England, the word **Indian** most often referred to persons from India, but the connection to sunworship here (lines 215–17) and in *Love's Labor's Lost* might also have suggested stories about the religious practices of natives of the New World.

2.1.154–59.
**He that of greatest works is finisher
Oft does them by the weakest minister.
So holy writ in babes hath judgment shown
When judges have been babes. Great floods have
    flown
From simple sources, and great seas have dried
When miracles have by the great'st been denied.**

Several passages from **"holy writ"** may lie behind these lines. As Naseeb Shaheen notes (*Biblical References in Shakespeare's Plays,* 1999), lines 154–55 seem to allude to 1 Corinthians 1.27: "God hath chosen the weake things of the world, to confound the mightie things." (See also Psalm 8.2: "Out of the mouth of very **babes** and sucklings hast thou ordeined strength.") In lines 156–59, writes Shaheen, "Shakespeare gives examples of God accomplishing mighty works by weak ministers." Shaheen sees lines 156–57 as "a reference to the righteous judgment of young Daniel, who saved innocent Susanna from death when all the elders of the people had condemned her" (citing, from the Apocrypha, Susanna 45—"The Lorde raised up the holy spirit of a yong childe, whose name was Daniel"—and Susanna 50). He cites as well Matthew 11.25: "thou hast hid these things from the wise and men of understanding, and hast opened them unto **babes.**" The words **"Great floods have flown from simple sources,"** writes Shaheen, refer "to Moses striking the rock at Horeb, causing water to gush forth" (Exodus 17.6, Numbers 20.8–11), and lines 158–59 refer "to the parting of the Red Sea at the time of the Exodus" (Exodus 14.16, 21–22). **"'The great'st'** would be Pharaoh, who repeatedly 'hardened his heart' in spite of the miraculous plagues that struck Egypt" (Exodus 7.22–23, and passim). While not all editors agree that the lines in this passage allude to the Bible, most accept the probability of the allusions.

4.2.32. **Jove's:** Jove seems an inappropriate deity by whom to **swear** faith in love, since **Jove's** adulterous escapades were the focus of many mythological tales. It is therefore possible that the word "God's" was replaced by (or because of) a censor. However, since the names of classical gods were used in the period in ways that seem strange today, we have allowed the Folio reading to stand.

4.3.16. **fleshes his will:** To flesh one's sword is to use it in battle for the first time, or to plunge it into flesh. This metaphorical use in turn derives ultimately from the hunting custom of rewarding a hawk or hound with a portion of the flesh of the prey in order to make it more eager to hunt.

4.5.22. **grass:** Following a long editorial tradition we emend the Folio's reading "grace" to **grass** in light of the biblical association between Nebuchadnezzar and **grass.** Yet the Folio's spelling of **grass** as "grace" may well reflect the fact that, as we know from other sources, the two words were still in Shakespeare's time pronounced so much alike that they could sometimes be spelled the same. Indeed, their similarity in sound, which provides the opportunity for a pun, appears to be the justification for the Fool's reference to **grass** in a verbal exchange about **herb of grace.** The interchangeability of **grass** and "grace" is also exemplified in Gerard's *Herball* of 1597, which lists the English names of **herb of grace** as "Grace of God, or S[t]. Johns Grasse."

5.1.6 SD. **Astringer:** The First Folio stage direction, *Enter a gentle Astringer,* appeared in the Second Folio of 1632 as *Enter a gentle Astranger* and in later folios as *Enter a Gentleman, a Stranger,* which in 1709 Rowe cut down to *Enter a gentleman.* When this character reappears in 5.3, the Folio calls him simply "a gentleman." Rowe's emendation is therefore attractive, especially because there is nothing in the dialogue that suggests that this particular character should be identified as a "keeper of goshawks." However, the Folio direction in its very strangeness seems worth preserving, in that it may have some meaning no one has yet discovered. We have thus incorporated it into our entrance direction, though our speech headings present him simply as a "gentleman," an expansion of the Folio's speech prefixes *Gent.* and *Gen.*

Textual Notes

The reading of the present text appears to the left of the square bracket. Unless otherwise noted, the reading to the left of the bracket is from **F,** the First Folio text (upon which this edition is based). The earliest sources of readings not in **F** are indicated as follows: **F2** is the Second Folio of 1632; **F3** is the Third Folio of 1663–64; **F4** is the Fourth Folio of 1685; **Ed.** is an earlier editor of Shakespeare, beginning with Rowe in 1709. No sources are given for emendations of punctuation or for corrections of obvious typographical errors, like turned letters that produce no known word. **SD** means stage direction; **SP** means speech heading; *uncorr.* means the first or uncorrected state of the First Folio; *corr.* means the second or corrected state of the First Folio; ~ stands in place of a word already quoted before the square bracket; ∧ indicates the omission of a punctuation mark.

1.1	0.	SD *Enter*] *Eneer* F
	1	*and hereafter in this scene.* SP COUNT-ESS] Ed.; *Mother* F
	3	*and hereafter in this scene.* SP BERTRAM] Ed.; *Ros.* F
	41.	promises. Her] ~ ∧ ~ F
	92.	me.] ~ ∧ F
	134.	got] F2; goe F
	164.	wear] F (were)
	178.	jarring∧ . . . discord∧] ~, . . . ~, F
1.2	4, 11, 23.	SP FIRST LORD] Ed.; *I. Lo. G.* F
	19.	SP SECOND LORD] Ed.; *2.Lo.E.* F

227

21. SD *1 line later in* F
23. Rossillion] F (*Rosignoll*)
47. obeyed] obey d F
49. And] Aud F
59. him!] ~∧ F
75. SP SECOND LORD] Ed.; *L. 2.E.* F
86. SD *They exit. Flourish.*] *Exit* | *Flourish.* F

1.3   0. SD *and hereafter. Fool.*] This ed.; *Clowne* F
        14 *and hereafter.* SP FOOL] This ed.; *Clo.* F
        20. I] w F
26, 40. o'] F (a)
        30. on by] onby F
        41. wife's] F (wiues)
        46. in] F (Inne)
        56. jowl] F (ioule)
75–76. With . . . stood, | With . . . stood,] F (With . . . stood, *bis*)
        84. o' th'] F (ath')
        88. or] Ed.; ore F
       115. Dian no] Ed.; *omit* F
       130. Even] Ed.; *Ol. Cou.* Euen F
       132. rightly] righlie F
       132. belong.] ~∧ F
       140 *and hereafter in this scene to line* 173. SP COUNTESS] Ed.; *Old Cou.* F
       154. wet,] ~? F
       171. Can 't] F (cant)
       177. mystery] F (mistrie)
       177. loneliness] Ed.; louelinesse F
       183. th' one to th'] F2; 'ton tooth to th' F
       212. intenible] intemible F
       212. sieve∧] ~. F
       248. Haply] F (Happily)

2.1   0. SD *Flourish cornets. Enter . . . Count Rossillion, and Parolles.*] Ed.; *Enter . . . Count, Rosse, and Parrolles. Florish Cornets.* F

    4. gain∧ all,] gaine, all∧ F

7, 20, 27, 39, 44, 53. SP FIRST LORD] Ed.; *Lord.G.* or *I. Lo. G.* F

    25. SP LORDS] F (*Bo.*)

    27. that] F ($\frac{t}{y}$)

29, 41, 45. SP SECOND LORD] Ed.; *2. Lo. E.* F

    31 *and hereafter in this scene.* SP BERTRAM] Ed.; *Rossill.* F

    44. Farewell] Farewll F

    49. with his cicatrice] Ed.; his sicatrice, with F

69, 71. SP LAFEW] Ed.; *L. Laf.* F

    70. fee] Ed.; see F

    107. SD *1 line later in* F

    126. two, more dear.] ~: ~ ~∧ F

    173. impostor] Impostrue F

    191. shame;] ~∧ F

    192. ballads,] ~: F

    193. nay] F (ne)

    213. heaven] Ed.; helpe F

    231. SD *They . . . assisted.*] *Exit.* F

2.2   1 *and hereafter in this scene.* SP COUNTESS] Ed.; *Lady., La.* F

    40. I] F3; *La.* I F

    60. An . . . sir.] And . . . sir∧ F

    66. legs] legegs F

2.3   1 *and hereafter to line* 101. SP LAFEW] Ed.; *Ol.Laf.* F

    9. SP BERTRAM] Ed.; *Ros.* F

29–30. facinorous] F (facinerious)

    35. minister.] ~∧ F

35–36. great transcendence] grear trancen-
dence F

42. Lustig] F (Lustique)

58. mistress∧] ~; F

72–73 choose; . . . refused,] ~, . . . ~; F

80. SD *printed in* F *at line* 64

102. her] F2; heere F

104. SP HELEN] F3; *La.* F

107. SP LAFEW] Ed.; *Ol.Lord* F

141. it] is F

151. tomb∧] ~. F

180. eyes.] ~, F

205. succeeding.] ~∧ F

222. thou'rt] th'ourt F

238. o'] F (a)

239. shalt] Ed.; shall F

264. o'] F (a)

281. SD *2 lines earlier in* F

282 *and hereafter to end of scene.* SP
BERTRAM] Ed.; *Ros.* F

308. detested] Ed.; detected F

316. SD *They exit.*] *Exit.* F

2.4   15. fortunes] Ed.; fortune F

34 + 1. PAROLLES . . .] *not in* F

49. o'] F (a)

57. SD *Parolles exits.*] F (*Exit Par.*)

58. SD *They exit.*] *Exit.* F

2.5   18. sir, 's] F (sirs)

27. End] Ed.; And F

29. one] F (on)

38. all, . . . custard;] ~: . . . ~, F

52. not] Ed.; *omit* F

55. SD *1/2 line later in* F

3.1   0. SD *French Lords*] Ed.; *Frenchmen* F

11. SP SECOND LORD] Ed.; *French E.* F

	20.	SP FIRST LORD] Ed.; *Fren.G.* F
	20.	nation] Ed.; nature F
	27.	to th'] F2; to 'th the F
3.2	9.	sold] F3; hold F
10, 17.		SP COUNTESS] Ed.; *Lad.* F
13, 14.		o'] F (a')
	18.	E'en] F (In)
	19.	SP COUNTESS *reads*] *A letter* F
	35	*and hereafter in this scene (except line 67).* SP COUNTESS] Ed.; *La.* F
	45	*and hereafter in this scene.* SP FIRST GENTLEMAN] Ed; *French E.* F

48, 53, 72, 74, 106. SP SECOND GENTLEMAN] Ed.; *French G.* F

	49.	you.] ~∧ F
	65.	SP SECOND GENTLEMAN] Ed.; *1.G.* F
	67.	SP COUNTESS] Ed.; *Old La.* F
	68.	engrossest∧] ~, F
	91.	Which] whlch F
	121.	still-'pearing] F (still-peering)
	137.	angels] F (Angles)
3.4	1	*and hereafter in this scene.* SP COUNTESS] Ed.; *La.* F
	4.	Saint] F (S.)
	10.	peace,] ~. F
	33.	worth] worrh F
3.5	0.	SD *daughter Diana*] Ed.; *daughter, Violenta* F
	31.	SD *1 line earlier in* F
36, 38, 112.		Saint] F (S.)
	75.	warrant] Ed.; write F
	87.	SD *1 line earlier in* F
	102.	jackanapes] Iacke an-apes F
	109.	SD *Bertram . . . exit.*] *Exit.* F
3.6	0.	SD *French Lords*] Ed.; *Frenchmen* F

1 *and hereafter in this scene to line 109.*
SP FIRST LORD] Ed.; *Cap. E.* F

3 *and hereafter in this scene to line 104.*
SP SECOND LORD] Ed.; *Cap. G.* F

36. his] Ed.; this F

37. metal] F (mettle)

37. ore] Ed.; ours F

67. magnanimous] magnimious F

83. thou 'rt] F (th'art)

112. SP FIRST LORD] Ed.; *Cap. G.* F

115, 122. SP SECOND LORD] Ed.; *Cap. E.* F

3.7 23. Resolved] Ed.; Resolue F

4.1 0. SD *French Lords*] Ed.; *Frenchmen* F

1 *and hereafter in this scene.* SP LORD]
Ed.; *I. Lord E. (Lor. E)* F

7. captain] Captaiue F

15. adversary's] F (aduersaries)

25. o'clock] F (a clocke)

63, 66. enemy's] F (enemies)

71 *and hereafter.* SP FIRST SOLDIER] Ed.;
Inter. F

105. SD *They exit*] F (*Exit*)

4.2 7. monument.] ~∧ F

17. o'] F (a')

46. may . . . snare] Ed.; make . . . scarre F

4.3 0. SD *Lords*] Ed.; *Captaines* F

1 *and hereafter in this scene.* SP FIRST
LORD] Ed.; *Cap. G.* F

3 *and hereafter in this scene.* SP SECOND
LORD] Ed.; *Cap. E.* F

34. measure] measurc F

77. SD *Servant*] Ed.; *Messenger* F

85. They] F3 (*Cap. G.*); *Ber.* They F

85. SD *1 line earlier in* F

86. Is 't] i'st F

102. has] ha s F
113. from] F (frō)
124. SP FIRST LORD Hush, hush. Hoodman]
     Ed.; hush, hush. *Cap. G.* Hoodman F
132. SP FIRST LORD] Ed.; *Cap.* F
147. SP BERTRAM, ⌐*aside*¬ All's one to him.
     What] Ed.; all's one to him. *Ber.* What F
169. o'] F (a)
171. but] Ed.; *omit* F
208. Lordship] Ed.; Lord F
212. o'] F (a')
237. *reads*] *Let.* F
255. our] Ed.; your F
281. him!] ~ ∧ F
297. cardecu] Cardceue F
305. o'] F (a')
335. SP BERTRAM] Ed.; *Count.* F

4.4 3. 'fore] F (for)
         9. Marseilles] F (*Marcellæ*)
        18. you] F4; your F

4.5 0. SD *Fool, Countess*] This ed.; *Clowne,
           old Lady* F
         6. advanced] aduanc d F
         8 *and hereafter in this scene.* SP COUNT-
           ESS] Ed.; *La.* F
        22. grass] Ed.; grace F
        40. name] Ed.; maine F
        47. of] F (off)
        82. Marseilles] F (Marcellus)
        86. It] Ir F

5.1 2. low.] ~, F
         6. SD *1/2 line later in* F

5.2 1. Monsieur] F (Mr)
        18. SD *1/2 line later in* F
        19. Here] Ed.; *Clo.* Heere F

33. her] F2; *omit* F
41. a] Ed.; *omit* F
41. Cock's] F (Cox)
50. office] offiee F
54. night.] ~, F

5.3   0. SD *Countess*] Ed.; *old Lady* F
5, 104, 175. SP COUNTESS] Ed.; *Old. La.* F
74. done] don,e F
80. SP COUNTESS] Ed.; *omit* F
106. life's] F (liues)
112. ungaged] Ed.; ingag'd F
118. Plutus] *Platus* F
131. falsely,] ~: F
132. conjectural] connecturall F
133. out.] ~, F
134. thou] rhou F
134. inhuman] F (inhumane)
140. tax] taze F
147. wrapped] wrap d F
147. SD *1 line earlier in* F
159. SP KING *reads*] Ed.; *A Letter* F
175. SD *3 lines earlier in* F
176. since∧] Ed.; sir, F
178. SD *Enter . . . Diana*] Ed.; *Enter Widdow, Diana, and Parrolles* F, *1/2 line later*
207. them. Fairer∧] ~∧ ~: F
220, 235. o'] F (a')
233 *and hereafter.* SP BERTRAM] Ed.; *Ros.* F
236. sickens∧] ~: F
246. infinite cunning] Ed.; insuite com-ming F
279. gentleman] F (Gent.)
358. are] Ed.; is F
377. Resolvedly] Resolduedly F

Ep.   6. SD *All*] F (omn.)

All's Well That Ends Well:
A Modern Perspective

David McCandless

On the simplest narrative level, *All's Well That Ends Well* is a play about a formidably obsessed young woman pursuing a truculently resistant young man. Although the question driving the play seems to be "Can she win him?" we are as likely, given the hero's defects, to inquire "Is he worth it?" or even "What's wrong with her?" Perhaps it is unsurprising, then, that the play has for so long been considered a "problem comedy" (along with *Measure for Measure* and *Troilus and Cressida*). No other comedy of Shakespeare's dramatizes such a startling romantic mismatch; no other comedy causes us to doubt the hero's merits and question the heroine's judgment quite so fretfully.

Even if, in the abstract, one can muster sympathy for a young man forced to marry against his will, the dramatic context all but precludes championing Bertram's cause. Helen dominates the play's early action, disarming the audience with heartfelt soliloquies, resourceful plotting, and a prodigious surmounting of obstacles: she risks death and performs a miracle to secure the power to choose Bertram as husband. By contrast, Bertram does not register sufficiently as a subject for us to take offense at his being treated as an object. In the play's first scene, he itches to leave for Paris; in the second he curries favor with the King; and in the fourth he indulges in some petulant whining about

235

having been excluded from the wars. Moreover, his strenuously contemptuous treatment of Helen ("A poor physician's daughter my wife? Disdain / Rather corrupt me ever!" [2.3.126–27]), combined with his headstrong defiance of the King, further inhibits sympathy. In addition, whereas Helen elicits nothing but praise and admiration from other characters, Bertram roundly provokes censure—even from his mother and his comrades-in-arms.

Helen, for her part, has exercised critics because of her confounding doubleness: she is at once studiously self-effacing and aggressively predatory. Traditional criticism has thus tended to portray her as either a long-suffering saint or a cunning vixen—either glossing over her audacious desire and celebrating her virtue, or reading her virtue as a mask for audacity and regretting or deploring her duplicity. Judgments of Helen—and of Bertram—perhaps follow inevitably from a focus on the play's "problematic" form, its apparent puncturing of the comic happy ending.

I would like in this essay to focus not on the play's "genre trouble," however, but on its "gender trouble."[1] The story of Helen's dogged pursuit of the disdainful Bertram is inextricably tied to the attempts of each to inhabit culturally imposed images of masculinity and femininity. Helen wants to become a woman by getting her man; Bertram wants to become a man by estranging himself from women, except insofar as they function as sexual objects. The inadequacy of these goals—as well as Helen's and Bertram's limited success in meeting them—discloses the inadequacy of gender as a marker of self and as a field for managing the complex interplay of power and desire. The powerful Helen proves ill-suited to the role of powerless object, while Bertram's ascension to powerful subject seems merely to sanction his intrinsic boorishness and narcissism. The play's exposure of the theatricality of gender makes its resolution—in which marriage seems to deliver our heroes to genders the play has already destabilized—even more problematic.

The performative base of Bertram's masculinity is personified by his mentor, the swaggering impostor Parolles. Bertram's identification with this cipher seems to validate Jacques Lacan's assertion that "the statement 'I am a man' . . . at most can mean no more than 'I'm like he whom I recognize to be a man.'"[2] In positioning Parolles as mirror of masculinity, Bertram turns away from the image of his father, whom the King and Countess urge him to imitate. The King implicitly characterizes Parolles and Bertram's father as rivals by recounting the Count's disparagement of meretricious fashionmongers who beget nothing but clothes ("whose judgments are / Mere fathers of their garments" [1.2.68–69]). Later Lafew implies that Parolles was begot *as* clothes, that he was not born but made by a tailor (2.5.16–19). Parolles functions as a symptom of the "tailoredness" of gender, performing a masculinity that impeaches the cultural norm it cites—for if masculinity can be successfully simulated, how can one confidently distinguish between acting like a *man* and *acting* like a man? In aiming to authenticate the glamorous masculinity that Parolles so speciously projects—a cartoon of the cultural ideal—Bertram aims to inhabit a fiction.

Helen could be said to perform femininity as much as Parolles performs masculinity. Throughout her campaign to win Bertram, she effaces her potentially transgressive desire with compensatory displays of exemplary submissiveness, presenting herself as an unoffending good girl who wants nothing more than to please her man, gratifying the cultural ideal of feminine subservience. Helen's much-discussed doubleness derives not so much from a cunning duplicity as from a kind of culturally induced schizophrenia, in which she must coexist with and strain to appease a second self aspiring to the feminine ideal, an ideal her own desire involuntarily sullies. Helen must therefore instantiate the image of innocent virgin that she herself constructs. She is, in a sense, her own Parolles.

The play's opening scene amply establishes Helen's doubleness; she proclaims her passion for Bertram even as she sadly disowns it, passively accepting an enforced chastity and the seemingly irrevocable loss of her beloved. In virtually no time, however, she boldly conceives a plan for winning Bertram. The unlikely agent of her conversion is Parolles, whose relentless testimonials to the naturalness of sex move her to ask, "How might one do, sir, to lose [virginity] to her own liking?" (1.1.156–57). Appalled by this implied transgression of feminine passivity, Parolles reminds Helen that, as a woman, she must be the chosen rather than the chooser. "Off with 't while 'tis vendible," he scolds, "answer the time of request" (160–61), essentially urging her to surrender her virginity to the first fellow who asks for it. Helen answers decisively if obscurely:

> Not my virginity, yet—
> There shall your master have a thousand loves,
> A mother, and a mistress, and a friend,
> A phoenix, captain, and an enemy,
> A guide, a goddess, and a sovereign,
> A counselor, a traitress, and a dear;
> His humble ambition, proud humility,
> His jarring concord, and his discord dulcet,

His faith, his sweet disaster, with a world
Of pretty, fond adoptious christendoms
That blinking Cupid gossips.

(171–81)

Modern editors have been inclined to assume a missing line between Helen's terse defense of virginity (171)
and her expansive list of lovers' endearments (172–81).
"There" is usually taken to mean "at the court," and the
speech is explained as Helen's anxious contemplation
of courtly rivals whose enchantments may well stir
Bertram's desire. But the speech can also be understood as a coded disclosure of Helen's sexual passion.
She will not part with her virginity "yet" because she is
saving it for Bertram (Parolles' "master") and, in the
act of giving it, she will release a powerfully creative
force bestowing a "thousand loves" on him. The obscu-
rity of her speech reflects the unspeakability of female
desire within a patriarchal culture that has tended to
silence it. Perhaps "at the court" has seemed the best
candidate for Helen's imagined "there" precisely
because virginity—or rather the unpenetrated female
territory it predicates—has been perceived not as a
"there" but as a "nowhere," a "nothing to be seen," in
Luce Irigaray's memorable phrase.[3]

The speech hints at Helen's problematic status as a
desiring subject in a culture that relegates women to
the role of desired object; yet it also affirms her urge to
become a desired object. The "thousand loves" that
Bertram will enjoy "there" may be seen as versions of
Helen, newly fashioned in the multiple guises of the
courtier's beloved. Her desire expresses itself as the
desire to be desired, the desire to fit herself to a con-
ventionally decorative, self-diminishing "femininity."

When choosing Bertram as husband, Helen explicitly constructs herself as normatively feminine, trading dominance for submission: "I dare not say I take you, but I give / Me and my service ever whilst I live / Into your guiding power" (2.3.110–12). Later, having succeeded in marrying Bertram, Helen savors feminine passivity as the reward for her masculine activity, embracing wifely subjugation with a fervor that mortifies Bertram. "Come, come, no more of that," he exclaims when she pronounces herself his "most obedient servant" (2.5.79, 78). Desiring a farewell kiss, Helen finds herself tongue-tied, once more disabled by the unspeakability of her desire. When Bertram finally demands, "What would you have?" she replies,

> Something, and scarce so much; nothing, indeed.
> I would not tell you what I would, my lord. Faith,
>   yes:
> Strangers and foes do sunder and not kiss.
>
> (92–96)

Helen's desire for a kiss is "something" that quickly becomes "nothing," something she would *not* tell. Although she shifts back into affirming it ("yes"), she then pauses, searching for a language expressive of her desire. As though confirming the impossibility of finding it, she proceeds to describe the desired kiss as something strangers and foes do *not* exchange. Hesitant to appear unfemininely forward, Helen secretes her desire to a negative space—a move habitually required of female subjects in a culture that equates their sexuality with "lack" and converts their biological difference into a symbolic cultural negation.

Bertram clearly upholds the cultural equation of women with nullity. Indeed, he positions himself as the self-actualizing hero for whom women represent the treacherous sirens' lure to feminized oblivion, transferring "lack" to men by afflicting them with an enslaving desire that arrests their pursuit of worldly power and sufficiency. Certainly Parolles figures women as dangerous emasculators, urging Bertram to "steal away" to the wars (2.1.34) and escape the unmanly bondage of marriage:

> He wears his honor in a box unseen
> That hugs his kicky-wicky here at home,
> Spending his manly marrow in her arms
> Which should sustain the bound and high curvet
> Of Mars's fiery steed.
>
> (2.3.295–99)

War, Parolles seems to say, offers a more manly sort of riding than marital sex. Whereas a man "sustains" masculine essence ("manly marrow") atop a horse in war, he "spends" it embracing a "kicky-wicky" in marriage. In such a context, the "box unseen" that conceals masculine "honor" becomes virtually synonymous with the receptacle into which a man "spends" his essence, allowing Parolles to negate crudely the female space whose generative powers Helen had celebrated.

Bertram effectively imprisons Helen in the land of "not" when annulling his marriage to her: "I have wedded her, not bedded her," he informs his mother, "and sworn to make the 'not' eternal" (3.2.20–22). He tries to "make the 'not' eternal" by imposing a seemingly impossible set of conditions for Helen's becoming his wife: once she has secured his ancestral ring, he tells her, and shown him a child he has begotten, "then call me husband. But in such a 'then' I write a 'never'" (60–62)—a proclamation that does indeed afflict Helen with an "eternal" *not*.[4]

Helen accedes all too readily to Bertram's negation, not only renouncing her desire but undertaking a pilgrimage for the sake of expiating it. She effectively colludes in her own erasure, refashioning herself as a guilt-ridden bad girl bent on disowning her "ambitious love" (3.4.5), an alteration which so enhances her status as good girl that the Countess is moved to compare her to the Virgin Mary (27–31). Helen seems intent on melding permanently with the self-nullifying "femininity" she has hitherto only fitfully performed.

Similarly, at the same point in the play, Bertram seems fixed on instantiating the image of fabulous warrior that Parolles has heretofore only projected. Bertram flourishes in the Florentine wars, garnering the military glory he coveted by ascending to the position of "general of our horse," dedicating himself to the war-god Mars ("Make me but like my thoughts, and I shall prove / A lover of thy drum, hater of love" [3.3.13–14]). He appears to actualize what Parolles can only simulate, enacting masculine potency more plausibly than the beribboned impostor could ever hope to.

But to the extent that cultural icons ("good girl," "fabulous warrior") can never be fully inhabited or authenticated, Bertram and Helen are also impostors: trading the complexity of self-formation for the simplicity of performance, extinguishing those aspects of themselves at odds with received myths of masculine power and feminine lack, becoming not so much icons as reductive caricatures—the chest-thumping warrior and the sexless madonna.

That Helen is only posing seems evident from the speed with which she ends the pilgrimage when opportunity affords her a second chance to win Bertram. In one sense, she trades the role of madonna for that of whore, anonymously supplying a body compliant with

Bertram's ecstatically impersonal love-making, desperately aiming to meld with the image of desirability that Bertram projects to (the absent) Diana. Yet the bed trick releases and affirms Helen's sexuality as much as it conceals and degrades it. Though, from one angle, she functions as a disposable receptacle—a "box unseen"—for Bertram's essentially autoerotic exercise, from another she functions as a dominant sexual agent, transforming him through trickery into a body compliant with her own desire.

One key indicator of Helen's dominance is the time frame she imposes on Bertram: "When you have conquered my yet maiden bed," Diana says on Helen's behalf, "Remain there but an hour, nor speak to me" (4.2.69–70). Helen phrases this command as a restriction, as though prohibiting Bertram from staying all night (an intention we might hesitate to ascribe to him), ostensibly because the morning light would discover her imposture. Still, if avoiding detection were her sole concern, she would presumably ask him to depart as soon as he had "conquered [her] bed" rather than an hour later. The same holds true if she were concerned only to satisfy Bertram's impossible conditions by having sex with him. So what is the point of this postcoital hour, of these lines that have absolutely no bearing on the plot?

The best answer is that they draw attention to Helen's control of the event. Regardless of what happens in that hour, it is Helen's time, in a way that the minutes devoted to the initial sex are not (as the image of having been "conquered" implies). "Helen's time" is irreducible to the temporal order of the play itself or to any order derived from logic or efficacy. It highlights a sexual agency that Helen has otherwise taken great pains to suppress.

Helen's creation of her time may express a desire for "something more," for satisfaction on her terms, for more sustained intimacy. In arranging the tryst with Diana, Bertram wishes for nothing beyond the performance of sex, a "trick" in another sense of the word. Helen not only offers him a different kind of trick but attempts to elicit a different kind of performance, one that transcends a merely performative sexuality. Helen's time confirms not only her sexual subjectivity but also her need to tame the beast, to transform a one-night stand into a foretaste of conjugal love.

In the aftermath of the bed trick, however, Helen seems rather to confirm Bertram's beastliness, marking him as "other," a creature from whom she is *estranged*:

> O, strange men,
> That can such sweet use make of what they hate
> When saucy trusting of the cozened thoughts
> Defiles the pitchy night! So lust doth play
> With what it loathes for that which is away.
> (4.4.23–27)

Still, by situating herself as object of conquest, Helen fulfills the conditions that enable her to conquer Bertram. By gratifying his fantasy, she aims to defeat it and decisively assimilate him to hers, trying once more to transform him from Beast to Prince Charming.

Bertram's humiliating exposure in the play's final scene is forecast by the parallel shaming of his discarded double, Parolles. The drum trick that ensnares Parolles, like the bed trick that entraps Bertram, depends on the victim's inability to communicate (Parolles cannot comprehend his comrades' gibberish, Bertram cannot speak), his intention to transgress (Parolles means to commit treason, Bertram adultery), his capacity for mistaking the familiar for the strange (Parolles takes his friends for his enemies, Bertram his wife for his lover), and his susceptibility to primitive drives (Parolles succumbs to fear, Bertram to lust). When put on trial, both Parolles and Bertram lie profusely in an effort to save themselves but are ultimately exposed as contemptible frauds. But whereas Parolles flexibly exchanges the role of military hero for that of fool, Bertram does not so readily reinvent himself as Prince Charming.

In the final scene Helen, though presumed dead, nevertheless continues to manifest her sexuality covertly, through surrogates and symbols. She embodies herself—and her desire—in two rings that, once introduced, decisively spoil Bertram's attempt to play the Prodigal Son. In a sense, both function as wedding rings. The first, which Helen places on Bertram's finger during the bed trick, signifies the consummation of her marriage, and the second, which Bertram surrenders to Diana in exchange for (he thinks) her sexual favors, betokens the fulfilled conditions that allow Helen to claim him as husband.

As tokens of Helen's persistently mystified sexuality, the rings have the effect of mystifying the play's characters—and spectators. In performance, one struggles mightily to differentiate the two or to discern their respective routes to Rossillion. The rings are too slippery, too indeterminate in origin and unstable in meaning to qualify as reliable agents of representation. The King may go so far as to suggest that Helen's ring possesses alchemical properties, multiplying owners as Plutus's "med'cine" multiplies gold (5.3.118–21).

Diana's evasions and equivocations concerning the rings further destabilize meaning, transporting the

King to the realm of "not": "It was not given me, nor I did not buy it. . . . It was not lent me neither. . . . I found it not. . . . I never gave it him" (5.3.307–14). Diana diverts the King from investigating Bertram's guilt to unraveling a riddle. In trying to explain her denial of that guilt, Diana makes the riddle explicit, evoking the hidden secrets of the bed trick:

> . . . he's guilty and he is not guilty.
> He knows I am no maid, and he'll swear to 't.
> I'll swear I am a maid, and he knows not. . . .
> He knows himself my bed he hath defiled,
> And at that time he got his wife with child.
> Dead though she be, she feels her young one kick.
> So there's my riddle: one that's dead is quick.
> And now behold the meaning.
> (5.3.329–31, 341–45)

Diana's coupling of opposites deranges the binary logic on which language—and representation—depends. Her words posit an impossible two-in-oneness, a meaning capable of uniting antonyms, of reconciling positive to negative. This assertion of doubleness proves an "abuse" to the King's ears until Helen steps forward and offers herself as the answer to the riddle, the "one" who dissolves all contradiction.

Yet Helen continues to be impenetrably double, calling herself, essentially, a wife and no-wife ("the shadow of a wife . . . / The name and *not* the thing" [5.3.350–51, emphasis mine]), thereby perpetuating rather than dissolving contradiction. Bertram affirms that she is both "name" and "thing" and begs her pardon, as though ready to accept her as wife and end her riddling self-division. But he follows his seemingly unequivocal affirmation with a more conditional one: "If she, my liege, can make me know this clearly, / I'll love her dearly, ever, ever dearly" (360–61). Characteristically, Helen affirms her claim to have met his conditions in negative terms: "If it appear not plain and prove untrue, / Deadly divorce step between me and you" (362–63)—once more raising the specter of a permanent *not*, the "never" of Bertram's original formulation. If Helen does indeed succeed in securing Bertram as husband, the marriage she makes can represent, at best, a double negative: she successfully negates Bertram's negation of her wedding. She proves herself not a not-wife. Whether she can truly achieve the status of wife remains provocatively questionable.

Equally questionable is precisely what it would mean to achieve it. What does "the thing" signify? The suspicion that "wife" connotes "safely nullified female" haunts the play's final scene. Given Helen's previous displays of obsequiousness, given the wife's submissive status in marriages of Shakespeare's time, one may plausibly conclude that becoming "the thing" of wife requires Helen to erase permanently those aspects of herself at odds with exemplary femininity, to end doubleness at the expense of self-negation. From this perspective, Helen's dominance of Bertram ultimately enables her to submit to him in marriage. She wins him only by putting him temporarily in her thrall so that she can put herself permanently in his. She resolves her doubleness by becoming "the one" she thinks he desires. The fulfillment of Helen's quest for womanhood depends on her helping Bertram to fulfill his quest for manhood, positioning herself as the woman awaiting him at the end of his heroic journey.

In order to do this, she must refigure him as a hero,

as Prince Charming, as one with whom to live happily ever after. Thus, she revises her reading of the bed trick, no longer affirming Bertram's difference ("O, strange men") but his likeness, his "kindness" ("O, my good lord, when I was like this maid, / I found you wondrous kind" [5.3.353–54])—a word that connotes kindredness as well as gentleness or generosity. Helen needs to claim Bertram as one of her own kind, to create him in her own image—the same image she has sought to impose from the start despite his obstinate assertions of "strangeness." She succeeds only to the extent that she elicits an apology and a capitulation that approximate and promote the kindredness she covets. The play, however, offers no assurances that Bertram has truly accepted his transformation from Beast to Prince Charming or that he can ever hope to match Helen's idealized vision of him.

Critics have long lamented the paltriness of Bertram's conversion speech, but the problems with the play's final scene run much deeper. Because Bertram has twice before falsely professed admiration for Helen (2.3.180–85, 5.3.52–63), no words of his, no matter how eloquently or torrentially penitential, could ever confirm his sincerity. Nor, for that matter, could his actions. Even the most extravagantly self-abasing gestures may be symptoms simply of feverish gratitude rather than of genuine conversion (after all, Helen has saved Bertram, a murder suspect, from possible execution). Helen may be able to work up feelings in Bertram that simulate and even enable love but do not actually generate it. And, of course, Bertram may simply cunningly simulate a penitential swoon. In either case, Helen manipulates Bertram into affecting a kindness that he may quickly discontinue after assuming his male prerogatives in marriage. It may be that for the second time in the play, Helen's goal eludes her even as she appears to achieve it.

Moreover, Helen's attempt to embrace normative femininity is scuttled not simply by Bertram's uncertain response but by her own unfeminine excess, her embodiment of a doubleness that resists reduction to a legible unity. On the one hand, Helen's pregnant body assimilates her sexuality to a reassuringly feminine, maternal image that evidences Bertram's potency and paternity.[5] On the other, it manifests her sexual power, serving as the text of Bertram's fulfilled conditions and thus as a spur to his capitulation. Moreover, because the astonished Bertram cannot yet "read" this text and comprehend his role as the author of Helen's physical transformation, her pregnant body also textualizes a mystery that further estranges her from the status of easily colonized feminine object.

Helen's pregnancy transforms her body into "something more," tangibly registering the secrets of the bed trick which, in turn, reflect the mystery of desire itself. Helen brings Bertram, however obscurely, new knowledge of herself, offering allusions to their time in bed and visible proof of their mutual gratification—allusions both tantalizing and confounding.[6] Her body claims knowledge of Bertram and attributes to him a knowledge of her that contradicts and challenges his lack of knowledge, sparking a desire to know more. When Bertram declares, "If she, my liege, can make me know this clearly," the "this" he wishes to know surely encompasses a good deal more than the details of Helen's fulfillment of his conditions: it must include the mystery of female difference, which transcends the reductive masculinist categories—madonna, whore, siren—to which he had previously consigned it.

The woman who awaits Bertram at his heroic journey's end turns out to be the one he abandoned along the way, the one he first mistook as an emasculating siren and then misused as a disposable plaything. The invisible object of the bed trick becomes formidably subjective and visible, returning in the person of a would-be wife, a once and future lover, who claims him as if she were an avenging spirit. To desire to know more of her is to desire *her*, to desire Helen as a riddle worth solving. The "this" that Bertram wishes to know becomes homologous with Helen's "there," suggesting that the performance of sex has solved his problem with sexuality. Yet this solution and the desire for knowledge that it predicates are simply intriguing possibilities. As the play ends, Helen remains elsewhere, suspended between known and not known.

The play's refusal to dissipate its tensions or confirm its tentative resolutions leaves its drama of sexual difference suspended, arrested in an unresolved but provocative and even poignant tension. Helen remains a mystery to be solved by the reader and spectator as well. So too does Bertram. Both characters aim to ground themselves in genders that the play suggests are groundless—or at least unstable, fluid, performative. Neither manages to forge a stable identity or secure a clear destiny.

The play itself also remains a riddle to be solved. It interrogates the happy ending it provisionally enacts by refusing to exorcise the doubts that have clouded Helen's pursuit of Bertram from the outset. It seems almost deliberately designed to force the audience to confront the implications of its need for a comic love story in which imperiled protagonists happily transcend all conceivable obstacles and vexations. Even as Helen finally secures Bertram as husband, the play stokes doubts about the sincerity of his conversion and the seemliness of their union. Does their reconciliation evidence the flourishing of mutual love or the wedding of delusion and opportunism?

In the play's epilogue, the actor/King declares, "The King's a beggar, now the play is done. / All is well ended if this suit be won, / That you express content" (Epi. 1–3). The play ends well if we say it does. And indeed, given its depiction of experiences not amenable to romantic idealization, we may wish to conclude that *All's Well That Ends Well* ends as well as it can.

---

1. *Gender Trouble* also happens to be the title of a very influential book by Judith Butler on the performativity of gender (New York: Routledge, 1990).

2. Jacques Lacan, "Aggressivity in Psychoanalysis," in *Écrits: A Selection*, trans. Alan Sheridan (New York: Norton, 1977), p. 23.

3. Luce Irigaray, "The Blind Spot of an Old Dream of Symmetry," in *Speculum of the Other Woman*, trans. Gillian C. Gill (Ithaca, N.Y.: Cornell University Press, 1985), p. 50.

4. I am indebted to Ralph Alan Cohen for pointing out the pervasiveness of the negative in the language of *All's Well* in "The (K)notty of Discourse of *All's Well That Ends Well*," a paper presented in the seminar chaired by Susan Snyder at the Shakespeare Association of America meeting in Atlanta in April 1993.

5. Given that one crucial condition of Bertram's accepting the marriage was that Helen show him a baby (3.2.59–60), it seems unlikely that she would claim to have fulfilled his demands without at least being visibly pregnant.

6. I use the phrase *"mutual* gratification" because of the belief circulating in Shakespeare's day that a woman could conceive only if she experienced an orgasm. See Thomas Laqueur, *Making Sex: Body and Gender from the Greeks to Freud* (Cambridge, Mass.: Harvard University Press, 1990), pp. 1–9.

Further Reading
All's Well That Ends Well

Abbreviations: *AWW* = *All's Well That Ends Well.*
Ado = *Much Ado About Nothing; Ant.* = *Antony and*
Cleopatra; MM = *Measure for Measure; MND* = *A Mid-*
summer Night's Dream; MV = *The Merchant*
of Venice; Oth. = *Othello; TN* = *Twelfth Night; Tro.* =
Troilus and Cressida; WT = *The Winter's Tale*

Adelman, Janet. "Marriage and the Maternal Body: On
Marriage as the End of Comedy in *All's Well That Ends*
Well and *Measure for Measure.*" In *Suffocating Mothers:*
Fantasies of Maternal Origin in Shakespeare's Plays,
"Hamlet" to "The Tempest," pp. 76–102, esp. pp. 79–86.
New York: Routledge, 1992.

Adelman reads *AWW* as an analysis of "male flight
from a woman who has become nearly indistinguish-
able from the mother and the desperate measures necessary to render her safe and pure." The most
desperate of those measures (and the one central to the
problematic nature of sexual relations in the play) is
the bed trick, which, Adelman maintains, serves to reg-
ulate Bertram's illicit desire, legitimizing and relocat-
ing it in the socially acceptable bond of marriage. By
presenting Bertram with "legitimate sexuality as a *fait*
accompli," the bed trick enables him to accept what he
feared was impossible—the compatability of marriage
and male desire. The final scene "depend[s] on something akin to a theatrical exorcism, where sexual con-
tamination is first attached to the supposedly violated

253

virgin . . . and then banished as the virtual [wife] return[s] and the truth is revealed." Having tried to separate himself from his mother at the beginning, Bertram comes full circle, finding himself restored to her through the extended maternal alliance linking the Countess with her surrogates (Helen, the Widow, and Diana).

Asp, Carolyn. "Subjectivity, Desire and Female Friendship in *All's Well That Ends Well*." *Literature and Psychology* 32.4 (1986): 48–63.

In this psychoanalytic study, Asp uses Lacan's ideas of the Imaginary and the Symbolic and intra- and interpersonal development to chart Helen's triumph over attitudes and theories of female deprivation and inferiority. Behind the masochistic femininity of the heroine's initial attitude toward Bertram, Asp detects a psychological form of sadism—"anger or rage at having been denied subjectivity by him and a willingness to inflict pain." Helen achieves independent womanhood by asserting desire in her choice of a husband, by refusing objectification, and by empowering herself through strong bonds of female friendship. *AWW* is unique in the Shakespeare canon because of its emphasis on the inadequacy of the male as subject and the challenge it poses to "both culture and theory which . . . subordinate the issue of woman-as-subject-of-desire to the question of male subjectivity and desire." Asp concludes that patriarchal order is modified, however slightly, as a result of the redefinition of gender prerogatives precipitated by Helen's single-minded action: "Fired by her desire, Helen refuses to submit to gender myths that link the female with loss unless that loss can be turned to gain." The conditional "wellness" of the play's ending reflects the fact that sexual relations will never be harmonious, "that psychic unity is tenuous at best."

Bradbrook, M. C. "Shakespeare's Hybrid: *All's Well That Ends Well.*" In *Muriel Bradbrook on Shakespeare*, pp. 84–98. Sussex: Harvester Press; Totowa, N.J.: Barnes & Noble Books, 1984. [Reprint of an essay that first appeared as "Virtue Is the True Nobility," *Review of English Studies* 26 (1950): 289–301; reprinted in *Shakespeare the Comedies: A Collection of Critical Essays*, edited by Kenneth Muir, pp. 119–32. Englewood Cliffs, N.J.: Prentice-Hall, 1965.]

Viewing the play within the context of Renaissance ideas of virtue, Bradbrook locates the governing theme of *AWW* in the question "Wherein lies true honour and nobility?" For Bertram, who represents false nobility, the answer lies in biological lineage and social rank; for Helen, an example of true nobility, in moral deeds and merit. Helen's vindication redeems Bertram and demonstrates that moral virtue is the chief criterion for real nobility. The poetic center of the play is found in Helen's confession speech to the Countess (1.3.201–27); its structural center lies in the King's speech on Helen's virtue (2.3.128–55). The play fails because the poetry of unrequited love does not suit a story structured around "the social problem of high birth versus native merit." In trying to write a play in the morality tradition, with Helen and Parolles functioning respectively as good and bad angels vying for Bertram's soul, Shakespeare the poet was at odds with Shakespeare the dramatist. "*AWW* expresses in its title a hope that is not fulfilled; all did not end well."

Brooke, Nicholas. "*All's Well That Ends Well.*" *Shakespeare Survey* 30 (1977): 73–84.

Unlike Leech and Rossiter (see below), who observe an unresolved tension between the play's realistic and romantic modes, Brooke argues that Shakespeare achieves a "consistently naturalistic presentation of traditional romance magic." In *AWW*'s terse, blunt, and unadorned language Brooke finds the perfect verbal complement to the reticence informing the entrapments and forced exposures that make up the dramatic action. Helen's exchange with Parolles on virginity in 1.1 and her unwilling exposure before the Countess in 1.3, along with the later entrapments of Parolles, Bertram, and Diana, demonstrate how the "uniquely bare" language makes "any romantic valuation of experience . . . superfluous." The interplay of romance conventions and a "severely naturalistic" treatment continues right up to the end when Helen's "resurrection," seen by the King and others as a "fairy tale miracle," becomes for the all-knowing audience "the springing of the final trap." For Brooke, the best moments of the play share a "striking bareness."

Calderwood, J. L. "Styles of Knowing in *All's Well That Ends Well*." *Modern Language Quarterly* 25 (1964): 272–94.

Calderwood describes the central "problem" of *AWW* as one of "knowing, both in the intellectual and in the sexual sense." Linked within the scope of this "knowing" motif are the play's major characters: Helen comes to know the uses of virginity and the complexities of passion; Bertram must understand Helen's virtues and Parolles' faults if he is to achieve self-knowledge; and the King, in trusting to Helen's proposed cure, must imitate "Him that all things knows," rather than "us that square our guess by shows" (2.1.167–68). Calderwood claims that Shakespeare's metaphoric fusion of the sexual act with the act of understanding allows us to see the two seemingly discrete fairy-tale episodes—the healing of the King and the bed trick—as more closely interrelated than previously thought. A focus on various styles of knowing results in a reading of *AWW* as "less the success story of an entirely virtuous maid bringing a recalcitrant young man to heel than the drama of two young persons, each with his share of virtues and faults, acquiring through trial and error the experience and moral insight needed for the revitalization of a moribund society."

Friedman, Michael D. " 'Service is no heritage': Bertram and the Ideology of Procreation." *Studies in Philology* 92 (1995): 80–101.

Focusing on the final scene of *AWW* as a performed text, with special attention to the moment of Helen's return, Friedman concentrates on the play's underlying conflict between two warring ideologies of procreation, both of which are embodied in Bertram: the individualistic code of military service interested only in the gratification of the soldier's sexual desire and the communal code of a civilian, patriarchal society concerned with the ethics of fatherhood and lineal heritage. Helen's climactic "resurrection" *seems* to resolve the conflict between individual desires and social pressures, for, by way of the bed trick and her resulting pregnancy, the heroine demonstrates to Bertram that "a man may love like a soldier and a father at the same time." The resolution is illusory, however, because the bed trick requires that Bertram's reconciliation to the civilian social order depend on "the facilitation of military 'service,' with which the Court's ideology of procreation is ultimately incompatible." Friedman turns to productions by Samuel

Phelps (Sadler's Wells, 1852), Tyrone Guthrie (Shakespeare Memorial Theatre, Stratford-upon-Avon, 1959), John Barton (Royal Shakespeare Company, 1967), Elijah Moshinsky (BBC TV, 1980), and Edward Gilbert (Huntington Theatre [Boston], 1989) to illustrate how performances gloss over the competing sexual ethics of the soldier and the father in order to achieve an imposed "resolution" of conflict. Performances have yet to provide a picture of Helen "as Bertram sees her [in the text], simultaneously his illicit lover and pregnant wife."

Haley, David. *Shakespeare's Courtly Mirror: Reflexivity and Prudence in "All's Well That Ends Well."* Newark: University of Delaware Press; London: Associated University Presses, 1993.

Haley observes in the plays written between 1597 and 1604 a focus on aristocratic identity and an epic self-consciousness or reflexivity that is intrinsically connected with "the courtier's obsession with praxis [action]." In *AWW* the exploration of courtly self-knowledge unfolds through a dialectic between courtly prudence and divine providence. What emerges from the debate as embodied in Bertram's search for honor is an implicit critique of the "court's secular humanism and its [public] mirror of honor," for the courtier's sense of self depends on the image he sees reflected back in the courtly mirror of prince and peers and thus implies that aristocratic self-knowledge is "perpetual agnosticism." In addition to analysis of Bertram's self-fashioning as a courtier and his final trial and exposure, the volume includes chapters on the melancholy nature of Helen's love and the collapse of her "providential design," the self-judgment and self-betrayal of Parolles, and the function of the Fool.

Hillman, Richard. *William Shakespeare: The Problem Plays.* New York: Twayne; Toronto: Maxwell Macmillan Canada, 1993.

Hillman uses recent studies in intertextuality, characterization, and subject construction to argue that the "contingency of genre and character" shared by *AWW, MM,* and *Tro.* marks these "radically unstable" plays as belonging to a period of major social and cultural transition. The chapter on *AWW* notes how the play "wrenches" the two-world pattern (court vs. natural or green world) found in the earlier romantic comedies "askew" by having Helen leave a position of "quasi-pastoral isolation for a court world that is contiguous with the masculine sphere of 'honor.' " Hillman approaches *AWW*'s fundamental split between romantic content and realistic style as part of a "metadramatic dynamism, at once the origin and object of play. The mixture of modes is a way of throwing control over the script up for grabs." The chief metadramatic manipulator of *AWW* is Helen, whose ambition is to achieve power, to refashion her world and its inhabitants to her own design. "She is simultaneously absent and present, passive and active, already inscribed within her text yet rewriting it—and with it, inevitably, herself—from the outside." To recognize that not only does Helen "never really *want* . . . Bertram any more than he wants her" but also she "never displays the slightest sign of caring whether or not *he* wants *her*" is to remove "the largest 'problem' in the way of reading the play in terms of romantic illusion and disillusion."

Hodgdon, Barbara. "The Making of Virgins and Mothers: Sexual Signs, Substitute Scenes, and Doubled Presences in *All's Well That Ends Well.*" *Philological Quarterly* 66 (1987): 47–71.

Asserting Helen's centrality to the "internal as well as the critical drama" of *AWW,* Hodgdon examines the play's erotic subtext primarily from Helen's point of view. Her rereading of the play addresses Shakespeare's transformation of Boccaccio's tale (particularly the implications of the heroine's name change from Giletta to Helen), the articulation of sexual signs in character and event, and the ways in which "substitute scenes and doubled presences function to sexualize [*AWW's*] narrative structure." Helen's name, evoking both the mythic, adulterous Helen of Troy and the lonely, virginal Helena of *MND,* economically "encompasses her sexual awareness, her obsessive desire and her virginity." The "resonant doublings" that Hodgdon observes include Helen/Diana, Helen/Fool, Helen/Maudlin, Helen's doubled cures of the King and Bertram, the doubled rings, and Bertram's double "winning" (5.3.357–59). Substitute scenes that articulate "the progress of offstage events" include 2.2—a narrative substitute for the King's reawakened sexual powers in which the Fool doubles as Helen and the Countess as the King—and 4.3, a substitute for the unseen bed trick in which the exposed Parolles doubles as Bertram and the report of Helen's death coincides with the moment of Bertram's (unknowing) consummation of the "lawful act" of marriage. The final scene "recalls and reproduces the whole narrative, transforming each repeated event in a series of astonishing volte faces." The tentative "wellness" of the ending, which acknowledges the problematic "ifs" of Helen, Bertram, and the King, "celebrates compromise, the text's final real-izing of romance."

Hunter, Robert Grams. *"All's Well That Ends Well."* In *Shakespeare and the Comedy of Forgiveness,* pp. 106–31. New York: Columbia University Press, 1965.

Hunter draws on a medieval dramatic tradition that emphasizes God's mercy toward sinful humanity to argue that *AWW* is best approached not as a romantic comedy but as a secular "comedy of forgiveness" informed by a Christian viewpoint. When Helen is seen as an agent of salvation and Bertram as a soul in need of reclaiming, the problems posed for critics by the play's troublesome "happy ending" disappear. Both sexually attractive and spiritually admirable, Helen functions as the human instrument of divine grace. Her combination of sacred and profane elements—even her name carries religious (St. Helena) and mythic (Helen of Troy) connotations—enables her to renew the dying world of the court and to lead Bertram to self-knowledge. The ending is "happy" not because of the marriage but because of Bertram's moral rebirth, achieved through the tenacity of Helen's redemptive love. When one understands that charity, not poetic justice, is essential to a comedy of forgiveness and when one views Bertram's conversion in light of the Renaissance belief in "the descent of grace upon a sinning human," the pardoning of Bertram becomes not only acceptable but formally required.

Jardine, Lisa. "Cultural Confusion and Shakespeare's Learned Heroines: 'These are old paradoxes.' " *Shakespeare Quarterly* 38 (1987): 1–18.

Whereas Wheeler (see below) deals with confused responses to Woman according to a psychoanalytic model and consequently sees them as internal to the individual subject, Jardine reads them as "culturally constructed and historically specific." Focusing on *MV* and *AWW*, she probes the ambivalent treatment of the "woman's place" in Renaissance intellectual life. Learned women like Portia (a student of the law) and

Helen (a student of medicine) reveal two incompatible views of the educated woman's expertise in traditionally male fields: one as essentially admirable and the other as "intrinsically indecorous." In *AWW* Helen's knowledge functions both as a symbol of female virtue and as a sign of unruly behavior (i.e., a disruptive threat to male autonomy). At the play's conclusion, having atoned for her earlier "forwardness," the actively knowing heroine becomes a "passively tolerant wife"—"a kind of wish-fulfillment solution" to the paradox of the learned lady as both civilizing and impudent.

Kastan, David Scott. *"All's Well That Ends Well* and the Limits of Comedy." *ELH* 52 (1985): 575–89.

Kastan examines the conclusion of *AWW* in light of comic theories and definitions that posit "happy endings" and the shaping of action to yield "comforting patterns of wish fulfillment." In *AWW* the ending fails to satisfy because the characters are too manipulative and conniving. Bertram is "crushed" by a plot, the bed trick is especially unpleasant, and the "predatory" Helen fails to see that love is something that cannot be compelled or earned. The numerous conditionals and qualifications running through the final scene and epilogue underscore the tentative and fragile nature of *AWW*'s "happy ending." Unlike the marriages that conclude *TN*—delightfully improbable unions manipulated by the playwright rather than by the dramatic agents themselves—the forced union of Bertram and Helen, achieved through a process humiliating to each, is a comic resolution that "does not release comic celebration." *AWW*, Shakespeare's "most insistent exploration" of comedy's limits in gratifying "fictive aspirations," makes us recognize "the inadequacy of a conception either of comedy or of ethical behavior that focuses exclusively on ends."

Lawrence, W. W. *Shakespeare's Problem Comedies.* New York: Macmillan, 1931.

In this seminal study of *AWW,* Lawrence argues that the play's so-called problems disappear when it is examined against the conventions of medieval romance and folklore, especially the motifs of "the healing of the king" (associated with tales involving a "clever wench") and "the fulfillment of the tasks" (associated with the "Virtue" stories showcasing the "faithful wife"). When viewed from this perspective, Helen's status as a noble, virtuous heroine is unqualified; Bertram's abrupt conversion becomes understandable; the unsavory aspects of Bertram, Parolles, and the Fool appear as requirements for dramatic contrast and motivation; and the ending becomes acceptable, for "no matter how harsh the treatment of the woman by the man, no matter how unsuited they may seem to each other, it is a convention of the Virtue Story that they 'live happily ever after.'" Lawrence contends that Shakespeare was not at liberty to make radical changes in stories that had become familiar through a long and rich oral tradition. To read the play ironically is to forget its source and the social and dramatic conventions of Shakespeare's time. The bed trick, for example, would not have bothered Elizabethan audiences, as it involved a wife lying with her husband. Moreover, they would have seen Helen's fulfillment of Bertram's condition as a clear demonstration that "virtue should stick at nothing in pursuing its course." Lawrence concludes that with the triumph of virtue over baseness, the play was appropriately named: all does end well.

Leech, Clifford. "The Theme of Ambition in *All's Well That Ends Well*." *ELH* 21 (1954): 17–29.

Because Shakespeare fails to harmonize a folktale plot with realistic elements, the total effect of *AWW* is "blurred." For Leech, the real-life atmosphere of the Countess's household and the King's court, the satiric treatment of the Florentine wars, and the "clumsy" ending make it "difficult to enter readily into the story of a half-magical cure or the story of apparent impossibilities brought to pass." The chief problem, however, lies with Helen, whose "intolerable and insolent" capacity for manipulation and willful determination to "lose" her virginity do not comport with the behavior of traditional heroines of romantic comedy and folktale. The bed trick, a device that can "hardly bring comfort," reveals the extent to which ambition taints her love for Bertram. Only Parolles shows signs of real growth; his acknowledgment that "Simply the thing I am / Shall make me live" (4.3.355–56) reveals "a certain humanity." For Leech, the main problem of the play is aesthetic, namely, a "failure in imagination."

Leggatt, Alexander. "*All's Well That Ends Well:* The Testing of Romance." *Modern Language Quarterly* 32 (1971): 21–41.

Leggatt describes *AWW* as "a play about testing, and a play which in itself is a test" between the worlds of romance and realism. The values of the former pass with receptive characters like the King, Lafew, and Helen; they fail with Bertram, Parolles, and the Fool. Each time romance seems to triumph (the curing of the King in Act 2 and the "miraculous" arrival of Helen in the final scene), reality intrudes in the person of Bertram (first in his rejection of Helen, thereby forcing her to abandon the idealism of romance for a pragmatic course of action, and later in his qualified acceptance of her). The tensions in *AWW* between the romantic and the realistic are never fully resolved, and its realities (fistulas, venereal disease, and bed-wetting) are more unpleasant than those found in the earlier comedies. Calling the play "an important dramatic experiment," Leggatt praises Shakespeare for daring to bring "two kinds of dramatic convention together, not in harmony . . . but in a positive and deliberate conflict."

McCandless, David. *"All's Well That Ends Well."* In *Gender and Performance in Shakespeare's Problem Comedies*, pp. 37–78. Bloomington: Indiana University Press, 1997.

In his study of the drama of sexual difference in *AWW*, *MM*, and *Tro.*, McCandless practices "a new mode of performance criticism keyed to a feminist *gestus*" that is specifically designed to "illuminate the tensions and contradictions intrinsic to phallocentric gender ideology." McCandless draws on *AWW*'s performance history and his own directorial vision to stage the erotic subdrama of the play's folkloric and fairy-tale motifs, pushing an underlying oedipal plot closer to the surface "for the purposes of tracing [*AWW*'s] provocative interrogation of gender." Deconstructing the folkloric device of the bed trick as both "an act of prostitution" (with Helen as object servicing Bertram's lust) and "a kind of rape" (with Helen coercing Bertram into having sex with her against his will), McCandless argues for performing what in the text is unperformed: a staged bed trick "demystifies and substantiates a female sexuality that the play elsewhere mystifies and evades." McCandless's "gestic strategy" attempts to reconcile Helen's "indomitable sexuality with her obsequious femininity," her "masculine" bold-ness with her "feminine" subservience. Even her visible pregnancy in the final scene sustains her "doubleness," since it speaks not only to Bertram's potency and pater-nity but also to her own desire and pleasure, thereby "reaffirming the active sexuality transgressively alien to the oedipal plot." Ultimately, both Helen and Bertram, "subjects-in-process," remain mysteries to be solved, for both try to "ground themselves in genders that the play suggests are groundless—or at least unstable, fluid, performative."

Mowat, Barbara A. "Shakespearean Tragicomedy." In *Renaissance Tragicomedy: Explorations in Genre and Politics*, edited by Nancy Klein Maguire, pp. 80–96. New York: AMS Press, 1987.

Mowat considers the problem plays (*AWW, MM,* and *Tro.*) experiments in tragicomedy as defined by Guarini in his 1601 *Compendio della poesia tragicomica:* a story in which tragic and comic parts are mixed, with per-sons of high rank approaching death but ultimately avoiding it, and a miraculously achieved "happy end-ing" that purges melancholy. In *AWW* Shakespeare places the comic action in a world of funerals, a dying king, and somber parental figures to achieve Guarini's essential requirement: the blending of "action, grave or comic, and speech 'tending toward commiseration or toward laughter.'" Throughout the play, comic events and situations are either presented seriously (e.g., Helen's disguise as a religious pilgrim) or tempered so as to modify the laughable (e.g., the morality-like qual-ity of Bertram's education in the Parolles subplot). In the opening scene, as lamentation gives way to the bawdy banter between Parolles and Helen on virginity, Shakespeare carefully orchestrates "the range of emotions to be explored in the play as a whole." Despite the ill will and "gratuitous unpleasantness" of the final scene, the technical "happy ending" meets—at least for the characters in the play—Guarini's requirements: "suspense, near-despair, and 'a credible miracle' which averts the expected catastrophe."

Neely, Carol Thomas. "Power and Virginity in *All's Well That Ends Well*." In *Broken Nuptials in Shakespeare's Plays*, pp. 58–104. New Haven: Yale University Press, 1985.
Neely's feminist reinterpretations of *Ado, AWW, Oth., Ant.,* and *WT* demonstrate how all five plays "embody the conflicts attendant on marriage by the incorporation of broken nuptials," which the author defines as "anything that disrupts the process of wooing, betrothal, wedding, and marriage." In *AWW*, broken nuptials in the form of delayed consummation, estrangement, and mock death express the individual anxieties, desires, and conflicts of Bertram and Helen as well as the social pressures placed on their union by parents, rulers, and the community at large. In the festive comedies the needs of the older generation are moderated to accommodate the individual wishes of the younger; in *AWW*, which "transforms the motifs" of the earlier comedies, youthful desire is "channeled to serve the social needs of both generations." Helen's pretended death while on a pilgrimage engenders Bertram's repentance and the mending of their ruptured nuptial; it also confirms her virtue. That ultimate vindication, however, comes at a cost: her patriarchal confinement in the "restrictive stereotype of chaste, loving, obedient, long-suffering wife." Neely maintains that the deliberate inconclusiveness of the final scene shows marriage "not as a happy ending but

as an open-ended beginning . . . with the potential for resolution."

Nevo, Ruth. "Motive and Meaning in *All's Well That Ends Well.*" In *Fanned and Winnowed Opinions: Shakespearean Essays Presented to Harold Jenkins,* edited by John W. Mahon and Thomas A. Pendleton, pp. 26–51. London: Methuen, 1987. [Reprinted in *Strands Afar Remote: Israeli Perspectives on Shakespeare,* edited by Avraham Oz, pp. 113–37. Newark: University of Delaware Press; London: Associated University Presses, 1998.]
A Freudian analysis of the "psychic space of evocation and resonance" shared by both audiences and dramatic characters leads Nevo to conclude that *AWW,* contrary to being a "problem play," is a "particularly interesting successor" to the festive comedies. Nevo attributes the "generic uneasiness" the play arouses in critics and audiences to their own "unaware masculine or feminine identifications[,] . . . defences and resistances." What gives the play its unique "richness and density" is the "intermesh" of the desires, fantasies, and memories of both older and younger generations. Concentrating on the "chiastic" doubling of Bertram and Helen—the former fearing a forbidden mother in his love and the latter seeking a forbidden father in hers—Nevo reads *AWW* as "a mode where three dreams cross [without ever harmonizing]: the dream of the elders, reliving their lives through their children, the dream of the young man escaping parental domination, and the dream of the young woman desiring a child and a father." Parolles is the "most brilliant dramatic invention" in the play. As Bertram's alter ego, he enables the audience to see the "rake's progress as an authentic reflection of masculine adolescence."

Price, Joseph G. *The Unfortunate Comedy: A Study of "All's Well That Ends Well" and Its Critics.* Toronto: University of Toronto Press, 1968.

In the first book devoted solely to *AWW,* Price provides an extensive critical and theatrical history of the play. The stage history addresses performances under the headings "Parolles and Farce (1741–1785)," "The Kemble Text: Sentiment and Decency (1794–1895)," "The Director and the Search for Unity (1916–1964)," and *"All's Well* in America and in the Minor Theatres (1799–1964)." The critical history is divided into sections labeled "The Spirit of Fantasy: Farce and Romance (1655–1840)," "Psychological Realism: Analysis of Failure (1840–1940)," and "The Reappraisal: A Pattern of Unity (1940–1964)." The survey of scholarship and productions reveals six major approaches to the play, each narrowly focusing on a single aspect: farce, romantic fable, melodrama, realism, satire, and symbolism. Rather than looking at these often contradictory aspects in isolation, and refusing to impose a tidy coherence by eliminating several of them, Price defends the play as a "tightly knit" blend of "seemingly jarring worlds." Through an elaborate system of parallels, parodies, anticipations, and commentaries, the theme of honor unfolds in symphonic variation. "If each of its elements is exploited rather than ignored," *AWW* emerges as "a very human play."

Rossiter, A. P. *"All's Well That Ends Well."* In *Angel with Horns and Other Shakespeare Lectures,* edited by Graham Storey, pp. 82–107. London: Longmans, Green, 1961.

Rossiter compares *AWW* with its source (William Painter's *The Palace of Pleasure,* a translation of Boccaccio's *Decameron* [Day 3, Story 9]) to focus his discussion of the play as a tragicomedy in which the Parolles subplot of "the seemer unmasked" casts a negative light on Bertram, a dupe and liar in his own right. Shakespeare's additions (the Fool, Lafew, Parolles, and the Countess), alterations (the King, Bertram, and Helen), and conversion of the denouement into "a species of Trial-scene" that is "thoroughly uncomfortable" result in a work filled with ambiguity of tone, plot, and character. The strange dichotomy of fairy-tale expectations and human reality psychologically exposed creates "off-notes" or "discords" that make the "feel" of *AWW* "uneasy." In a postscript Rossiter claims that analysis of Helen's inconsistent character "only results in confusion."

Snyder, Susan. *"All's Well That Ends Well* and Shakespeare's Helens: Text and Subtext, Subject and Object." *English Literary Renaissance* 18 (1988): 66–77.
    Snyder uses *MND*—the only other play in the canon with a woman (similarly named) who aggressively pursues a nonreciprocating beloved—as a subtext for filling in "the silences and suppressions" surrounding the speech and action of *AWW*'s Helen (e.g., her surprisingly sophisticated "mental image of court love life" at 1.1.172–83 and the mystery surrounding her journey to Florence). The Helena of *MND* and the Helen of *AWW* are linked by a name—Helen of Troy—"that ironically contradicts its prototype [as the 'archetypal desired object'] and thus underlines their peculiar situation as subject . . . of active desire, rather than . . . as pursued object." Although the later comedy can be read "safely" as depicting a providential force propelling the action, Snyder proposes a more subversive interpretation rooted in psychology rather than religion, one that

assigns agency to Helen's desire, not God's. In contrast to *MND*, where bonds of female friendship are never fully recovered and "culturally constituted sexual identities" are ultimately reasserted in a fully orthodox patriarchal order, female solidarity increases in *AWW* and proves empowering as Helen and Diana manipulate the King and Bertram. The uncertainty of the "happy ending" is not surprising given the play's enactment "by disjunction, indirection, and suppression" of the difficulties and conflicts "of imagining a woman as active, desiring subject."

Snyder, Susan. " 'The King's not here': Displacement and Deferral in *All's Well That Ends Well.*" *Shakespeare Quarterly* 43 (1992): 20–32.

Snyder considers the Marseilles scene (5.1), with its absent king and (in his place) a representative telling about his sudden departure, to be emblematic of *AWW*'s "persistent tendency . . . toward displacement and (more or less inadequate) substitution." Her Lacanian interpretation of the play as an enactment of desire, "the fulfillment [of which] is forever beyond," concentrates on the unseen bed episode (the play's central substitution) and the many deferrals and displacements generated by the final scene (e.g., Helen is replaced by Maudlin, who is displaced by Diana, who herself was a surrogate). "Falsified by the absent term of Diana," the bed trick involves both Helen and Bertram "in a kind of 'reference back' to the woman who isn't there, highlighting the lack that propels desire." Helen's pregnancy, a departure from the source in which her counterpart arrives on the scene with twins, exemplifies the pattern of postponed fulfillment that is characteristic of the ending and the play as a whole. Snyder perceives a Lacanian connection between Helen and Bertram and the Poet and Young Man of the Sonnets: both Helen and the Poet get "at best . . . flawed, imperfect substitute[s] for the image[s] that drive . . . [them]."

Styan, J. B. *All's Well That Ends Well.* Shakespeare in Performance Series. Manchester: Manchester University Press, 1984.

This study of how *AWW* has been realized in production concentrates on twentieth-century performances spanning the years 1916 to 1981. Following an introductory overview of the play's "perfunctory and fitful" performance history through the eighteenth, nineteenth, and first part of the twentieth century, Styan discusses realistic versus romantic stagings, the "spectrum of possibilities" available to actresses playing the role of Helen, the difficulties posed by Bertram's character, the Parolles subplot, and such topics as male-female relations, class snobbery, and intergenerational tensions. The volume provides a scene-by-scene analysis of the play with extensive reference to specific performances for purposes of illustration. These productions include those of Tyrone Guthrie (Stratford, Ontario, 1953; Stratford-upon-Avon, 1959), Michael Benthall (Old Vic, 1953), John Houseman (Stratford, Connecticut, 1959), John Barton (Stratford-upon-Avon/Aldwych Theatre, London, 1967/68), Jonathan Miller (Greenwich Theatre, 1975), Elijah Moshinsky (BBC TV, 1980), and Trevor Nunn (Stratford-upon-Avon/Barbican Theatre, London, 1981/82).

Wheeler, Richard P. "Imperial Love and the Dark House: *All's Well That Ends Well.*" In *Shakespeare's Development and the Problem Comedies: Turn and Counter-Turn,* pp. 34–91. Berkeley: University of California Press, 1981.

Wheeler makes extensive use of Freudian and contemporary psychoanalysis in his study of the problem comedies and where they fit in Shakespeare's development. The chapter on *AWW* examines the play in relation to the lovers and the festive endings of the earlier comedies, the "anguished adoration" of the Sonnets (Helen corresponding to the humiliated poet and Bertram to the insensitive young man), and the miraculous recoveries central to the late romances. Arguing that *AWW* "belongs to a phase of Shakespeare's development when the forceful presence of a woman is often perceived, or misperceived, as a deep threat to a tragic hero's manhood," Wheeler locates Bertram's rejection of Helen in a son's oedipal desires and fears of female domination: "marriage to Helena means for Bertram accepting a sexual bond made repugnant by its incestuous associations and abandoning the possibility of achieving masculine identity independent of infantile conflict." A focus on Bertram helps identify the play's unresolved tensions between comic form and deep psychological conflict.

Shakespeare's Language

Abbott, E. A. *A Shakespearian Grammar.* New York: Haskell House, 1972.

This compact reference book, first published in 1870, helps with many difficulties in Shakespeare's language. It systematically accounts for a host of differences between Shakespeare's usage and sentence structure and our own.

Blake, Norman. *Shakespeare's Language: An Introduction.* New York: St. Martin's Press, 1983.

This general introduction to Elizabethan English discusses various aspects of the language of Shakespeare and his contemporaries, offering possible meanings for hundreds of ambiguous constructions.

Dobson, E. J. *English Pronunciation, 1500–1700.* 2 vols. Oxford: Clarendon Press, 1968.
This long and technical work includes chapters on spelling (and its reformation), phonetics, stressed vowels, and consonants in early modern English.

Houston, John. *Shakespearean Sentences: A Study in Style and Syntax.* Baton Rouge: Louisiana State University Press, 1988.
Houston studies Shakespeare's stylistic choices, considering matters such as sentence length and the relative positions of subject, verb, and direct object. Examining plays throughout the canon in a roughly chronological, developmental order, he analyzes how sentence structure is used in setting tone, in characterization, and for other dramatic purposes.

Onions, C. T. *A Shakespeare Glossary.* Oxford: Clarendon Press, 1986.
This revised edition updates Onions' standard, selective glossary of words and phrases in Shakespeare's plays that are now obsolete, archaic, or obscure.

Robinson, Randal. *Unlocking Shakespeare's Language: Help for the Teacher and Student.* Urbana, Ill.: National Council of Teachers of English and the ERIC Clearinghouse on Reading and Communication Skills, 1989.
Specifically designed for the high-school and undergraduate college teacher and student, Robinson's book addresses the problems that most often hinder present-

day readers of Shakespeare. Through work with his own students, Robinson found that many readers today are particularly puzzled by such stylistic devices as subject-verb inversion, interrupted structures, and compression. He shows how our own colloquial language contains comparable structures, and thus helps students recognize such structures when they find them in Shakespeare's plays. This book supplies worksheets—with examples from major plays—to illuminate and remedy such problems as unusual sequences of words and the separation of related parts of sentences.

Williams, Gordon. *A Dictionary of Sexual Language and Imagery in Shakespearean and Stuart Literature.* 3 vols. London: Athlone Press, 1994.

Williams provides a comprehensive list of the words to which Shakespeare, his contemporaries, and later Stuart writers gave sexual meanings. He supports his identification of these meanings by extensive quotations.

Shakespeare's Life

Baldwin, T. W. *William Shakspere's Petty School.* Urbana: University of Illinois Press, 1943.

Baldwin here investigates the theory and practice of the petty school, the first level of education in Elizabethan England. He focuses on that educational system primarily as it is reflected in Shakespeare's art.

Baldwin, T. W. *William Shakspere's Small Latine and Lesse Greeke.* 2 vols. Urbana: University of Illinois Press, 1944.

Baldwin attacks the view that Shakespeare was an uneducated genius—a view that had been dominant among Shakespeareans since the eighteenth century. Instead, Baldwin shows, the educational system of Shakespeare's time would have given the playwright a strong background in the classics, and there is much in the plays that shows how Shakespeare benefited from such an education.

Beier, A. L., and Roger Finlay, eds. *London 1500–1700: The Making of the Metropolis*. New York: Longman, 1986.

Focusing on the economic and social history of early modern London, these collected essays probe aspects of metropolitan life, including "Population and Disease," "Commerce and Manufacture," and "Society and Change."

Bentley, G. E. *Shakespeare's Life: A Biographical Handbook*. New Haven: Yale University Press, 1961.

This "just-the-facts" account presents the surviving documents of Shakespeare's life against an Elizabethan background.

Chambers, E. K. *William Shakespeare: A Study of Facts and Problems*. 2 vols. Oxford: Clarendon Press, 1930.

Analyzing in great detail the scant historical data, Chambers' complex, scholarly study considers the nature of the texts in which Shakespeare's work is preserved.

Cressy, David. *Education in Tudor and Stuart England*. London: Edward Arnold, 1975.

This volume collects sixteenth-, seventeenth-, and early-eighteenth-century documents detailing aspects of formal education in England, such as the curriculum, the control and organization of education, and the education of women.

De Grazia, Margreta. *Shakespeare Verbatim: The Reproduction of Authenticity and the 1790 Apparatus.* Oxford: Clarendon Press, 1991.

De Grazia traces and discusses the development of such editorial criteria as authenticity, historical periodization, factual biography, chronological development, and close reading, locating as the point of origin Edmond Malone's 1790 edition of Shakespeare's works. There are interesting chapters on the First Folio and on the "legendary" versus the "documented" Shakespeare.

Dutton, Richard. *William Shakespeare: A Literary Life.* New York: St. Martin's Press, 1989.

Not a biography in the traditional sense, Dutton's very readable work nevertheless "follows the contours of Shakespeare's life" as he examines Shakespeare's career as playwright and poet, with consideration of his patrons, theatrical associations, and audience.

Fraser, Russell. *Young Shakespeare.* New York: Columbia University Press, 1988.

Fraser focuses on Shakespeare's first thirty years, paying attention simultaneously to his life and art.

Schoenbaum, S. *William Shakespeare: A Compact Documentary Life.* New York: Oxford University Press, 1977.

This standard biography economically presents the essential documents from Shakespeare's time in an accessible narrative account of the playwright's life.

Shakespeare's Theater

Bentley, G. E. *The Profession of Player in Shakespeare's Time, 1590–1642.* Princeton: Princeton University Press, 1984.

Bentley readably sets forth a wealth of evidence about performance in Shakespeare's time, with special attention to the relations between player and company, and the business of casting, managing, and touring.

Berry, Herbert. *Shakespeare's Playhouses.* New York: AMS Press, 1987.

Berry's six essays collected here discuss (with illustrations) varying aspects of the four playhouses in which Shakespeare had a financial stake: the Theatre in Shoreditch, the Blackfriars, and the first and second Globe.

Cook, Ann Jennalie. *The Privileged Playgoers of Shakespeare's London.* Princeton: Princeton University Press, 1981.

Cook's work argues, on the basis of sociological, economic, and documentary evidence, that Shakespeare's audience—and the audience for English Renaissance drama generally—consisted mainly of the "privileged."

Greg, W. W. *Dramatic Documents from the Elizabethan Playhouses.* 2 vols. Oxford: Clarendon Press, 1931.

Greg itemizes and briefly describes many of the play manuscripts that survive from the period 1590 to around 1660, including, among other things, players' parts. His second volume offers facsimiles of selected manuscripts.

Gurr, Andrew. *Playgoing in Shakespeare's London.* Cambridge: Cambridge University Press, 1987.

Gurr charts how the theatrical enterprise developed from its modest beginnings in the late 1560s to become a thriving institution in the 1600s. He argues that there were important changes over the period 1567–1644 in the playhouses, the audience, and the plays.

Harbage, Alfred. *Shakespeare's Audience*. New York: Columbia University Press, 1941.

Harbage investigates the fragmentary surviving evidence to interpret the size, composition, and behavior of Shakespeare's audience.

Hattaway, Michael. *Elizabethan Popular Theatre: Plays in Performance*. London: Routledge and Kegan Paul, 1982.

Beginning with a study of the popular drama of the late Elizabethan age—a description of the stages, performance conditions, and acting of the period—this volume concludes with an analysis of five well-known plays of the 1590s, one of them (*Titus Andronicus*) by Shakespeare.

Shapiro, Michael. *Children of the Revels: The Boy Companies of Shakespeare's Time and Their Plays*. New York: Columbia University Press, 1977.

Shapiro chronicles the history of the amateur and quasi-professional child companies that flourished in London at the end of Elizabeth's reign and the beginning of James'.

The Publication of Shakespeare's Plays

Blayney, Peter W. M. *The First Folio of Shakespeare*. Hanover, Md.: Folger, 1991.

Blayney's accessible account of the printing and later life of the First Folio—an amply illustrated catalog to a 1991 Folger Shakespeare Library exhibition—analyzes the mechanical production of the First Folio, describing how the Folio was made, by whom and for whom, how much it cost, and its ups and downs (or, rather, downs and ups) since its printing in 1623.

Hinman, Charlton. *The Norton Facsimile: The First Folio of Shakespeare.* 2nd ed. New York: W. W. Norton, 1996.

This facsimile presents a photographic reproduction of an "ideal" copy of the First Folio of Shakespeare; Hinman attempts to represent each page in its most fully corrected state. The second edition includes an important new introduction by Peter W. M. Blayney.

Hinman, Charlton. *The Printing and Proof-Reading of the First Folio of Shakespeare.* 2 vols. Oxford: Clarendon Press, 1963.

In the most arduous study of a single book ever undertaken, Hinman attempts to reconstruct how the Shakespeare First Folio of 1623 was set into type and run off the press, sheet by sheet. He also provides almost all the known variations in readings from copy to copy.

Key to
Famous Lines and Phrases

'Twere all one
That I should love a bright particular star
And think to wed it, he is so above me.
[*Helen*—1.1.90–92]

Withal, full oft we see
Cold wisdom waiting on superfluous folly.
[*Helen*—1.1.109–10]

Our remedies oft in ourselves do lie
Which we ascribe to heaven. The fated sky
Gives us free scope, only doth backward pull
Our slow designs when we ourselves are dull.
[*Helen*—1.1.222–25]

. . . he must needs go that the devil drives.
[*Fool*—1.3.30–31]

If ever we are nature's, these are ours. This thorn
Doth to our rose of youth rightly belong.
Our blood to us, this to our blood is born.
[*Countess*—1.3.131–33]

'Tis often seen
Adoption strives with nature, and choice breeds
A native slip to us from foreign seeds.
[*Countess*—1.3.147–49]

Thus, Indian-like,
Religious in mine error, I adore
The sun that looks upon his worshipper
But knows of him no more.

[*Helen*—1.3.214–17]

Good alone
Is good, without a name; vileness is so;
The property by what it is should go,
Not by the title.

[*King*—2.3.139–42]

The web of our life is of a mingled yarn, good
and ill together.

[*First Lord*—4.3.73–74]

All's well that ends well. Still the fine's the crown.
Whate'er the course, the end is the renown.

[*Helen*—4.4.39–40]

. . . whose words all ears took captive . . .

[*Lafew*—5.3.20]